FORUM
An Imprint of Prima Publishing
3000 Lava Ridge Court
Roseville, California 95661

DISCLAIMER: Nothing in this book constitutes legal advice or any kind of professional counsel whatsoever. The references, citations, quotations, and discussions of statutes and case decisions are for general information purposes only. Although great efforts were made to ensure the accuracy of the information supplied in this book, neither the author nor the publisher can assume any legal responsibility for how the information might be used or the reliance that any person might place on the information. Before drawing any legal conclusions or making any legal decisions in any individual case, a person must consult a qualified lawyer.

All persons who possess and use firearms or any other weapons should learn and practice safe handling techniques. Nothing in this book should be taken as advocating or encouraging any person to violate any law or to commit any crime. Whether a particular action will be considered lawful self-defense depends upon the specific facts and the local law. This book offers no advice about such matters. A qualified lawyer must be consulted for advice in individual cases.

Library of Congress Cataloging-in-Publication Data

Poe, Richard
The seven myths of gun control : reclaiming the truth about guns, crime, and the Second Amendment / Richard Poe
p. cm.
Includes bibliographical references and index.
ISBN 0-7615-2558-0
1. Gun control—United States. 2. Violent crime—United States. I. Title.
HV7436 .P64 2001
323.4'3'0973—dc21 2001033469

01 02 03 04 HH 10 9 8 7 6 5 4 3 2 1
Printed in the United States of America

THE SEVEN MYTHS OF GUN CONTROL

Reclaiming the Truth About Guns, Crime, and the Second Amendment

Richard Poe

FORUM
An Imprint of Prima Publishing

To my wife, Marie

"If ye love wealth greater than liberty, the tranquility of servitude greater than the animating contest for freedom, go home from us in peace. We seek not your counsel, nor your arms. Crouch down and lick the hand that feeds you. May your chains set lightly upon you; and may posterity forget that ye were our countrymen."

Samuel Adams, 1776

"They that can give up essential liberty to obtain a little temporary safety deserve neither liberty nor safety."

Benjamin Franklin, 1759

CONTENTS

FOREWORD

In 1999, a six-year-old walked into a Michigan classroom with a loaded handgun and shot and killed five-year-old Kayla Robbins. There was an immediate public outcry from predictable quarters about "gun violence." President Clinton held a press conference deploring the tragedy and calling for legislation that would require mandatory trigger locks on all handguns.

The key to unlocking most political puzzles is making a distinction between fantasy and reality. In the fantasy world of liberal gun-control advocates, Kayla Robbins might be alive today if a trigger-lock requirement had been added to the 20,000-plus gun laws already on the books. In the real world, the little boy who shot Kayla Robbins lived in a crack house run by his uncle who was a career criminal with three outstanding warrants for his arrest. He was living with his criminal uncle because his father was in jail and his drug-addicted mother was out of the picture. Is there any law that government can design that this "family" would feel compelled to obey?

The six-year-old killer did not buy the murder weapon at a gun-show to avoid "loopholes" in the existing laws. He did not buy the gun at all. He picked it up, already loaded, from its resting place on a bed in the crack house where he lived. Focusing on *this* reality—or rather this set of realities—would dispose of the idea that a trigger-lock law would have saved Kayla Robbins's life.

Extend the proposition. Criminals kill people. But, being criminals, they don't obey the law.

Or put the proposition another way: More than 50,000 people a year are killed by automobiles. Should we outlaw these vehicles to save those lives?

In the fantasy world, guns cause violence and laws are obeyed. In the real world, individuals pull the triggers and it is they who cause the violence. If they are individuals who are likely to use guns on innocent victims, they are individuals who by definition do not obey laws. Including gun laws.

Hence, gun control is really about controlling law-abiding citizens. It is about disarming law-abiding citizens in the face of those who would do them harm. As Richard Poe's indispensable book shows, citizen-endangering crimes such as "hot" burglaries—burglaries that occur while the victims are home—are much higher in countries like England, which outlaw guns, than they are in the United States, which so far does not.

In the real world, gun-control liberals usually live in safe neighborhoods and low-crime areas. If they live in big cities, they have access to private security systems because they know that law enforcement agencies are over-worked and understaffed. In contrast, the only security available to the welfare mother who lives in a high-crime area is what she can store in her night-table drawer.

Richard Poe's richly informative and superbly argued book pierces the veil between fantasy and reality and sets the record straight. It is the needed guide to political good sense in an area that affects the security of ordinary Americans in more ways than they know.

David Horowitz

AUTHOR'S NOTES

IN THE CLIMACTIC SCENE of *Saving Private Ryan*—Steven Spielberg's eulogy to the fighting men of World War II—the dying Captain Miller draws Ryan close and gasps, "Earn this."

Every baby boomer in the theater wondered: "Have I earned it?"

Do we deserve the freedoms that our parents bequeathed to us? Would we have fought as they did? Would we have had the guts?

Maybe not, says Tom Brokaw. In his book *The Greatest Generation*, Brokaw implies that the shoes our parents left are too big for us.

Our parents proved themselves at Iwo Jima and Omaha Beach. We lose our composure if the NASDAQ hiccups. Next to them, it seems, we are Lilliputians. Or so Brokaw implies.

How strange, then, to find ourselves confronting a threat far more personal and immediate than anything our parents faced—the disarming of the American people.

When the Greatest Generation came marching home from World War II, many carried captured enemy weapons from the battlefield.

No guards stood at the border to confiscate these trophies. America trusted its fighting men to keep them.

Like the Greek warriors of old, who kept their spears and armor at home, Americans were a free people, armed and ready to defend their liberty against any threat, internal or external.

For many black Americans, the right to keep and bear arms—like so many other rights—came later and harder.

During the War Between the States, many black Americans served in the Union Army. In many cases, they kept the rifles that they had borne in battle. But these were often confiscated when they returned home to the South, along with any other arms they might have.

Ku Klux Klan nightriders and state militiamen systematically ransacked the homes of black people, confiscating their weapons and leaving them helpless against lynch mobs.

In testimony before Congress, Union General Rufus Saxton reported that the state of South Carolina sought "a disarmed and defenseless" black population. He said:

> It is reported that in some parts of this State, armed parties are, without proper authority, engaged in seizing all fire-arms found in the hands of the freedmen. Such conduct is in clear and direct violation of their personal rights as guaranteed by the Constitution of the United States, which declares that "the right of the people to keep and bear arms shall not be infringed."

General Saxton charged that such disarmament "would subject them to the severest oppression, and leave their condition no better than before they were emancipated, and in many respects worse than it was before."[1]

As constitutional scholar Stephen P. Halbrook explains in *Freedmen, The Fourteenth Amendment and the Right to Bear Arms, 1866–1876*, such testimony helped push through passage of the

Fourteenth Amendment, which forbade state governments from infringing upon basic constitutional liberties—among them, the right to keep and bear arms.

Gun rights continued to play a vital role in African American life during the Civil Rights struggles of the 1950s and '60s.

Modern civil rights mythology emphasizes Martin Luther King's nonviolent teachings. However, John Salter, a professor at Tougaloo College and an NAACP organizer in the early '60s, wrote, "No one knows what kind of massive racist retaliation would have been directed against grassroots black people had the black community not had a healthy measure of firearms within it."[2]

Salter personally defended his home against nightriders on several occasions, exchanging shots with them and driving them off.

Civil rights workers in the early '60s were often protected by armed patrols of the Deacons for Defense and Justice—a private black militia based in churches, with chapters in more than 60 southern cities.

"If only the government has guns, only the people the government cares to protect are safe," notes former New York City prosecutor David B. Kopel in his book *The Samurai, the Mountie, and the Cowboy*. "In America, black communities have often been denied effective protection."[3]

Today, as in the past, law-abiding African Americans probably need firearms more than most. It is they who are most likely to encounter dangerous criminals, looters, and rioters in their neighborhoods. Yet they are the least likely to be allowed to purchase a firearm legally.

Just as in the Old South, minorities are singled out by today's gun control movement.

Consider the hue and cry over "Saturday Night Specials"—a nickname for the sort of inexpensive pistols that minorities in high-crime areas can most likely afford. Major cities, where crime is highest, often have the strictest gun laws. Permits to carry guns are costly and are frequently issued on subjective grounds, granted readily to the rich and famous, but denied to the poor and nonwhite.

In 1994, President Bill Clinton attempted to push through a nationwide program in which police would be empowered to conduct "gun sweeps" through public housing projects, systematically entering and ransacking every apartment, without search warrants, in their quest for illegal arms.

Many black civil rights leaders have jumped on the gun-control bandwagon, lured by the power and money that comes from playing ball with the government. Instead of fighting for their people's right to bear arms, many call for disarmament as vehemently as did the Ku Klux Klan during the Reconstruction era.

Instead of giving African Americans something they need in the present day—the ability to defend themselves against criminal violence—many self-styled civil rights leaders focus on issues more relevant to the last century, such as the display of the Confederate flag.

In regard to this nostalgic tendency of today's would-be liberators to fight last century's battles, Myles Kantor, one of our columnists at FrontPageMagazine.com, brought up a 1910 quote by G. K. Chesterton.

Chesterton wrote, "We often read nowadays of the valor or audacity with which some rebel attacks a hoary tyranny or an antiquated superstition. There is not really any courage at all in attacking hoary or antiquated things, any more than in offering to fight one's grandmother. The really courageous man is he who defies tyrannies young as the morning and superstitions fresh as the first flowers."[4]

The Confederate flag and the regime it symbolizes have been impotent for generations. To fight them is like fighting one's grandmother.

But antigun hysteria is vital and strong today, as "young as the morning" and as "fresh as the first flowers."

Unlike Confederate nostalgia buffs, the gun-ban lobby has behind it all the power of government, courts, media, and academia. It has behind it millions of starry-eyed followers who believe in its doctrines as fervently as millions once believed in slavery, Nazism, or witch-burning.

The loss of our gun rights will affect every American, regardless of race, class, or political party.

In World War II, we managed to put aside our differences. Blacks and whites fought side by side. Their grudges against each other were bitter and deep. Yet they pulled together against a common foe, lest America herself be lost.

The Dutch have a saying:

> *Waar twee honden vechten om een been, loopt de derde ermee heen.* (When two dogs fight for a bone, the third one will walk away with it.)

Let us not be like those foolish dogs. The gun-ban lobby can succeed only if it divides American against American, black against white, man against woman, young against old.

I am not a hunter, a gun hobbyist, or a gun enthusiast.

I wrote this book not out of any personal zest for firearms, but out of a sense of duty as a journalist and citizen. I could no longer stand silent while my Constitution was shredded. If the Second Amendment can be snatched away, how long before the rest of the Bill of Rights will follow?

We all learned in the 2000 election that our voting system is flawed. Yet I have faith in America, faith in our ability to clean up our electoral process, and faith that we will win back our liberties through the lawful and peaceful exercise of our voting rights.

Americans of every color and creed must search their hearts today and decide where they stand.

It is easy to wax nostalgic over a videocassette of *Saving Private Ryan*, to heap praise on our parents' generation, and to savor their courage from afar, as one might savor a rich latte from Starbucks.

But our parents' struggle is over. The enemies they faced are gone. Now it is our turn to show who we are.

ACKNOWLEDGMENTS

ABOVE ALL, I wish to thank my wife, Marie, whose contribution to this and all my other books cannot be measured. I thank Christopher Ruddy for publishing the original series of articles on which this book is based, between November 1999 and December 2000, on his NewsMax.com Web site. Thanks also to my boss, David Horowitz, for his great patience during the writing of this book, his inspiration, and for his considerable help in making *The Seven Myths of Gun Control* a success.

Others who have helped, in large ways and small (sometimes without knowing it) include Steve Martin; Ben Dominitz; Libby Larson; Lloyd Jassin; David Yeagley; Tanya Metaksa; John Perazzo; Roy and Niger Innis; Aaron Zelman; Sarah Thompson, M.D.; Richard W. Stevens; Stephen P. Halbrook; David Theroux; John R. Lott Jr.; Duncan Maxwell Anderson; Scott Rubush; Jennifer Kabbany; Tephanie Carpenter and her brave family; my mother, Lillian Poe; and my late father, Alfred Poe.

INTRODUCTION

THE MARCH TOWARD GUN ABOLITION

FOR FOURTEEN-YEAR-OLD Jessica Carpenter, the morning of August 23, 2000, began like any other. Her father had left for work. Her mother had taken the car to get the brakes checked. Jessica had been left in charge, to look after the four other children, Anna, 13; Vanessa, 11; Ashley, 9; and John, 7.

Although the day started normally, it was not destined to end that way. It would turn out to be the most terrifying day of Jessica's life.

Shortly after her mother left, Jessica heard noises from the living room. It sounded as if someone were moving furniture around. Still half asleep, Jessica assumed that it must be her mother.

But it wasn't.

She heard the phone ring down the hall and someone answered it. "I wonder what time it is," thought Jessica sleepily. Her grandmother was coming at nine to pick them up. She rose from bed and went to the kitchen, where the clock on the range showed that it was already after nine. Better wake up the others, Jessica thought.

Then she noticed something strange. The sliding glass door in the living room had been blocked with furniture. The shades were shut, leaving the house in gloom. Why would her mother do that?

Jessica froze. A sudden chill gripped her stomach. At first, she did not want to believe what she was seeing, but she could not deny the evidence of her own eyes. A man was in the living room. A strange man. He was stark naked and appeared to be trying to pull on his shorts.

Something Dreadful

"Hey!" the man shouted.

Startled and embarrassed, Jessica fled back to her bedroom and locked the door. Her mind raced, seeking a reasonable explanation for what she had seen.

Perhaps the man was a friend whom her father had invited over to the house to change clothes, she thought. But then why had he been moving furniture around, blocking the door? Jessica's heart sank as she slowly came to grips with the fact that something dreadful was happening.

A knock came at her bedroom door.

"Who is it?" asked Jessica.

No one answered. The knock came again. And again.

Jessica, knowing that her mother had a cell phone, picked up the phone to try to call her. But there was no dial tone. When Jessica's grandmother had called earlier, the intruder had lifted the receiver and left it off the hook.

Safe Storage

Cold terror began to seep into Jessica's bones. She wished that she had a gun. Her father had taught Jessica and the other children to shoot. Jessica had passed her hunter safety course and received her certificate at age twelve. She knew that her Dad always kept a .357 Magnum in his bedroom.

In deference to California's safe storage laws, however, Mr. Carpenter kept the pistol high up on a closet shelf, unloaded, and out of reach of the children. Even if she could somehow get to the other end of the house to retrieve it, Jessica knew she would have to climb up on something to reach the gun, scramble around for the bullets, and then load them. The man would be on her before she had a chance.

Mr. Carpenter had always taught the children that in an emergency, such as a fire in the house, they should open a window, push out the screen, and climb outside. She proceeded to do that.

From another part of the house, Jessica heard a cry that sounded like one of her sisters. But she put it out of her mind. "I knew I shouldn't go to investigate and I should go and get the police," Jessica later told reporters.

She slipped out the window and set off barefoot across an open field, cutting her feet as she ran.

A "Spooky" Man

The intruder was twenty-seven-year-old Jonathon David Bruce. The Carpenter family did not know him, but he lived in their small town of Merced, California, where he worked as a part-time telemarketer.

Bruce's strange behavior had long worried his neighbors. He slept all day, emerging only at night. "He was spooky," said neighbor Dawn Carter. "He would walk up and down the sidewalks talking to himself. Talking to the trees. He did a lot of wandering."

Bruce hated children. Neighbors had begun keeping their kids indoors when he was around. "He yelled about the children mostly," recalls Ray Adams, a neighbor. "He didn't like kids. And any little noise bothered him."

The police were frequent visitors to Bruce's house. He had spent a week in jail for resisting arrest, assaulting an officer, and being under the influence of methamphetamine.

Bruce's live-in girlfriend had left him several months before, with her two sons, ages four and five. After that, "he just sort of went downhill," said Adams. Bruce was evicted from his duplex apartment in August, just before he broke into the Carpenter home.[1]

To this day, no one knows why he picked on the Carpenters. We only know that, on the morning of August 23, Bruce armed himself with a pitchfork and entered their home, barricading himself inside with the five Carpenter children. Jessica managed to escape through her bedroom window. But her little brother and three younger sisters were left behind to face the madman.

A Scene of Terror

Thirteen-year-old Anna was the first victim. When Bruce failed to get into Jessica's room, he proceeded to Anna's bedroom, ordering her to lie on the bed. Then he began jabbing at her with his pitchfork, taunting her and yelling a stream of profanities while Anna screamed and tried to fend off the attack.

"He looked possessed," Anna later told reporters.

The only thing that saved Anna's life that morning was her little sister Ashley, age nine. Ashley appeared at her sister's bedroom door just as the man was pressing the pitchfork to Anna's forehead. Anna could feel the cold metal against her skin. She knew that, in another moment, she was going to die.

"Stop it!" Ashley yelled. "Don't hurt my sister!"

Bruce turned slowly to look at Ashley, the metal prongs of his pitchfork scraping along Anna's forehead. "Shut up!" he snapped.

But Ashley would not shut up. Over and over, she screamed at the man to leave Anna alone. He advanced toward her, pitchfork poised, looking—in Anna's words—like a lion about to pounce on its prey.

Ashley backed away into her bedroom as he came toward her. It almost seemed as if she were deliberately leading the man away from Anna. "It was like she knew she had to back into her room to get him away from her sisters," says Tephanie Carpenter, the mother.

Guardian Angels

Vanessa followed the two into Ashley's room. What she saw made her blood run cold. The man pushed Ashley against the wall and began stabbing her. She bounced off the wall and grabbed his ankles, biting and hitting him while he stabbed her again and again.

At one point, the man caught Ashley's head between his legs. The two sisters' eyes met. Blood was spraying out of Ashley from every direction. With her hand, she motioned for Vanessa to go. That was the last time Vanessa saw her sister.

The hallway was barricaded with furniture. Vanessa had to vault over these obstacles to make her getaway. Behind her, she heard Ashley screaming, "GO! GO! GO!" and she knew that the man must be close behind her.

She met Anna in the kitchen. The two girls looked back. To their horror, they saw that the man was right on their heels. Yet something appeared to be slowing him down.

"The girls both noticed that he was slow and clumsy all of a sudden," Tephanie Carpenter relates. "It was as though he was having to push his way through a football team. He actually fell onto the bar and was swinging the pitchfork in the air like he was fighting his way through a brick wall. We believe that there was a team of guardian angels at work."

Howling Like a Beast

The intruder had barricaded every exit from the house. The back door was blocked by a coatrack full of coats, an oak chair, and a heavy oak bookcase. Somehow, the girls managed to squeeze alongside the bookcase and coats and climb over the chair to gain access to the laundryroom.

As Vanessa pulled the wounded Anna through the door, Anna felt the wind from Bruce's hand on her leg. They shut the door behind them just in the nick of time.

But there was no lock. Vanessa held the door shut, knowing that she didn't have the strength to keep the man out. She braced for a struggle. Instead of trying to force the door, however, the man just knocked.

"Let me in," he said. "I won't hurt you. I'll be nice now."

They could hear Ashley screaming down the hall. Gradually, her screams went silent. In her heart, Anna knew that her sister was gone.

At last, the girls got the window open. They slipped out into the sunlight. Behind them, the man howled like a wild animal. "They said it sounded like the beast in *Beauty and the Beast*," said their mother.

911

Outside, the two girls met Jessica, who had already run to one neighbor's house and found it empty. Together, the three girls ran to another neighbor's house—a man named Juan Fuentes—and pounded on his door.

Covered with blood and growing weaker by the moment, the wounded Anna pleaded with Fuentes to get his gun and "take care of this guy." But he declined. Instead, he allowed them to use his phone to call 911.

The sheriff's deputies came quickly, but they arrived too late. John and Ashley were already dead. Seven-year-old John had been killed while he slept. When the deputies entered the house, the intruder charged them with his pitchfork. Whatever had made the man slow and awkward as he chased the girls down the hallway no longer seemed to affect him. Bruce sprang at the deputies, as swift and limber as a wild predator.

They shot him thirteen times, killing him on the spot.

CENSORED

MOST PEOPLE reading this book will never have heard of the Carpenter family or their ordeal. Unlike the school massacres and office shootings that seem to saturate network news coverage these days, the Carpenter tragedy received little national attention.

I first learned of the event months after it occurred. Like most Americans, I did not see it on the evening news or read about it in my daily newspaper. Instead, I heard Professor John Lott, the Yale economist who wrote the book *More Guns, Less Crime*, discussing the case on the Sean Hannity radio show on WABC in New York.

Professor Lott argued that the case revealed the fallacy of safe storage laws. By forcing people to keep their guns unloaded and out of children's reach, he said, the law prevents both children and adults from using firearms to defend themselves.

The Carpenter story made this clear. But most Americans never heard the message, said Lott, because all mention of guns and gun laws had been surgically removed from the story by the newswires. Lott says that an early account of the bloodbath distributed by one news service mentioned that guns were in the house, that the children were trained and ready to use them, and that the guns had been put out of reach, in order to comply with the law. But subsequent accounts failed to include this information.

As a journalist, I was intrigued by Professor Lott's observation. I ran a Nexis search and discovered that, with the exception of two local news stories in the *Fresno Bee* and two opinion columns—one by well-known gun rights advocate

Vyn Suprynowicz and another by Professor Lott himself—no accounts of the incident remained in the public record that so much as mentioned the gun angle.

No Heroes Allowed

"John Carpenter's children are probably dead because John obeyed the laws of the state of California," says Reverend John Hilton, the great-uncle of the Carpenter children. In Hilton's view, the tragedy could have been prevented had the children been provided with easy access to a loaded gun. Many of Hilton's friends and neighbors quietly agree.

Hilton—who is pastor of a Pentecostal church in Merced—recalls that when he was growing up, his father always kept a loaded Colt .45 in a holster fastened to the pantry wall.

"He was away a lot of the time, working on construction jobs," says Hilton. "But he made sure that gun was available to us, if we needed it. Without even looking, you could reach over and get hold of the handle."

In those days, it was common to let children use firearms. They learned to use them early, safely, and responsibly. And there were no school shootings. Ever.

Hilton, who is now sixty-six years old, says that he shot his first deer at age seven. By the time he was ten, he was proficient with the Colt .45 and capable of defending his family with it. Nowadays, Hilton's father would be putting himself at risk of imprisonment by giving children access to a loaded gun. California law imposes criminal penalties on gun owners if children are injured or injure others while using their guns.

Technically, if Jessica or any of the other Carpenter children had managed to get hold of their father's .357 Magnum and had gunned down the killer, their father could have faced criminal charges. It was for fear of the law that John Carpenter kept his gun unloaded and hidden on a high closet shelf.

"He's more afraid of the law than of somebody coming in for his family," Hilton told the *Fresno Bee.*

Likewise, the neighbor who refused to intervene may well have hesitated out of fear or uncertainty about the law. In today's legal environment, heroism is not encouraged. The way to stay out of trouble is to sit back and wait for the police—even if innocent children are being slaughtered right next door.

No Moral

According to their mother, all of the surviving Carpenter children have vowed that they would have shot the killer if only they had had a gun handy. In fact, the wounded girl Anna told her father that when she saw the man go after her sister Ashley, "I could have shot him right in the back of the head."

The children's bravery and fighting spirit were not considered newsworthy. These elements were left out of the story by the wire services. Instead, the Carpenters' ordeal was reduced to a depressing yarn of five helpless children attacked by a maniac, a tale without meaning, moral, or purpose.

MEDIA BIAS

THE CARPENTER CASE is but one example of a larger problem—the problem of media bias. In the Carpenters' case, their tale ended tragically. But many similar stories have a happier resolution. By some estimates, Americans use firearms successfully to defend themselves against criminals more than 3 million times each year. These incidents are rarely reported in the news.

Instead, we are immersed in images of mass shootings by psychotic killers. Each time such an incident occurs, spin doctors from antigun groups such as Hand-Gun Control Inc.

make the talk-show rounds. But no comparable outpouring of *progun* commentary can be heard in the wake of incidents such as the Carpenter family massacre.

Major news organizations show a clear bias in favor of gun control. A study by the Media Research Center released in January 2000 showed that television news stories calling for stricter gun laws outnumbered those opposing such laws by a ratio of ten to one. When it comes to guns and gun rights, we are hearing only one side of the story. Small wonder that few Americans are equipped to debate the issue intelligently.

"Where the press is free, and every man able to read, all is safe," wrote Thomas Jefferson in 1816. But when the press aligns itself with special interests—such as the antigun lobby—critical information is censored, and liberty itself hangs in the balance. "If a nation expects to be ignorant and free . . . it expects what never was and never will be," warned Jefferson.

Don't Blame Liberal Journalists

Many are quick to blame "liberal journalists" for the antigun slant they see in the media. Perhaps they are *too* quick.

It is undeniable that most journalists hold left-of-center views. A 1996 survey of working journalists by the Roper Center and the Freedom Forum showed that 89 percent had voted for Bill Clinton in 1992 (compared to only 43 percent of Americans overall who voted for Clinton). Only 4 percent of the journalists surveyed identified themselves as Republicans and only 2 percent as conservatives. Journalists clearly favor the Left.

Yet their "liberal" opinions probably have less impact on the media's gun coverage than most people assume. Rank-and-file journalists in large news organizations actually have little control over the political slant of their stories. It is management that decides how a network or newspaper will spin a particular issue. Ordinary journalists have little opportunity to vent their personal views.

The *New York Post*, for example, is generally recognized to be a conservative paper. Yet when I worked there in the mid-1980s, I found the newsroom filled with liberals. They grumbled constantly about the paper's conservative slant, but they did as they were told because it was company policy.

Liberal news organizations are no different. Political bias comes from the top. Rank-and-file reporters simply follow orders. The antigun bias permeating our mass media comes not from individual journalists but from the owners and senior managers of multibillion-dollar media conglomerates.

Don't Blame Liberal Politicians Either

"Liberal" politicians are another favorite scapegoat of gun-rights advocates. But in government, as in media, the forces promoting gun control appear to be larger than any party or faction.

It was President George Bush Sr. who banned the import of "assault weapons" in 1989 and promoted the view that Americans should only be allowed to own weapons suitable for "sporting purposes."[2]

It was Governor Ronald Reagan of California who, in 1967, signed the Mulford Act, which prohibited the carrying of firearms in public or in a vehicle. The law was aimed at stopping the Black Panthers, but affected all gun owners.[3] Twenty-four years later, Reagan was still pushing gun control. "I support the Brady Bill," he said in a March 28, 1991, speech, "and I urge the Congress to enact it without further delay."[4]

One of the most aggressive gun control advocates today is Republican Mayor Rudolph Giuliani of New York City, whose administration filed suit against twenty-six gun manufacturers in June 2000.

In March of that same year, New York City police commissioner Howard Safir—presumably with Giuliani's encouragement—put forth a nationwide plan for gun licensing, which would require owners to bring in their weapons once a year for "safety" inspections. The real purpose of the inspection, Safir admitted, was to keep tabs on guns and monitor whether or not they had been sold.[5]

Another Republican, New York State Governor George Pataki, on August 10, 2000, signed into law what the *New York Times* called "the nation's strictest gun controls," a radical program mandating trigger locks, background checks at gun shows, and "ballistic fingerprinting" of guns sold in the state. It also raised the legal age to buy a handgun to twenty-one and imposed a ban on "assault weapons," the sale or possession of which would now be punishable by seven years in prison. "This is something the rest of the nation should take a look at," said Pataki. "I hope this serves as a model."[6]

George W. Bush has kept a low profile regarding Pataki's gun crackdown. But when the program was first announced in March 2000, a Bush spokesman said, "The governor . . . wants to review it, but his initial response was positive."[7]

Journalist William Safire asked Richard Nixon, back in 1969, what he thought about gun control. "Guns are an abomination," Nixon replied. According to Safire, Nixon went on to confess that "Free from fear of gun owners' retaliation at the polls, he favored making handguns illegal and requiring licenses for hunting rifles."[8]

GUN ABOLITION—THE REAL GOAL

TODAY'S GUN-CONTROL promoters seem to share a view of gun rights every bit as restrictive as that of Richard Nixon. The ongoing case of *United States of America v. Timothy Joe Emerson* has helped make this clear.

In the midst of a bitter divorce fight, Dr. Emerson—a Texas physician—was hit with a restraining order from his wife. Unbeknownst to Dr. Emerson, federal law prohibits anyone under a restraining order from keeping a gun. He was arrested for unlawful possession of a firearm—even though he had legally owned the firearm in question for years.

A federal judge dismissed the charges, partly on the grounds that they violated Emerson's Second Amendment rights. But the U.S. Justice Department appealed. Arguing before a three-judge panel on June 13, 2000, Justice Department attorney William B. Mateja dropped an unexpected bombshell, revealing the government's true—but seldom stated—position on gun rights.

According to Mateja, the Constitution does not ensure ordinary citizens the right to keep and bear arms. Those rights stipulated in the Second Amendment apply only to members of a state "militia," Mateja claims. In today's terms, that would mean the National Guard. So if you're not a Guardsman, says the government, you have no right to own a gun. Any kind of gun.

Evidently stunned by Mateja's position, Judge William L. Garwood sought clarification. "You are saying that the Second Amendment is consistent with a position that you can take guns away from the public?" asked the judge. "You can restrict ownership of rifles, pistols and shotguns from all people? Is that the position of the United States?"

Mateja answered, "Yes."

The judge probed further. "Is it the position of the United States that persons who are not in the National Guard are afforded no protections under the Second Amendment?"

"Exactly," said Mateja.[9]

Dr. Emerson's case is now before the Fifth U.S. Circuit Court of Appeals. Whatever its outcome, it has clarified, beyond doubt, that our government—or at least powerful elements within it—recognizes no right to keep and bear arms on the part of ordinary Americans.

Most gun-control advocates swear that they have no intention of challenging the basic right to own a gun. But these soothing assurances should be measured against the reality of Mr. Mateja's words.

A Global Movement

The ongoing debate over the meaning of the Second Amendment is important. Yet forces beyond our shores may ultimately carry more weight in the battle over gun rights than our own Constitution. Year by year, our government is ceding more of its sovereignty to international courts and global regulatory bodies. Americans may soon find that foreign bureaucrats have more influence in defining our gun rights than did the Founding Fathers.

For instance, the United Nations, of which we are a member, actively promotes and coordinates efforts to ban or severely restrict firearms all over the world. At a UN conference in Cairo in 1995, the Japanese government proposed formulating "a common strategy for effective control of firearms at the global level." Since then, the UN has moved aggressively in that direction.

One 1998 resolution by the UN Panel of Governmental Experts on Small Arms (Report to the Secretary-General on "Measures to Regulate Firearms" #E/CN. 15/1998/4) recommends, among other things, that no person be allowed to own more than one gun, that hunters must store their firearms in sporting clubs, and that gun ownership should be denied to the elderly.[10]

To the extent that such measures are adopted globally, there will be intense pressure on the United States to conform, regardless of what our Constitution says.

THE SEVEN MYTHS

WITH SUCH powerful forces arrayed against gun rights, we should not be surprised that so little progun information manages to filter down to the public. Ignorance about guns has reached pandemic proportions. Children are not taught the history or meaning of the Second Amendment in school, nor do they learn later as adults. Much of what Americans think they know about guns is false.

The antigun case rests almost entirely on a set of deeply erroneous assumptions. I call them the Seven Myths of Gun Control. They are:

1. Guns increase violent crime.
2. Pulling a gun on a criminal endangers you more than the criminal.
3. Guns pose a special threat to children.
4. The Second Amendment applies only to militiamen.
5. The Second Amendment is an obsolete relic of the frontier era.
6. We should treat guns the same way we treat cars, requiring licenses for all users.
7. Reasonable gun-control measures are no threat to law-abiding gun owners.

We stand at a crossroads today. For the first time since our Constitution was drafted, a major component of the Bill of Rights—the right to keep and bear arms—is in danger of being jettisoned.

We must decide, as a people, whether or not we will allow this process to continue. Ignorance, fear, and hysteria are poor foundations upon which to base such a weighty decision. I hope the following discussion of the Seven Myths of Gun

Control will help clarify the issue of gun rights in the minds of those for whom it still remains cloudy.

Readers will notice that I have devoted considerably more space to Myth 1 than to the other myths. In many respects, Myth 1 is the most important, for it is in this section that I have sought to lay out the moral and political justification for an armed society, laying the groundwork for the discussions of other myths that follow.

MYTH 1

GUNS INCREASE VIOLENT CRIME

"THERE IS A lamentable streak of violence in the American character," writes journalist Jack Anderson in his book *Inside the NRA*, ". . . a lawless streak . . . a tendency to carry our freedoms to the extreme and flirt with chaos."

What does Anderson mean by this? Just how have Americans flirted with chaos, in his view? He offers such examples as the Whiskey Rebellion; the Civil War; decades of labor unrest; the assassinations of Presidents Lincoln, McKinley, and Kennedy; the riots of the '60s; and the fabled gunplay of the Old West.

In Anderson's view, these episodes distinguish America greatly from other nations. Violent as we are, he opines, allowing us to have guns is like pouring gasoline on the flames. The only logical solution is to take our guns away. Without them, the violence will abate. That, at least, is the view promoted by Anderson and his fellow gun-controllers.

Are they correct?

Anderson's argument rests upon four key assumptions:

1. America is more violent than other nations.
2. The United States has more guns per capita than any other developed country.

3. Lax U.S. gun laws encourage violence.
4. Countries with fewer guns and stricter gun laws have less violence.

Let us examine these assumptions one by one.

ASSUMPTION 1

America Is More Violent Than Other Nations

ON JANUARY 22, 1905, a crowd of between 120,000 and 200,000 men, women, and children marched on the Winter Palace in St. Petersburg, the capital of Imperial Russia, led by a socialist priest named Father George Gapon. Their plan was to present the Tsar with a list of demands that included an eight-hour work day, a minimum wage, an income tax, universal suffrage and education, amnesty for political prisoners, the convening of a constituent assembly, and so on.

The palace guard was forewarned. No sooner did the protesters arrive than soldiers opened fire, killing about five hundred and wounding thousands more. The incident—which became known as "Bloody Sunday"—helped spark the 1905 Revolution.

When I was a boy, my father was fond of pointing out to me the huge difference in scale between the Bloody Sunday massacre and our own Boston Massacre, in which only four men were killed by British soldiers. He found it absurd that Americans should refer to the killing of four men as a "massacre."

My father's parents were Russian Jews who had lived through three revolutions, a World War, and a Civil War before finally emigrating to America. They were luckier than most. Those who stayed behind in Russia suffered much worse in later years.

The one thing that always struck me about my grandfather was the deep, brooding depression from which he never seemed to emerge. He had had many adventures in the old country, including serving in the Russian army during World War I. As a boy, I was naturally curious to know more about these episodes. But Grandpa refused to discuss them. He greeted any and all questions about those years with a sad shake of his head. My grandmother, too, had suffered in Russia. Her frequent nightmares about that part of her life continued until the day she died.

My mother's parents came from a different part of the world, but they, too, knew war and oppression. They were not Jews but Mexican Catholics, who came to the United States as refugees, fleeing Mexico to escape the depredations of Pancho Villa. An estimated two million people died in the Mexican Revolution that raged from 1910 to 1920. By contrast, America's War Between the States—the bloodiest conflict in our history—claimed about 620,000 lives.

My grandparents—Russian and Mexican alike—would have laughed at the idea of calling America a violent nation. They knew what real violence was, even if Jack Anderson and his fellow gun-controllers do not.

A STORY WITH A MORAL

In September 1941, German SS troops, assisted by Ukrainian militiamen, gunned down 34,000 Jews at a place called Babi Yar. It is not far from where my grandfather grew up. When I was studying at Leningrad University in the summer of 1978, I visited Babi Yar with a group of my fellow American students. Strolling across the well-manicured lawns that now cover the site, I could not help wondering how many of the people buried there might be named Pogrebissky, my grandfather's surname before he changed it to Poe.

Historians tell us that the executioners at Babi Yar worked around the clock for two days straight. The victims were brought in batches, stripped naked, beaten, forced to lie face-down in a ditch, then machine-gunned. A few shovelfuls of earth were thrown on their bodies, and then the next batch was brought forward and made to lie down on the bodies before them.

Some armchair historians, with the courage that comes from 20/20 hindsight, have criticized the victims of Babi Yar for going to their deaths like sheep. But it is not so easy for unarmed families of men, women, and children to stage a spontaneous uprising against soldiers bearing submachine guns.

As Abram L. Sachar writes in *The Redemption of the Unwanted*, "This, the most appalling massacre of the war, is often alluded to as a prime example of utter Jewish helplessness in the face of disaster. But even the few desperate attempts, almost completely futile, to strike back served as a reminder that *the difference between resistance and submission depended very largely upon who was in possession of the arms* that back up the will to do or die" (emphasis added).

As citizens of the Soviet Union, the victims of Babi Yar were not allowed to keep or bear arms. Contrary to the views of Jack Anderson and company, the strict gun control enforced by Stalin's regime, and subsequently by the Nazi occupiers, did not spare the people of that region from violence.

Gun control never eliminates guns. It never stops violence. There are always plenty of firearms available, in every society, and plenty of people willing to use them. The only question is who has access to the guns and who does not. That question, in large part, determines who lives and who dies.

DEATH BY GOVERNMENT

SOME READERS may object to these examples. They may argue that events such as the massacre at Babi Yar are rare, while random gun crimes such as we experience in the United States are common. But the facts show otherwise. Around the world, many times more people are murdered in cold blood by organized government actions than are killed by any other cause, including combat. More people die violently in countries with strict gun control than in countries without it.

The world's foremost expert on mass killing is Rudolph J. Rummel, now Professor Emeritus of Political Science at the University of Hawaii. In his 1994 book, *Death by Government*, Rummel coined a new word to describe government-orchestrated mass murder. He called it "democide"—from the Greek word *demos* (people) and the Latin *cida* (killing).

Rummel's democide statistics do not include the number of people killed in combat. He counts only unarmed civilians murdered in cold blood, either by execution or other means, such as deliberately imposed mass starvation. Shockingly, Rummel found that the number of democide victims during the twentieth century (or at least until 1987, when his study ends) was four times the number killed in combat—nearly 170 million compared to 38.5 million killed in battle. Rummel writes:

> In total, during the first eighty-eight years of this century, almost 170,000,000 men, women, and children have been shot, beaten, tortured, knifed, burned, starved, frozen, crushed, or worked to death; or buried alive, drowned, hung, bombed, or killed in any other of the myriad ways governments have inflicted death on unarmed, helpless citizens or foreigners. The dead even could conceivably be near 360,000,000 people. This is as though our species has been devastated by a modern Black Plague. . . . The souls of this monstrous pile of dead have created a new land, a new nation, among us. Let in Shakespeare's words "This Land be called The field of Golgotha, and dead men's Skulls."[1]

DEMOCIDE U.S.A.

HOW DOES AMERICA rank on the scale of worldwide violence? Quite low, says Rummel. True, an estimated 583,000 civilians may have been killed by U.S. forces overseas during the twentieth century (mostly through aerial bombing). However, organized government violence against unarmed civilians has been rare on our soil.

Looking strictly at the twentieth century, lynchings and vigilantism by groups such as the Ku Klux Klan—often with the complicity of local government—have constituted the worst of it, accounting for an estimated 6,000 deaths since 1900. Another 6,000 Americans may have been killed in what Rummel calls "collective or intergroup violence," yielding a grand total of about 12,000 killed in the twentieth century. Tragic as this death toll may be, Rummel points out that it "hardly makes the United States the 'most violent country in the world,' as some journalists and academics contend."[2]

On the contrary, the United States does not even come close to qualifying for Rummel's list of the top seventeen democidal states of the twentieth century. Even if we count foreign civilians killed overseas—such as the Germans, Japanese, Rumanians, and Hungarians killed by U.S. strategic bombing in World War II—America's death toll pales before the 61 million innocent people killed by the Soviet Union, the 35 million murdered by the Communist Chinese, and even the 1 million killed by Yugoslavia's Tito regime.

GUN CONTROL AND MASS MURDER

AARON ZELMAN and Richard W. Stevens have written a book called *Death by Gun Control*, which largely builds upon Rummel's research. Unlike Rummel, who ignored the effect of gun laws on government-sponsored killing, Zelman and

Stevens confront the issue head-on. They found a direct correlation between gun control and mass murder. Indeed, according to these authors, every government that has set out to commit mass murder in the twentieth century has first disarmed its intended victims.

"'Gun control' laws cleared the way for seven major genocides between 1915 and 1980," says Zelman, who heads the organization, Jews for the Preservation of Firearms Ownership (JPFO) in Hartford, Wisconsin.[3]

To illustrate the thinking of tyrants, Zelman points to a remark Hitler made in 1942: "The most foolish mistake we could possibly make would be to permit the conquered Eastern peoples to have arms," said Hitler. "History teaches that all conquerors who have allowed their subject races to carry arms have prepared their own downfall by doing so."[4]

A Holocaust Survivor Speaks

On his Web site, jpfo.org, Zelman features an interview that he conducted with Theodore Haas, a Jewish survivor of the Dachau concentration camp. Asked whether camp inmates ever speculated about whether they might have resisted the Nazis had they been armed, Haas responded:

> Many, many times. Before Adolph Hitler came to power, there was a black market in firearms, but the German people had been so conditioned to be law abiding, that they would never consider buying an unregistered gun. The German people really believed that only hoodlums own such guns. What fools we were. It truly frightens me to see how the government, media, and some police groups in America are pushing for the same mindset. . . .
>
> There is no doubt in my mind that millions of lives could have been saved if the people were not "brainwashed" about

> gun ownership and had been well armed. Hitler's thugs and goons were not very brave when confronted by a gun. Gun haters always want to forget the Warsaw Ghetto uprising, which is a perfect example of how a ragtag, half starved group of Jews took up 10 handguns and made asses out of the Nazis.[5]

Actually, the Warsaw Ghetto rebels initially had "a few dozen pistols and hand grenades," according to author Stephen Halbrook. With these meager arms, they managed to keep 2,000 German soldiers and police, armed with tanks and artillery, busy for three days. Subsequently, the fighting escalated, with about 1,500 Jewish resistance fighters facing some 12,000 Germans. The rebels held out for twenty-eight days. "The Jews have actually succeeded in making a defensive position of the Ghetto. Heavy engagements are being fought there . . . ," ranted Joseph Goebbels in his diary. "It shows what is to be expected of the Jews when they are in possession of arms."[6]

Zelman suggests that America's traditionally permissive gun laws have so far helped spare us from the sort of bloodshed that runs rampant in other countries. Interested readers can purchase Zelman's and Stevens's book, *Death by Gun Control*, through the jpfo.org Web site, or by calling (800) 869-1884.

A "CULTURE OF VIOLENCE"

DESPITE THE EVIDENCE of history, the myth persists that America is more violent than other nations. Foreign lands may suffer war, dictatorship, and genocide on a scale unimaginable to Americans. Yet in the eyes of gun controllers, the high crime rate in our cities and the occasional eruption of armed psychotics in our schools and shopping malls somehow mark us as a singularly bloodthirsty people.

When a crazed gunman shouting antireligious epithets killed seven people in a Fort Worth church, in September 1999, *Washington Post* pundit E. J. Dionne Jr. was moved to write a column entitled "A Culture of Violence."

"We need to face the fact that we are an exceptionally violent nation," he fretted. "There is no developed country like ours when it comes to killing. . . . There is a lethal combination in our country of a violence-prone culture and gun laws that are more permissive than in any comparable nation."[7]

Predictably, Dionne put much of the blame on movies and television. But, more to the point, he argued that "the frontier spirit we revere as part of our history and culture may have a dysfunctional side when it comes to shaping our current lives in cities and suburbs."

In other words, Americans are cowboys at heart. And cowboys don't mix with cities. What we need, Dionne implied, is to become less like America and more like Europe, that fairy-tale land where a happy confluence of strict gun laws and tame people has supposedly given rise to a veritable garden of peace and civility.

The Myth of the Wild West

Dionne is here giving voice to the Myth of the Wild West—the notion that America's western frontier was a place of uncontrolled barbarism. Gun controllers lean heavily on the Hollywood image of the Old West to make their point. They claim that our high rate of gun violence today is a lingering vestige of the frontier culture. And they say that today's concealed-carry laws—which permit people to carry weapons on their person, in some states—threaten to bring back the chaos of frontier days.

However, the Old West may not have been nearly as wild as Hollywood portrays it. The dueling gunfighters, train robbers,

Indian fighters, and impromptu "necktie parties" familiar to us from the silver screen may have had their place on the frontier, but they were far less representative of Old West culture than decades of John Wayne and Clint Eastwood films may have led us to believe.

COWBOYS AND INDIANS

The worst violence in the Old West arose from conflicts between settlers and Indians. The death toll was high, yet probably lower than most people assume. "Although cowboy and Indian movies leave the impression that Indians were massacred by the tens of thousands, actual body counts show otherwise," states Rummel. To give just a few examples, anywhere from 70 to 600 Cheyenne may have been killed in the Sand Creek massacre of 1864, about 103 Cheyenne were slaughtered at Washita in 1868, 250 Shoshoni were murdered at Bear River in 1863, and perhaps 146 Sioux at Wounded Knee in 1890. Other massacres occurred, but these are considered some of the worst.

"Taking all the army–Indian battles and massacres into account, probably no more than some 3,000 Indians were killed in the years 1789 to 1898," writes Rummel. "Settlers and vigilantes likely killed a thousand more." When we add the death toll from harsh living conditions and other mistreatment imposed by the white conquerors—such as the forced march of the Cherokees in the winter of 1838–1839, called the "Trail of Tears"—Rummel estimates that a grand total of as many as 25,000 Indian victims may have perished from democide by 1900. This is a large number but still hardly comparable to the death tolls common in other countries.

The biggest killer of Indians was not the bullets of the white man but his diseases. By some estimates, as many as 95 percent of the Indians of North, Central, and South America may have perished from measles, smallpox, and other epidemics brought from the Old World. This was a tragedy of unspeakable proportions. But it was not a democide.

Fair Fights

War brings out the worst in people. We should not be surprised that fighting between whites and Indians gave rise to atrocities, on both sides. But Dionne said more than that. He said that America was "an exceptionally violent nation," to the point of being "dysfunctional." If true, we should see some evidence of this in the way that whites in the Old West behaved toward each other.

In recent years, a number of scholars have studied guns and violence on the Western frontier and have drawn a surprising conclusion. It appears that ordinary citizens may have been safer in the Old West than in modern cities such as New York, Detroit, and Washington. The findings of these scholars are summarized in a 1994 paper by Clayton E. Cramer and David B. Kopel.[8]

The paper cites historian Roger D. McGrath, whose book *Gunfighters, Highwaymen and Vigilantes* analyzes historical records from Aurora and Bodie, two nineteenth-century mining towns in the Sierra Nevada.

These were not typical towns. McGrath selected them specifically for their violent reputations. The populations of both towns were overwhelmingly male—90 percent, in Bodie's case. The brothels, bars, and gambling houses were busy every night of the week. Virtually everyone carried a gun. Aurorans preferred the Colt Navy .36 six-shot revolver, while Bodie-ites favored the Colt Double Action Model, nicknamed the "Lightning."

Just as in the movies, the drunken quarrels of young men in these towns would often be settled through "fair fights," in which the combatants would square off and draw their pistols.

They murdered each other at rates that sometimes exceeded the homicide rate of modern Washington, D.C.

An Armed Society Is a Polite Society

However, McGrath found that the violence in Bodie and Aurora was almost wholly confined to drunken young men in saloons. Death and violence came to those who welcomed and invited it. But decent citizens who avoided the saloons were left unmolested.

McGrath reports that the per capita robbery rate in Aurora and Bodie was only 7 percent that of modern New York City, while the burglary rate was 1 percent of New York's. Women were never robbed. There were only two allegations of rape in the recorded history of both towns, both against prostitutes.

McGrath quotes one long-time Bodie resident:

> One of the remarkable things about Bodie, in fact, one of the striking features of all mining camps in the West, was the respect shown even by the worst characters to the decent women and children. Some of the best families in town lived in the immediate neighborhood of Chinatown and the red-light district, and the women and children could not move out of their houses without passing saloons and all sorts of terrible places. Yet I do not recall ever hearing of a respectable woman or girl in any manner insulted or even accosted by the hundreds of dissolute characters that were everywhere. In part, this was due to the respect that depravity pays to decency; in part, to the knowledge that sudden death would follow any other course.[9]

The bit about "sudden death" is perhaps the most telling. The wild young men of Bodie and Aurora knew that they would be shot dead if they molested innocent townspeople, virtually all of whom were armed.

The Real Dodge City

Bodie and Aurora were noteworthy for their violence. Crime was far less common in other Western cities. The name "Dodge City" is analogous, in modern minds, with wanton gunslinging. Yet a 1968 study by Robert A. Dykstra showed that the combined murder rate in Dodge City, Abilene, Ellsworth, Wichita, and Caldwell—all notorious, wide-open cattle towns—was minuscule by modern standards, less than two murders per year for all five towns combined.[10] This pattern was repeated throughout the Old West.

Cramer and Kopel write:

> During the 1870s, Lincoln County, New Mexico was in a state of anarchy and civil war. Homicide was astronomical, but (as in Bodie and Aurora) confined almost exclusively to drunken males upholding their "honor." Modern big-city crimes such as rape, burglary, and mugging were virtually unknown. A study of the Texas frontier from 1875–1890 found that burglaries and robberies (except for bank, train, and stage coach robberies) were essentially non-existent. People did not bother locking doors, and murder was rare, except of course for young men shooting each other in "fair fights" in which they voluntarily engaged.

In short, as historian W. Eugene Hollon concludes, "the Western frontier was a far more civilized, more peaceful, and safer place than American society is today."[11]

THE NEW FRONTIER

In the suburbs of Syracuse, New York, where I grew up, many families owned firearms for hunting and self-defense. My father owned three. Firearms were plentiful in our community, but gun violence was completely unknown.

Later, I moved to New York City and took up residence in Alphabet City, a largely Hispanic neighborhood on the Lower East Side of Manhattan, notorious for drug trafficking. There I encountered a level of violence that I had never before witnessed.

On one occasion, I was nearly stabbed in the stairwell of my apartment building, when I walked inadvertently into the middle of a knife fight between two drug dealers. On another occasion, my wife and I had to take cover in a doorway when a gun fight broke out between drug dealers in front of our building.

As in Aurora and Bodie, the violence in Alphabet City was largely confined to a select group of people. In Aurora and Bodie, the troublemakers were miners and prospectors. In Alphabet City, they were black and Hispanic young men involved in drug trafficking.

THE END OF CHIVALRY

UNFORTUNATELY, TODAY'S gunslingers do not exhibit the same respect for innocent men, women, and children as did our frontier forebears. "In modern Washington, D.C.," write Cramer and Kopel, "criminals sometimes murder drivers who have stopped at a traffic light, simply for the pleasure of watching them die."

And, unlike the gunslingers of old, they have no fear that such actions will bring "instant death." As Cramer and Kopel put it:

> The Washington, D.C. government, which cannot protect those drivers (or anyone else) forbids the law-abiding populace to possess a handgun in their car, in their home, or on their person. . . . Bodie, Aurora, and the rest of the Old West had little high culture, and their streets were made of dirt and littered with horse manure. But a woman could walk alone

safely after dark in those towns; good people did not cower in fear and allow predatory thugs to terrorize the innocent.[12]

THE REAL "CULTURE OF VIOLENCE"

IF SUCH A THING as a "culture of violence" exists in America, then its modern exemplars would appear to be inner-city minorities, especially African Americans. According to U.S. Justice Department figures from 1992, white Americans commit murder at a rate of 5.1 per 100,000. For black Americans, the rate is 43.4 per 100,000—eight times that of whites.[13] In his book, *The Myths That Divide Us: How Lies Have Poisoned American Race Relations*, John Perazzo makes these observations, based upon 1995–1996 data:

> According to the *Uniform Crime Reports* prepared annually by the FBI, blacks, who make up roughly 13 percent of the U.S. population, commit some 42 percent of all violent crimes—including 40 percent of weapons violations, 59 percent of robberies, 42 percent of rapes, and 54 percent of murders. These offenders are particularly concentrated among the young. Contemporary black males aged fourteen to twenty-four are among the most dangerous demographic groups in American history. Constituting just 1 percent of our country's population, they commit at least 30 percent of its murders each year.[14]

Most black criminals target other blacks. "Though whites outnumber blacks by nearly six to one, black criminals account for 94 percent of homicides [against blacks] and 81 percent of all other violence against blacks," writes Perazzo.[15]

However, black violence also spills over into other communities. African American criminals prey on whites at a far higher rate than white criminals do on blacks. Justice Department figures show that in nearly 90 percent of all interracial crimes, a white person turns out to be the victim and a black person the perpetrator—a proportion that has remained remarkably steady for two decades (the figure was 87.49 percent in 1981 and 87.83 percent in 1999).[16]

YOUTH VIOLENCE

YOUTH VIOLENCE has received a great deal of media coverage lately. What has not received much attention are the different rates of violence that prevail among black and white youth in America.

Sensational media reports of suburban school shootings give the impression that Main Street, USA, is seething with potential violence. Yet Mike A. Males, a researcher for the Center on Juvenile and Criminal Justice at the University of California, Santa Cruz, has calculated that the murder rate among white American teenagers in 1995 (that is, the rate at which white youth, ages twelve to seventeen, were killed) was "virtually identical" to that of Canadian youth. By contrast, the murder rate among nonwhite youth in the United States was eight times higher than among Canadian youth in 1998.[17]

KIDS AND GUNS

Gun control advocates frequently point to Canada as a model of strict firearms regulation. Yet, even with our looser laws, white American teenagers are hardly more inclined to engage in gun violence than Canadian youth. Writing in the leftwing journal *In These Times*, Males points out that, in California, "where white households are the most likely to harbor guns . . . the gun death rate among white teens (three per 100,000) is as low as Sweden's or Canada's."[18]

A similar phenomenon can be observed nationwide. Males notes that the proportion of youth murders committed with guns in Canada is much smaller than that in the United States. Yet, when Canadian youth are compared specifically with *white* American teenagers, the difference narrows considerably. "The U.S. white-teen [gun] murder rate is pretty close to Canada's," notes Males. "Nonwhite youth are a different story: 180 murders, 147 by guns, in 1998, a rate five and eight times higher than for California white or Canadian youth."[19]

Race and Class

In keeping with his leftwing views, Males emphasizes the role of class in these differential murder rates. He contends that blacks commit more murders because, overall, they have less money. Males's figures do show that poor and affluent groups within the same race exhibit different levels of violence.[20] (Interested readers can download Males's book, *Kids and Guns: How Politicians, Experts and the Press Fabricate Fear of Youth*, at http://www.commoncouragepress.com/males_guns.html.)

Males's research notwithstanding, there are clearly cultural factors at work in the American crime wave of the last forty years that cannot be explained by income alone. As Perazzo points out, "During the Great Depression of the 1930s, when poverty and hopelessness plagued American life as never before or since, violent crime rates were far lower than today—for whites and blacks alike. Indeed, it was not until the 1960s, a period of economic prosperity, that crime rates soared."[21]

A TALE OF TWO NEIGHBORHOODS

African American author, talk-show host, and columnist Larry Elder made this observation in April 1999:

> A recent article in *U.S. News & World Report* compared two impoverished areas outside of Boston—South Boston,

predominantly white, vs. Roxbury, predominantly black. Both have high levels of unemployment, approximately the same percentage of children born to single-parent households and roughly the same number of people living in public housing. But the violent crime rate in Roxbury is four times higher than that of South Boston. What explains the discrepancy? Well, we know that poverty and single-parent status do not. This sort of leaves values, doesn't it?[22]

MEDIA DISTORTION

MANY READERS will be surprised to learn that violence among black Americans is so disproportionately high. The news media tend to give an opposite impression. If a white teenager shoots up his school, the event will be top news for a week. But the extreme violence that wracks some inner-city neighborhoods on a daily basis is ignored.

When I worked at the *New York Post* in the mid-1980s, around six murders per day would come in over the police wire. Virtually every case involved black or Hispanic people, killing each other over drug deals or domestic squabbles, almost always in certain predictable neighborhoods. We were instructed to ignore these cases. Only if a crime involved a white person—either as victim or perpetrator—did we spring into action. Killings among blacks and Hispanics were so common that they were not considered news.

GEORGE WILL'S PRESCRIPTION FOR AMERICA

"TWO STAGGERING FACTS about today's America are the carnage that is a consequence of virtually uncontrolled private ownership of guns, and Americans' toleration of that carnage," wrote *Newsweek* columnist George Will in 1991.

Once again, a leading "conservative" was speaking out against gun rights.

Will opined that it might be time to repeal the Second Amendment of the U.S. Constitution. "The Bill of Rights should be modified only with extreme reluctance," he wrote, "but America has an extreme crisis."

Will was pessimistic, however, about the possibility that Americans would take his advice. Why? Because the violence was almost wholly confined to poor, inner-city communities. "More teen-age males die from gunfire than from all natural causes combined," he wrote, "and a black male teen-ager is 11 times more likely than a white counterpart to be killed by a bullet. If sons of the confident, assertive, articulate middle class, regardless of race, were dying in such epidemic numbers, gun control would be a national imperative."[23]

In effect, Will was saying that middle-class Americans would only support gun control if their own children were being gunned down. His words turned out to be oddly prophetic. Only five years after he wrote them, America got exactly what Will said we needed: an epidemic of violence among white, middle-class teenagers. Or so it seemed.

REVENGE OF THE NERDS

IN FEBRUARY 1996, fourteen-year-old Barry Loukaitis entered his algebra class in Moses Lake, Washington, dressed in a black trench coat. He opened fire with a hunting rifle, killing a teacher and two students. Loukaitis was seemingly the first of a new breed—nerdy, small-town, white adolescents who shot up their schools at random, for no apparent reason. His act was duplicated, over the next few years, in several rural and suburban schools throughout America, culminating in the Columbine High School massacre in Littleton, Colorado, in which two teenage boys killed fifteen people.

No doubt, George Will was just as dismayed by these events as anyone. But they could not possibly have been better tailored to meet his prescription for America. Major networks gave saturation coverage to these massacres. Pundits went out of their way to emphasize the fact that the perpetrators were white and, in many cases, middle-class.

THE EPIDEMIC THAT WASN'T

ACCORDING TO MIKE MALES, however, the scare over killer white kids was largely a media fabrication. Random school shootings by white kids had been a rare but regular occurrence for decades.

In the past, national news organizations had shown little interest in such incidents. That changed in the mid-1990s, when white suburban shooters were singled out for lavish national coverage. All the attention notwithstanding, the actual numbers of such shooters remained statistically insignificant.

Males notes:

> It was a year between Springfield and Columbine, then two years between Columbine and Santee, in a secondary school institution that serves 25 million students (17 million of them white) daily. Mathematically, what zero to three students in a population of 17 million do in a given year is a long, long way from charting a 'trend.' Even 100 times that number would be impossible to analyze even as 'rare events.'
>
> . . . Frankly, given that the media and officials have announced they will award massive, permanent recognition to a white youth who shoots other white youths at school, I'm shocked such shootings don't occur every week.[24]

Law and Order?

Males has his own theory as to why the mass media have chosen to shine such a disproportionate spotlight on white suburban youth violence. In *Kids and Guns*, he writes:

> The law-and-order lobby faced a formidable problem. In the late 1990s, real urban gang violence had plunged. From their early-decade peaks, murder rates among Los Angeles's black, Hispanic and Asian youths fell by 85%, reaching three-decade lows by 1999. . . . As fears waned that mobs of ghetto "superpredators" would pillage pristine suburbs, *The [Los Angeles] Times*, along with other major media and authorities, cranked up a relentless crusade to convince suburban folks that they now were in dire peril from their own murderous, drugged-out kids. . . . Hence the creation of the suburban teen killer.[25]

In fact, youth violence declined sharply during the 1990s, not only among inner-city minorities, but also among all races. According to the U.S. Justice Department, the juvenile arrest rate for murder, rape, robbery, and aggravated assault fell by 36 percent between 1994 and 1999. The 1999 homicide arrest rate for juveniles was the lowest since 1966.[26]

Yet it was precisely during this period that media coverage of youth violence exploded. According to Males, the purpose of the scare campaign was to push a "law and order" agenda. However, the nature of the coverage itself—which has tended to focus obsessively on alleged "loopholes" in the gun laws—suggests that pushing gun control was more important to the scaremongers than the more nebulous goal of "law and order."

KILLER WHITE KIDS

DESPITE THE LACK of statistical support, network news broadcasts, cable talk shows, and even stand-up comedy routines relentlessly promoted the notion that killer white kids had become a major menace to society. In July 1999, three months after the Columbine massacre, black comedian Chris Rock joked on HBO that school shootings were getting so bad, he jumped out of a hotel elevator the other day when two white teenagers got on.

"If you are white and under 21," he said, "I am running for the hills." Rock predicted that pretty soon, "You're gonna have little white kids saying, 'I want to go to a black school, where I'm safe.'"[27]

On a more serious note, Rev. Jamal Harrison Bryant, director of the youth and college division of the National Association for the Advancement of Colored People (NAACP), observed that the school shooting epidemic proved that "youth violence is not a black issue. If you look at the school shootings that have happened around the country in recent years, all of them were done by Caucasian perpetrators. Yet America still thinks of violence with a black face."[28]

BLAMING GUNS

OF COURSE, all of this was just grandstanding. The NAACP was well aware that violence remained overwhelmingly concentrated among inner-city minorities. On July 12, 1999, it issued a press release stating: "Firearm homicide has been the leading cause of death among young African American males for nearly 30 years."

In that release, the NAACP blamed the problem on guns. "Easily available handguns are being used to turn many of our communities into war zones . . . ," said NAACP president Kweisi Mfume. "Urban communities have sadly become so accustomed to the prevalence of firearms in their neighborhoods that they are no longer shocked at the sound of gunfire."

Mfume failed to note that guns were plentiful not only in black neighborhoods but also in everyone else's neighborhood. Nearly half of all U.S. households own at least one gun. One in four keeps them loaded at all times.[29] Yet only in black and Hispanic urban communities has abuse of firearms become widespread.

Mfume announced that the NAACP intended to sue the gun industry for "negligent marketing," by which he meant "dumping firearms in oversaturated markets," such as black urban communities. He thus sought to fight black crime by making it harder for all Americans to obtain guns, even the vast majority, of all races, who are peaceful, law-abiding citizens.

BREAKING THE TABOO

THE MASS MEDIA failed to question the logic behind the NAACP's lawsuit. Indeed, the press seemed to applaud Mfume's move. But one man spoke out. He was author and columnist David Horowitz.

In an August 16, 1999, column in Salon.com, entitled "Guns Don't Kill Black People, Other Blacks Do," Horowitz systematically defied every journalistic taboo surrounding race and guns in America.

Regarding the NAACP lawsuit, Horowitz asked, "Am I alone in seeing this as an absurd act of political desperation by the civil-rights establishment? What's next? Will Irish Americans sue whiskey distillers, or Jews the gas company?"

The lawsuit, said Horowitz, was feeding into "a fantasy in which African-Americans are no longer responsible for anything negative they do, even to themselves."

He denounced the NAACP's "racist insinuation that whites are somehow the cause of those 'disproportionate' violent deaths [among black males], just as whites are the implied cause of nearly every other social pathology that afflicts the African-American community."

"A Real, Live Bigot"

This is not the sort of op-ed piece that you are likely to read in your local paper. Guns, race, and violence in America are seldom addressed with such candor. In view of what happened to Horowitz next, it is not hard to understand why. Only a week after his article appeared, Horowitz was denounced as a "bigot" in *Time* magazine.

In a column entitled "A Real, Live Bigot," black pundit Jack E. White wrote, "Last week . . . I ran across a column by a prominent right-wing ideologue named David Horowitz. . . . It reminded me that blatant bigotry is alive and well, even on one of the Internet's otherwise most humane and sophisticated websites. So many racists, so little time!"[30]

While conceding that Horowitz might have had a point in criticizing the NAACP's antigun crusade, White took exception to what he called Horowitz's "blanket assault on the alleged moral failures of African Americans. . . ."

"Well, what does Horowitz want us to do, go back to Africa?" he asked rhetorically.

STONEWALLED

In Stalin's Russia, the mere suggestion that you might be a *vrag naroda*—an enemy of the people—was enough to get you dragged from your home in the middle of the night and shot in the back of the head. In seventeenth-century Salem, Massachusetts, all it took was for someone to call you a witch.

The charge of racial bigotry has acquired a similar power in our society. The charge need not be true. It can be made recklessly and groundlessly. Yet it still has the power to destroy. A denunciation such as that directed at Horowitz in *Time* magazine might have ruined a lesser man. But Horowitz fought back.

He fired off a letter to *Time* editor Walter Isaacson, in which he called White's column "an outrage" and criticized "*Time*'s failure to exercise responsible editorial control. . . ."

"The question I ask you is: 'How do I get my reputation back?'" wrote Horowitz.

Time refused to apologize. Moreover, its letters editor declined to print a letter of protest that Horowitz had written, unless he agreed to allow it to appear in a tightly edited form that made it appear whiny and defensive.

"This is unacceptable," Horowitz told her. "I want a retraction and an apology."

"I don't think you're going to get one," she responded.

In an interview with *New York Press*, Horowitz observed, "I would really be dead meat if it weren't for the Internet." Salon.com allowed Horowitz to post an open letter of protest against *Time*, and cyber-journalist Matt Drudge defended him on his popular Drudge Report Web site. At least, said Horowitz, "My case is out there."

Time never did apologize. But the magazine's unfairness had been publicly exposed. *Time* went out of its way to make clear to Horowitz that it did not share White's view of him as a "bigot." And—perhaps not coincidentally—when Horowitz's next book, *Hating Whitey and Other Progressive Causes* was released, *Time* gave it an unexpectedly good review.

A LIFELONG OBSESSION

I HAVE SOMETHING of a personal stake in the events described here, for David Horowitz is my boss. Since June 2000, I have had the honor of serving him as editor of his Web site, FrontPageMagazine.com.

It is hard to imagine any charge less appropriate to level against this man than that of "bigot." For his entire life, Horowitz has been brooding over the question of how to heal America's racial wounds.

In his book *Radical Son*, Horowitz describes his upbringing as a "red-diaper baby," born in 1939 to Jewish parents in New York City, both of whom were dedicated Communists. In the radical activist culture that pervaded his family, the cause of the American "Negro" held the status of holy crusade. Horowitz writes:

> In our political catechism, the suffering of the Negro people was always a central image. The crime against the Negro was like an American crucifixion, and we constantly used it to pierce the veil of American benevolence, revealing the inequality and oppression underneath.[31]

Consequently, the black singer and Communist activist Paul Robeson—whom Horowitz calls "the enduring hero of my political youth"—held exalted status in the eyes of the leftist community. Horowitz remembers that "a palpable reverence filled the air" when Robeson sang at political rallies. His "sonorous bass was like a great bell that made your bones resonate with its sound. . . . Its sound filled every bosom in the room with a glow of satisfaction, as though his presence confirmed our truth."[32]

The Chosen People

Horowitz's early indoctrination in the cause of black liberation helped shape the course of his life and, indeed, that of his whole generation. He writes:

> Robeson's presence as a god in our midst seems prophetic to me now. In my radical generation, blacks would replace the proletariat in our imaginations as the Chosen People. People who were going to lead the rest of us to the Promised Land.[33]

Horowitz was only nine years old in 1948 when he attended his first civil rights rally, in support of equal employment opportunities for blacks. He joined the campus NAACP at Columbia. After moving to Berkeley in 1968 and becoming coeditor of *Ramparts*—a leading radical magazine—Horowitz befriended Black Panther leader Huey Newton and became a moving force behind the scenes in the Panther organization. Among other things, he organized—and raised $100,000 for—the Oakland Community Learning Center, a Black Panther school for inner-city children that was to become one of the group's leading public relations triumphs.

Turning Point

But the closer Horowitz got to the center of the Black Power movement, the more clearly he saw its corruption. In the Black Panther Party, violent, unstable leaders reigned over a criminal empire of drug dealing, prostitution, and other rackets. They maintained discipline through beatings, torture, sexual abuse, and murder.

In 1974, the Panthers told Horowitz that they needed an accountant. Still naïve about the full scope of the danger involved, he recommended a friend, Betty Van Patter. She appears to have learned too much. Van Patter went missing in December 1974, and her body was found two weeks later in the San Francisco Bay, her head bashed in with a heavy object.

It was widely assumed that the Panthers had murdered her, and, indeed, private investigators later concluded that she was killed for having learned too much about the Panthers' drug and prostitution rackets.[34]

When Horowitz called Black Panther leader Elaine Brown after Van Patter's disappearance, she acted evasive and belligerent. Though she denied any wrongdoing, she told Horowitz angrily that "[Betty Van Patter] went around sticking her nose into everything, asking everybody questions. She knew all our little secrets."[35]

Neither the press nor police seemed interested in pursuing the matter. One local news reporter said that she would not touch the story unless black reporters did it first. The police said bluntly, "You guys have been cutting off our balls for the last ten years. You destroy the police and then you expect them to solve the murders of your friends."[36]

Overwhelmed with guilt, Horowitz collapsed into depression and anxiety. "Every day in the spring after Betty's death," he wrote, "tears would well uncontrollably in my eyes and blades of pain spike at my chest, as morning approached, until I would bolt awake in a futile effort to escape the visions of my broken life."[37]

Enemy of the People

The more Horowitz tried to talk about Van Patter's murder to other leftists, the more they turned against him. He wrote: "I spoke to some of my personal friends who were concerned about me and seemed genuinely saddened by Betty's death. But their questions quickly showed that they were equally concerned about the Panthers and even more about the political impact of what I might reveal."[38]

Horowitz began to wonder if his fellow leftists might even be reporting his words to the Panthers themselves, an act that could easily result in his assassination. He realized he could trust no one. It was wiser to keep his mouth shut. Horowitz experienced what he later called "the loneliness that closed around a person identified as an 'enemy of the people.'"[39]

Another white activist named Fay Stender was gunned down by an operative of Panther leader George Jackson. She was shot five times at point-blank range. Though she survived, Stender was paralyzed from the waist down. She subsequently committed suicide. As with Van Patter, the Left's response to her death was muted. Some even speculated that she must have been an agent or informer and that she had gotten what she deserved.

Horowitz himself had been accused of being a CIA agent by Panther leader Elaine Brown. After Stender's death, he finally took the hint. Horowitz realized that he was a marked man. "I went out and bought a gun," he writes. "It was a .38 Ruger, the first weapon I had ever owned."[40]

Man with a Mission

Horowitz never had to use that gun. The power of the Panthers faded soon afterward. Yet deep in his heart, he had declared war on the Left. Horowitz's conversion from Marxism was a slow process. He shed its teachings one by one, but eventually, he shed them all. By the early '80s, Horowitz had become a powerful spokesman for the conservative movement and one of the Left's sternest critics.

"I had schooled myself in Hegel and Marx, and where had they led me?" he later wrote. "I had worshipped the gods of reason, and they had delivered me into the company of killers."[41]

Horowitz vowed that he would never again hold his tongue in the face of evil. He has kept that promise. His bluntness in criticizing black leaders today has earned him widespread hatred on the Left.

When African American novelist Ishmael Reed accused him of racial insensitivity, Horowitz responded in these words:

> I have three black granddaughters for whom I want the absolute best that this life and this society have to offer. My extended black family, which is large and from humble origins in the Deep South, contains members who agree and who disagree with my views on these matters. But all of them understand that whatever I write on the subject of race derives from a profound desire for justice and opportunity for everyone in this country, including my extended black family. It springs from the hope that we can move towards a society where individuals are what matters and race is not a factor at all.[42]

The discussion of race, guns, and violence in this chapter may rub some people the wrong way. Yet it is offered in the same spirit and with the same earnest hope expressed by Horowitz in the passage above. I have learned from him that there is little to be gained by evasion and euphemism. If there is any salve by which our wounded society may be healed, candor would appear to be its first ingredient.

ON LIBERTY

IN COLLEGE, during the late 1970s, I read a book called *For a New Liberty* by Murray Rothbard. It persuaded me to become a libertarian. The term has grown fashionable of late. Everyone from the far right to the far left seems to be rushing to claim "libertarian" status. But few seem to understand what the word really means.

Like the Founding Fathers of this country, a libertarian believes that each and every citizen is endowed with the right to liberty. Basic rights and freedoms are not granted by the government in exchange for good behavior. They are ours by right, God-given and unalienable, which means that no government may take them away, for any reason, under any circumstance.

Even many defenders of gun rights fail to understand this simple concept. They approach the gun rights debate as if the American people are guilty until proven innocent, as if we are somehow obliged to prove our worthiness to keep and bear arms.

The Framers of the Constitution never intended that basic rights should be subject to this sort of debate or negotiation. They knew that once such a debate started, it would never end. One excuse after another would be found to chip away at our rights, until all had finally disintegrated.

The Real Question

A large part of the gun debate involves back-and-forth argument between progun and antigun college professors, each side armed with its own statistics. One side argues that guns increase violence. The other argues that guns in the hands of honest citizens reduce violence, by serving as a deterrent.

My sympathies are with the latter. In the pages ahead, I will present many statistics to support that view.

However, the debate over statistics begs a more important question. Suppose the antigun side should eventually win the statistics battle. Suppose it could be shown that the net effect of allowing citizens to keep and bear arms is that more people are killed. Would the government then be justified in repealing the Second Amendment and confiscating all arms?

A libertarian would always answer no to this question. Since rights are not granted in exchange for good behavior, they cannot be withdrawn for bad behavior. That is what it means for a right to be unalienable.

(I should make clear, by the way, that the libertarian perspective I am about to offer is my own. FrontPageMagazine.com is not committed to that philosophy, nor is David Horowitz, as far as I know. But the libertarian view, in my opinion, shines the clearest light into the murk of today's gun rights debate.)

THE UTILITARIAN TRAP

MANY PEOPLE TODAY have come to believe that rights are conditional. They believe, for instance, that if people are posting hateful or dangerous material on the Internet, then the Internet must be regulated. They believe that if people are making bad use of guns, then guns must be restricted.

Murray Rothbard gave a name to this sort of thinking in his book *For a New Liberty*. He called it "utilitarianism"—the notion that rights and freedoms take second place to utilitarian or practical concerns. In other words, if your rights are felt to conflict, in some way, with the greater good of society, then your rights can be taken away. He writes:

> Suppose a society which fervently considers all redheads to be agents of the Devil and therefore to be executed wherever found. Let us further assume that only a small number of redheads exist in any generation—so few as to be statistically insignificant. The utilitarian-libertarian might well reason: "While the murder of isolated redheads is deplorable, the executions are small in number; the vast majority of the public, as non-redheads, achieves enormous psychic satisfaction from the public execution of redheads. The social cost is negligible, the social psychic benefit to the rest of society is great; there-

fore it is right and proper for society to execute the redheads."[43]

A true libertarian would recognize that the rights of redheads are just as unalienable as everyone else's rights. Likewise, a libertarian recognizes the irrevocability of gun rights—including those of black and Hispanic gun owners—regardless of how poorly those rights may have been used, up till now.

A CHANCE ENCOUNTER

WHILE TAKING IN the sights of Moscow, during my student days in 1978, I ran into an elderly couple from New Jersey. "What a wonderful country!" the woman exclaimed. "There's no crime. You can walk the streets after dark without being afraid."

No crime? The irony of her statement was not lost on me. I knew that the Soviets had murdered tens of millions of people (61 million, according to Rummel). Surely this qualified as a "crime" of some sort. But I held my tongue politely.

Arguing would have seemed insensitive. I knew that, back home in New Jersey, elderly people such as they were prime targets for muggers and burglars. Who was I to begrudge them whatever small pleasure they might glean from strolling Red Square unmolested, under the watchful gaze of gray-uniformed *militsionyeri*?

Yet I wondered how deep their admiration for Brezhnev's police state really went. Did those dreamy looks on their faces mean they actually preferred Soviet dictatorship to our own system? I tried not to think about it.

TRADING LIBERTY FOR SAFETY

That chance encounter in Moscow returned to haunt me years later, when I stumbled across two disheartening statistics. The first was nationwide poll results showing that 83 percent of African Americans would support a ban on all gun sales, except by special police permit.[44] The second came from a Department of Housing and Urban Development survey of public housing residents, indicating that 68 percent believe that allowing police to conduct random searches for guns, without warrants, would improve safety in their projects.[45]

Like those elderly tourists in Moscow, black Americans are clearly fed up with crime. And who can blame them? Fully 50 percent of all murder victims in the United States are black. But like those short-sighted tourists, many African Americans appear dangerously willing to tolerate police-state tactics, in exchange for safer streets.

An authoritarian crackdown might well succeed in curbing crime. Did not Mussolini get the trains running on time? But African Americans would be naïve to expect our government to continue working in their best interests, once it has stripped them of their liberties.

A CONTRARY VIEW

WITH THE NAACP suing gun manufacturers and Jesse Jackson stumping for stricter gun laws, black leaders seem to have fixed their crosshairs squarely on the Second Amendment. But not all African Americans are cheering them on.

Niger Innis certainly isn't. Growing up in Harlem, Innis lost two brothers to gun-wielding killers. But these tragedies only deepened his conviction that an armed and vigilant citizenry is the best curb on lawlessness.

"Not every cop can be everywhere at all times," says Innis, who is national spokesman for the New York–based Congress of Racial Equality (CORE). "Decent men and women with families need to be able to defend themselves and their property. It's that simple."

More to the point, Innis sees gun control as a slippery slope toward outright gun confiscation. Loss of Second Amendment rights, he says, would leave both whites and blacks vulnerable, not only to criminal violence but to other forms of tyranny as well.

Disarmed and Disenfranchised

"Traditionally, when governments want to disenfranchise people, the first thing they do is disarm them," says Innis. "That was the case in Nazi Germany, when the Jews were disarmed. That was the case in the American South, after slavery."

Innis is correct, on both counts. On November 7, 1938, a seventeen-year-old Jewish refugee named Herschel Grynszpan shot and killed a German diplomat in Paris. The highly publicized shooting gave the Nazis the excuse they needed for a major crackdown.

German newspapers whipped up hysteria over the threat of Jewish terrorism. Then, on November 11, the Nazi government ordered Jews to surrender all firearms, clubs, and knives. Without weapons, the Jews were easily herded into concentration camps.[46]

Slaves and Guns

Southern slaveowners also understood the need to keep their victims helpless and unarmed, as gun-law expert Stephen P. Halbrook documents in his book *That Every Man Be Armed.*

"No slave shall go armed with a gun, or shall keep such weapons," declared an 1854 law of North Carolina. Violators received thirty-nine lashes.[47]

After the Civil War, white southerners tried to maintain their monopoly over firearms. Many states barred African Americans from owning guns. Local police, state militias, and

Ku Klux Klansmen rode from house to house, demanding that blacks turn in their weapons. Once disarmed, they were helpless against lynch mobs.

"Before these midnight marauders made attacks upon peaceful citizens," Representative Benjamin F. Butler of Massachusetts informed the U.S. Congress in 1871, "there were many instances in the South where the sheriff of the county had preceded them and taken away the arms of their victims."[48]

On the other hand, freedmen who kept their guns were able to fight back. Representative Butler described an incident in which armed blacks successfully resisted a Klan attack.

"The colored men then fired on the Ku Klux, and killed their leader or captain right there on the steps of the colored men's house. . . . There he remained until morning when he was identified, and proved to be 'Pat Inman,' a constable and deputy sheriff. . . ."[49]

CONTROLLING BLACKS

According to Halbrook, the Fourteenth Amendment temporarily stymied the gun-control efforts of white southerners. It forbade the states from passing any law that would deprive citizens of their constitutional rights, including the right to keep and bear arms.

But in the 1960s, fear of armed blacks soon got the ball rolling again. Race riots spread from city to city. The Black Panther Party urged African Americans to arm themselves for revolution.

The response from white America was swift and predictable. As liberal antigun crusader Robert Sherrill put it in his 1973 book *The Saturday Night Special*, "The Gun Control Act of 1968 was passed not to control guns but to control blacks. . . ."

In their fear of black unrest, white Americans had given birth to a Frankenstein's monster. The machinery of gun control set up in the 1960s is now being turned against its creators—a case of "the chickens coming home to roost," as Malcolm X would have put it.

Warrantless Searches

A glimpse of what may lie in store for white America can be seen in some of the extreme measures that have already been used against blacks.

In the early '90s, some cities experimented with "sweeps" of public housing projects, in which police, without warrants, would systematically enter and search every apartment for weapons. Bill Clinton praised the program, urging its adoption nationwide.

Project residents were divided in their opinions about the sweeps. Referring to Chicago Housing Authority chairman Vince Lane, who spearheaded the program in that city, one tenant told the *Chicago Sun-Times:* "He's using the Southern, Jim Crow, Ku Klux Klan method on his own people."[50]

Other residents declared themselves more than willing to give up their rights, if it would bring peace. "Sometimes you got to sacrifice your rights to save your life," Daisy Bradford told the *New York Times.* "As far as I'm concerned, the Constitution needs to be changed. The innocent people are being violated by the criminals."[51]

A federal judge struck down warrantless sweeps in 1995, calling them a clear violation of the Fourth Amendment. But in view of their popularity among public housing residents, it seems only a matter of time before some pretext is found to bring them back.

THE CIVIL RIGHT NO ONE TALKS ABOUT

Niger Innis believes that blacks are being hoodwinked by their leaders.

"The Jesse Jacksons and the NAACPs are mouthpieces of the liberal establishment and the gun prohibitionist crowd," he charges. "They are not serving their constituents within the black community. They're serving their masters within the liberal Democratic party."

According to Innis, the right to keep and bear arms is a fundamental freedom. Yet of all the major civil rights organizations, CORE is the only one defending it.

"My father [CORE national chairman Roy Innis] is a lifetime member and a board member of the National Rifle Association," says Innis. "We and the NRA are kindred souls, when it comes to the Second Amendment."

GOOD SAMARITAN

IN 1990, CORE defended Kenneth Mendoza, a nineteen-year-old Hispanic resident of East Harlem hailed in the press as a "Good Samaritan." Mendoza had rescued his pregnant neighbor from a knife-wielding intruder.

The woman called Mendoza her hero. But after gunning down the assailant with a .38 pistol, Mendoza was charged with murder and possession of an unlicensed weapon. CORE general counsel Mel A. Sachs managed to get both charges dismissed.

"No other civil rights organizations have spoken in defense of Good Samaritans," Sachs laments. Yet about 80 percent of Good Samaritans are minorities, he observes. CORE routinely defends such cases in court.

Shortly after Mendoza's arrest, the *New York Times* interviewed the "Good Samaritan's" neighbors, finding strong support for Mendoza's action. "There is a code of law we live by in this neighborhood: people have to survive," said Ralph Vello, twenty-five. "He did the right thing."[52]

The Right to Self-Defense

The code to which Vello referred is not unique to East Harlem. It is a timeless principle, enshrined in common law: the right to self-defense.

Since ancient times, society has recognized the right of free men to arm themselves in defense of their lives, homes, and families. Slaves, however, were often denied this right. Under the laws of William the Conqueror, the difference between free men and slaves was actually defined by ownership—or nonownership—of weapons.

"If any person is willing to enfranchise his slave," said the Norman law code, "let him . . . deliver him free arms, to wit, a lance and a sword; thereupon he is a free man."[53]

Innis believes that black Americans have an intuitive grasp of the link between guns and freedom, an understanding that will eventually force them to part ways with the Jesse Jackson crowd.

Referring to public housing tenants such as Daisy Bradford, who have supported warrantless sweeps, Innis remarks, "People in a housing project that is under siege might not care about an esoteric right, like the right not to be searched without a warrant.

"But those individuals damn well know what the right of self-defense is. And they know the power of having a gun on the premises.

"I'll bet if we were to go into that project right now, there would be many law-abiding, decent citizens that have guns in their households, and they are branded as criminals because of unfair gun laws. Those people in that project have a desire to protect themselves more than anybody else. And they'll do it by any means necessary."

HISTORY WILL JUDGE

Speaking in defense of gun sweeps, back in 1994, Bill Clinton dismissed the charge that warrantless searches violated people's freedom. "The most important freedom we have in this country is the freedom from fear," he declared before the tenants of a violence-plagued Chicago housing project.[54]

Clinton's words got a respectful hearing from those shell-shocked tenants. But our founding fathers would have seen right through them.

"They that can give up essential liberty to obtain a little temporary safety deserve neither liberty nor safety," chided Benjamin Franklin.

In the end, history will judge whether our generation cared more about saving its freedom or saving its skin. Should we manage to retain any semblance of our constitutional liberties, it will be thanks to the courage of men such as Roy and Niger Innis, who dared to speak out when all around them were silent.

A LIBERTARIAN APPROACH

TO SUM UP, it appears that the United States is far from being "the most violent nation on earth," as Jesse Jackson once called it.[55] By world standards, it is a relatively peaceful land. Yet we do have some extremely violent minority populations.

A "utilitarian" approach to this problem would be to enact different gun laws for different racial and ethnic groups—precisely the approach that was taken in the Old South and also, de facto, in public housing projects during the Clinton era. White people were not generally the targets of Clinton's warrantless gun sweeps.

But such a race-based approach would be fatal to liberty. It would violate the God-given rights of minorities. And it would soon be expanded to apply to everyone. In time, the chickens would come home to roost, as Malcolm X might put it.

The libertarian approach is to trust in freedom. Just as goods traded freely in a free market can be relied upon to find the right price, so a people allowed to keep and bear arms in a free society will eventually find equilibrium—a way to live in peace together. That is the faith upon which our country was built. I see no reason to abandon it now.

As we move on to explore the more practical pros and cons of gun rights in the pages ahead, I ask readers to keep this single, guiding principle in mind.

ASSUMPTION 2

The United States Has More Guns Per Capita Than Any Other Developed Country

IN APRIL 1999, an employee named Masaharu Nonaka burst into the office of Yoichiro Kaizaki, president of Bridgestone Corporation in Japan. Before the president's horrified eyes, Nonaka pulled out a kitchen knife, ripped away his shirt, and disemboweled himself, in the ancient ritual known as *seppuku.*

"The Japanese public was shocked by Nonaka's suicide . . . ," wrote Michael A. Lev, Tokyo correspondent for the *Chicago Tribune*. "But if there was a collective second emotion in Japan, it was relief that Nonaka only had access to a knife instead of a gun."

Lev implied that had the incident occurred in America, Nonaka—a thirty-two-year Bridgestone veteran angry about being forced into early retirement—might have entered the building with an AK-47 rather than a knife.

THE JAPANESE MODEL

THE HEADLINE of Lev's May 16, 1999 article—"Feeling a Bit Safer Under Japan's Gun Laws"—summed up his point of view. "Without guns," he enthuses, "the daily burden of paranoia one must carry around in a big American city is significantly diminished. So is the death toll." Lev's view is shared by many gun controllers today, who see Japan as the model of the future—an advanced, urban, technological society that has managed to control gun violence through its enlightened policies.

In Japan, it is completely illegal to buy a rifle, a handgun, or even a sword. Sportsmen may obtain shotguns for hunting and skeet or trap shooting, but only if they have a license. Without one, Japanese citizens are forbidden even to *hold* a firearm.

Getting a license is an exhausting process that can take months. After attending special classes, you must pass a written test, a shooting test, a safety exam, and a mental health screening, to ensure that you are psychologically stable and not addicted to drugs. Then you and your relatives must submit to a background investigation by the police. Among the factors that would disqualify an applicant are membership in any disapproved political or activist group.

Should you succeed in getting a gun license, you must store your weapon in a locker at all times, and your ammunition must be locked away separately. Moreover, you must provide the police with a map of your apartment showing the exact location of your firearm, just in case they might feel the need to stop by and confiscate it sometime in the future.[1]

Low Gun Crime

While the Japanese have done an efficient job of keeping guns out of the hands of ordinary citizens, Japanese criminals naturally have little problem obtaining what they need. About 1,500 gun crimes occur in Japan each year, perpetrated mainly by professional criminals with illegal, unlicensed weapons.

Even so, gun controllers are correct in pointing out that gun violence is low in Japan. If you are not a gangster, your chance of encountering it is almost nonexistent.

Police State

Should America become more like Japan? Before we jump to take the gun controllers' advice, we might first want to consider what life is really like there. As David B. Kopel documents in his book *The Samurai, the Mountie and the Cowboy*, Japan is essentially a police state. The cops keep full dossiers on every citizen. Twice a year, each Japanese homeowner gets a visit from a local cop to update the files on who lives there, how they are related to each other, what work they do, whether they work late, what sorts of cars they own, how much money they have, and so on.

Japanese police keep a sufficiently close eye on the community that they are able to include, in their year-end reports, detailed statistics on the sex lives of people under their charge. For instance, they report data on "Background and Motives for Girls' Sexual Misconduct," as well as data on how many juveniles are smoking, staying out late, or exposing themselves to "unsound companionship." Any groups that are perceived as critical or antagonistic toward the government—including environmental activists—are viewed as subversive and are closely monitored.[2]

"It Is No Use to Protest Against Power"

In Japan, a citizen has no right to trial by jury. If you are arrested, you can be held without bail for twenty-eight days, without ever seeing a judge. During that time, the police may interrogate you for twelve hours a day and may forbid you to stand up, lie down, or lean against the wall of your cell. Sometimes, when the twenty-eight days are over, the police simply arrest you on another charge and start the cycle over again. You may end up in jail for months, without ever being brought before a judge.

According to the Tokyo Bar Association, suspects in police custody are routinely tortured and beaten in order to obtain confessions. Sometimes prisoners attempt to disavow these confessions later. But Japanese judges have a habit of disregarding their pleas, even when they have the bruises to prove they were abused. Not surprisingly, the confession rate of Japanese prisoners is 95 percent. The conviction rate is 99.91 percent. One Tokyo police sergeant explained the high confession rate in these words: "It is no use to protest against power."

Amnesty International has declared the Japanese police custody system to be a "flagrant violation of United Nations human rights principles." Kopel writes, "To an American, especially an American concerned about civil liberties, the breadth of Japanese police powers is horrifying."[3]

In view of these facts, it is not hard to understand why crime is so low in Japan. Guns are not the only things kept under lock and key. People are, too.

The Sword Hunt

The harsh attitude of the Japanese toward gun rights—and, indeed, toward human rights in general—dates back many centuries to the samurai era. In the sixteenth century, a peasant soldier named Hideyoshi rose up through the ranks of the army of Lord Oda Nobunaga—a feudal warlord who had managed to conquer most of Japan. After Nobunaga's death, Hideyoshi took command of his army and finished the conquest. He became supreme ruler of the entire country.

In 1588, Hideyoshi proclaimed a "Sword Hunt"—*taiko no katanagari*. All commoners were commanded to turn in their swords and firearms, ostensibly so they could be melted down to provide nails and bolts for a temple housing a giant image of Buddha. A report by Jesuit missionaries noted that Hideyoshi "is depriving the people of their arms under the pretext of devotion to religion."[4]

Permission to Kill

However, the actual wording of Hideyoshi's decree revealed its true purpose. It announced:

> The people in the various provinces are strictly forbidden to have in their possession any swords, short swords, bows, spears, firearms, or other arms. The possession of unnecessary implements makes difficult the collection of taxes and tends to foment uprisings. . . . Therefore the heads of provinces, official agents, and deputies are ordered to collect all the weapons mentioned above and turn them over to the government.

Only the samurai or noble classes were allowed to retain their arms. No sooner had the peasants complied with Hideyoshi's order than the betrayal began. Rather than building a temple to Buddha, as he had promised, Hideyoshi used the melted arms to cast a huge statue of himself. He then forbade all peasants to leave their land without permission, reducing them to a status hardly better than slaves.

Hideyoshi's successor, Ieyasu, went a step further. He granted his samurai the right to execute any peasant on the spot, for any reason. It was called *kiri-sute gomen*—permission to kill and depart.[5]

The New Samurai

Japan's feudal system lasted until the late nineteenth century, when it was abolished by the Emperor Meiji, as part of a nationwide modernization and industrialization program. Many ex-samurai subsequently joined the new National Police Academy. The samurai aura has clung to Japan's police force ever since. "In modern Japan," writes Kopel, "the police are considered the new samurai, full of *Nihon damashii* (Japanese spirit)."[6]

Like the peasants of feudal Japan, today's Japanese are imbued, from earliest childhood, with a spirit of submission and conformity. They use the same word, *chigaau*, to mean both "different" and "wrong." A well-known Japanese proverb says, "The nail that sticks out will be pounded down."[7]

As Kopel notes, the low murder rate in Japan seems to arise from its culture, rather than from its gun laws. Murder rates are high in American prisons, even though the prisoners have no guns. In Japan, murder among prisoners is almost unknown. Robberies even *without guns* occur more than seventy times more frequently in the United States than in Japan.[8] Kopel also notes that crime was high in the former Soviet Union, though its gun laws were strict and its police far more ruthless than Japan's. He attributes the difference to the fact that "Japan has the socially accepted and internalized restraints on individual behavior that the Soviets lacked."[9]

The Global Samurai

Most Americans would not voluntarily submit to a system as authoritarian as Japan's. But in the area of gun rights, we may have such a system imposed on us whether we like it or not. The Japanese have been pressing hard, for a number of years, to sell their model of gun control to the rest of the world. And they are making progress.

In 1995, at the Ninth United Nations Congress on the Prevention of Crime and Treatment of Offenders in Cairo, Japan proposed the development of a global gun control strategy. The UN appointed an "experts group" to study the issue.

As columnist Tanya Metaksa notes in FrontPage Magazine.com, "The 11 so-called experts, including 3 Canadians, 2 Japanese, and 1 Russian, were chosen for their bias in favor of global gun control. The first item on the group's agenda was to quickly begin gathering governmental and non-governmental organizations (NGOs) in support of their position that citizens should not be allowed to possess personal firearms for self-protection."[10]

Over the next fourteen months, the group conducted a worldwide study of guns and gun laws in sixty-nine different countries. Not surprisingly, the study concluded that countries with stricter gun laws had less violent crime. Released in 1997, the UN International Study on Firearm Regulation gave a big boost to the Japanese antigun agenda.

MORE GUNS, MORE CRIME

USING 1994 FIGURES, the study showed that the U.S. homicide rate was 9 per 100,000—of which 70 percent involved the use of firearms—while the homicide rate in England was only 1.4 per 100,000 (of which 9 percent involved firearms).

Citing figures such as these from many different countries, the study concluded that there was a direct correlation between guns and crime. Countries with looser gun laws such as the United States had a bigger problem with violent crime than countries, such as England, that had strict gun laws. In other words, the more guns available in a country, the more crime that country suffered.

A SIGNIFICANT OVERSIGHT

It seemed an open-and-shut case. But constitutional scholar Stephen P. Halbrook noticed some significant holes in the UN experts' reasoning.

"Such comparisons can be dangerous," he cautioned in a June 4, 1999, article in the *Wall Street Journal*'s European edition.

"In 1900, when England had no gun controls, the homicide rate was only 1.0 per 100,000. Moreover, using data through 1996, the U.S. Department of Justice study 'Crime and Justice' concluded that in England the robbery rate was 1.4 times higher, the assault rate was 2.3 times higher, and the burglary rate was 1.7 times higher than in the U.S. This suggests that lawfully armed citizens in the U.S. deter such crimes."

Even more significantly, the UN researchers had completely overlooked an important European country whose statistics turned their theory on its ear. Halbrook wrote: "The U.N. study omits mention of Switzerland, which is awash in guns and has substantially lower murder and robbery rates than England, where most guns are banned."

Indeed, noted Halbrook, "More per capita firepower exists in Switzerland than in any other place in the world, yet it is one of the safest places to be."[11]

ARMED NEUTRALITY

MANY READERS will be surprised to learn that Switzerland—not the United States—has the highest per capita firepower in the world. We associate Switzerland with peace, neutrality, and pacifism. And rightly so.

Switzerland is one of the few European countries that has managed to stay out of both World Wars and to avoid dictatorship, invasion, and revolution. In tribute to its longstanding neutrality and stability, Switzerland is frequently asked to play host to major peace conferences.

Yet no country in the world is more heavily armed, man for man, than Switzerland. It can be argued that the peace and freedom enjoyed by generations of Swiss may be a direct result of that country's long tradition of what it calls "armed neutrality."

William Tell

According to legend, the Swiss nation came into being in 1291. At that time, the mountain tribes of the Alps were ruled by the Hapsburg emperors of Austria. Governor Gessler of Uri, a Hapsburg puppet, tried to impress his authority on the Swiss by placing a hat atop a pole at Altdorf and commanding that anyone who passed must doff his own hat in respect, exactly as if Gessler himself were standing there.

A local man named William Tell persistently failed to do it. One day, he was arrested and brought before Gessler. As punishment for his insolence, he was sentenced to shoot an apple from the head of his six-year-old son at 120 paces, with his bow. If he refused, both father and son would be executed.

Expert archer that he was, Tell hit the apple dead-on. Gessler then asked him why he had a second arrow in his quiver. Tell explained that, had the first arrow hit his son, he would have shot the second right into Gessler's heart.

The Uprising

The legend relates that Gessler, infuriated by this threat, took back his word and condemned Tell to life in prison. But Tell escaped and caught Gessler in an ambush, shooting that second arrow into the tyrant's heart, just as he had promised. Tell's act inspired an uprising against the Austrians. The three cantons of Uri, Schwyz, and Unterwalden formed an alliance, which became the basis of the Swiss Confederation.

No one knows to what extent the legend of William Tell is true. Some even argue that the man never existed. Whether he did or not, the story of Tell's defiance symbolizes Switzerland's 200-year struggle to free itself from Austrian rule. His indomitable spirit and perfect marksmanship inspire Swiss fighting men to this day.

No Kings or Presidents

Centuries before Lexington and Concord, the Swiss decided that they would never again bow before any king. They have kept their vow. During their 200-year struggle against Austria, they developed a system of self-rule that remains, to this day, the most democratic of any nation.

In Switzerland, power resides in the local cantons, or states, which presently number twenty-six. There is no strong central government and no president.[12] There is not even a general to command the army. In time of war, the Swiss appoint a temporary general. To allow any one man to hold such power in peacetime is regarded as dangerous and undemocratic.[13]

Citizen Soldiers

The Swiss really have no army at all, in the conventional sense. The people themselves are the army. In Switzerland, every able-bodied man between the ages of twenty and forty-two serves in the active militia. Swiss law requires its citizen soldiers to store their gear at home, ready for action. Every man keeps a Sturmgewehr 90 assault rifle with ammunition in his closet.

Switzerland has only about 1,500 full-time soldiers. But an army of 650,000 militiamen can be mobilized in twenty-four hours—a force larger than all U.S. forces stationed in Europe. That is what the Austro-Hungarian diplomat Klemens Fürst von Metternich meant when he remarked, during the Napoleonic era, that "Switzerland does not have an army; it is an army."

Unconquerable

Switzerland's militia system has made it virtually unconquerable. Other neutral countries, such as Holland and Belgium, are routinely invaded whenever war breaks out between their larger neighbors. But Switzerland is left in peace.

It is not only the huge numbers of its army that discourages conquerors but also their expertise. By law, every militiaman must join a rifle club. Target shooting is one of the favorite weekend pastimes of Swiss men, women, and children. Thanks to constant practice, from childhood on, Swiss marksmanship rivals that of the legendary William Tell.

"Shoot Twice"

Soldiers in other countries cannot make the same boast. Most never hold a rifle before basic training. This puts them at a great disadvantage when facing skilled marksmen, such as the Swiss.

In 1916, while World War I raged in Europe, the U.S. Senate published a report on the Swiss militia entitled *The Military Law and Efficient Citizen Army of the Swiss.* It included this comment by American attaché Eric Fisher, regarding the shooting skills of French soldiers: "The only shooting that they had ever done was gallery shooting at a range of about 40 yards, and they were singularly poor even at this." The German soldiers, he said, "shoot poorly from an American standpoint, but do better than the French."[14]

By contrast, Swiss militiamen were trained to hit a target at 300–400 meters.[15] In mountain fighting, Swiss snipers perched on every ledge could pick off invading troops at their leisure.

In the saber-rattling years before World War I, German generals pondered the idea of marching through Switzerland to outflank the French. But they never followed through. A popular postcard of the era showed Kaiser Wilhelm II asking a Swiss militiaman what he would do if half a million German soldiers marched against the quarter-million-strong Swiss army. "Shoot twice," the militiaman replied.[16]

It was largely because the Germans knew there were teeth behind such threats that they abandoned their invasion plan.

Their Finest Hour

The greatest threat to Swiss liberty in modern times came during World War II. As Stephen Halbrook describes in his book *Target Switzerland*, it was the militia system, once again, that saved the day.

From the moment Hitler took power in 1933, the Nazis made clear that they viewed Switzerland as a long-lost German province. With 70 percent of the Swiss population speaking German, the Nazis believed that its proper place was within the Reich. The Swiss disagreed.

In April 1940, the Germans stationed fifteen Wehrmacht divisions on the Swiss frontier. Their plan was to outflank the French army, with one pincer advancing through Belgium and Holland in the north and another through Switzerland in the south.

No Surrender

The Swiss commander, General Henri Guisan, broadcast an order by radio to the entire country, instructing the militia to fight to the death. There would be no surrender. Indeed, even if it should appear that the government itself was surrendering, said Guisan, the militia should fight on, ignoring any orders to lay down their arms. The order stated:

> If by radio, leaflets or other media any information is transmitted doubting the will of the Federal Council or of the

> Army High Command to resist an attacker, this information must be regarded as lies of enemy propaganda. Our country will resist aggression with all means in its power and to the bitter end.

Only a self-sufficient militia of citizen soldiers could carry out such a command, for only they had the equipment, training, and decentralized organization to fight on their own, without government support. And the Germans knew it.

Indeed, the German minister in Bern, Otto Kocher, reported to his superiors that junior officers within the Swiss militia had resolved that if, "in an invasion, a commanding officer showed signs of giving way before overwhelming enemy forces, these officers have mutually pledged themselves to shoot such a commander on the spot."

The threatened German invasion never came.[17] Had the French, Dutch, Belgians, Norwegians, Danes, and other European nations showed such stoutness, World War II might never have occurred.

A Warrior Culture

Switzerland's warrior spirit did not materialize out of thin air. It is carefully cultivated in the young, from the earliest age. Children learn respect for firearms in the intimacy of their homes, where they grow up watching their fathers cleaning and maintaining their assault fires at the kitchen table. Stephen Halbrook writes:

> By car or train, you see shooting ranges everywhere. . . . If there is a *Schuetzenfest* (shooting festival) in town, you will find rifles slung on hat racks in restaurants, and you will encounter men and women, old and young, walking, biking and taking the tram with rifles over their shoulders, to and from

> the range. They stroll right past the police station and no one bats an eye. (Try this in the U.S., and a SWAT Team might do you in.)
>
> [T]here have been no school massacres in Switzerland, where guns and kids mix freely. At shooting matches, bicycles aplenty are parked outside. Inside the firing shelter, the competitors pay 12-year-olds tips to keep score. The 16-year-olds shoot rifles with men and women of all ages. In fact, the tourist brochure "Zurich News" recommends September's *Knabenschiessen* (boy's shooting contest) as a must-see: "The oldest Zurich tradition . . . consists of a shooting contest at the Albisguetli (range) for 12 to 16 year-old boys and girls and a colorful three-day fun-fair." The event has been held since 1657, and attracts thousands of teenage participants and spectators.[18]

The True Swiss Is Armed

Guns remain at the core of Swiss experience through adulthood. Every able-bodied man undergoes 118 days of basic training around age twenty. He trains with people from his own canton. This is important in a country with four official languages (German, French, Italian, and Romansch). The men he trains with speak his language and will likely be his friends and neighbors for life.

"The recruit school brings the young men of the country together at a very impressionable age . . . ," writes American scholar Carol Schmid. "Besides civic instruction which stresses the Swiss national position and attitude, it introduces Swiss, from whatever linguistic group, to the varied landscape of their country, and gives them something to talk about for the rest of their lives."[19]

It also connects them with the traditions of their warrior ancestors. "The true Swiss is armed," writes Jonathan Steinberg in *Why Switzerland?* "Popular culture has been saturated with military activities, with rifle competitions, with gun lore, with a certain Alpine bellicosity, with the wrestling, the drinking and the ponderous camaraderie. . . . The modern Swiss army still has a vestigial atmosphere which goes back to the unruly crowd of armed, free peasants who slaughtered the flower of Burgundian chivalry by flailing at them with five-foot pikes."

An old Swiss folk song says:

Was bruucht e rachte Schwyzerma
nes subers Gwehril a der Wand,
nes heiters Lied furs Vaterland.

What does a true Swiss man need?
A clean little gun on the wall
And a cheerful song for the Fatherland.

So fundamental is the warrior spirit to the true Swiss—or *rechter Schweizer*—that, for centuries, every free man has been required to bring a sword to the *Landsgemeinde*, or town hall meeting, as a token of his citizenship. The tradition is observed to this day.[20]

A TOKEN OF POWER

In the sixteenth century, the Florentine savant Niccolo Machiavelli traveled through Switzerland and marveled at its citizen's militia. He noted in 1532 that a "republic armed with its own citizens is less likely to come under the rule of one of its citizens than a city armed with foreign soldiers." He further observed that "the Swiss are most armed and most free" *(armatissimi e liberissimi)*.

The Swiss understand as clearly as did Machiavelli that they owe their freedom to their arms. "If weapons are a token of power," goes one Swiss dictum, "then in a democracy they belong in the hands of the people." The Swiss are also fond of saying: "If the government cannot trust the people, the people cannot trust the government."[21]

Happily for the Swiss, their government bestows total trust in its people. There are virtually no restrictions on the purchase of weapons for law-abiding citizens. Indeed, the government does all in its power to encourage people to acquire arms and ammunition.

Guns for All

"There is no real impediment to the Swiss buying any type of gun," writes Kopel. With a population of about seven million people, Swiss citizens own approximately two million guns, including half a million pistols and 600,000 fully automatic assault rifles. Militiamen keep their rifles when they retire from active service. And when the government upgrades its military rifles, it sells off the old ones to the public. Ammunition is sold by the government at cost, to encourage people to engage in target practice. People may buy any type of ammunition, including hollow-point bullets. In addition, the government sells antitank weapons, howitzers, antiaircraft guns, cannons, and various types of machine guns to the public.

Permits are required to buy military arms and ammunition, and fully automatic weapons must be registered with the government. However, permits are easily obtainable by every law-abiding citizen. They are a mere formality, quite unlike the cumbersome registration, waiting-period, and background-check procedures now being introduced in the United States, which are specifically designed to discourage and disqualify as many people as possible from buying arms.

In Switzerland, no permit is required to buy semiautomatic rifles. Dealers do not even record sales of hunting rifles or small-bore rifles. In twenty-one out of Switzerland's twenty-six cantons, sales of guns from one individual to another are completely unregulated. The government imposes no restrictions on carrying long guns in any canton, and—in eleven cantons—there are none on carrying handguns either.

STILL FREE

ONE OF THE most stunning falsehoods put forth by America's antigun lobby is its portrayal of Switzerland as a practitioner of strict gun control. Handgun Control Inc. circulates a pamphlet called "Handgun Facts," which cites Switzerland as a model for the United States to follow. However, as David Kopel points out, the pamphlet "is wrong about every single fact it mentions concerning Switzerland." He continues:

> If Handgun Control really approves of the Swiss system, the organization ought to reverse a number of its current policies. First, [it] should oppose handgun prohibition laws in Washington, D.C., Chicago, and other cities. . . . Second, [it] should work to repeal laws that prohibit Americans from owning howitzers, anti-aircraft guns, and other military weapons. . . . Lastly, [it] should reverse its policy and work for repeal of America's ban on the possession of fully automatic firearms manufactured after 1986. Handgun Control should push to adopt the Swiss policy: having the government sell automatics at discount prices to anyone with an easily obtained permit.[22]

Despite attempts by the antigun lobby to obscure the issue, Switzerland is incontestably the most heavily armed nation on earth, per capita. As in Machiavelli's day, the Swiss remain "most armed and most free."

Crime and Violence

They also remain remarkably nonviolent. The murder rate in Switzerland is approximately the same as in Japan, where guns are all but banned. It is much lower than the murder rate in England, Canada, Australia, and New Zealand.[23] In 1997, 1.2 homicides occurred per 100,000 people in Switzerland and 546 armed robberies. "Almost half of these crimes were committed by non-resident foreigners, whom the locals call 'criminal tourists,'" writes Halbrook.[24]

Political violence is even rarer among the Swiss. In 1918, socialist revolution and labor disorders struck nearly every country in Europe. Switzerland, too, experienced a general strike. But there was no shooting. The Swiss strikers left their military rifles at home.[25]

Those "Dull" Swiss

During the 1994 congressional debate over an "assault weapons" ban, Democratic Senator Bill Bradley of New Jersey—one of the sponsors of the ban—appeared on a talk show. The host asked him why Switzerland had so little crime, when every male citizen was armed with an assault rifle.

Bradley replied that the Swiss "are pretty dull."[26]

What Bradley meant is not entirely clear. Perhaps he regards fatherless, feral children running the streets in youth gangs to be "interesting." By that standard, I suppose one would have to call Switzerland "dull."

Family life there is remarkably stable. The percentage of children born outside of wedlock was 8.7 percent in 1998—the lowest in Europe. The percentage of women who work outside the home is also lower in Switzerland than in any other European country. Families spend much of their free time together, skiing, swimming, or shooting at the rifle range. Studies have shown that Swiss teenagers prefer the company of their parents to that of their peers.[27]

A Multiethnic Nation

Many Americans argue that the Swiss system would not work here. They say it can only work in an ethnically homogenous nation such as Switzerland. Yet Switzerland is far from homogenous. It is divided into several distinct ethnic regions, each speaking its own language.

In fact, Switzerland recognizes four official languages. About 70 percent of the Swiss speak German, 20 percent French, 4 percent Italian, and less than 1 percent Romansch, an obscure tongue related to Latin. The population is also divided between Catholics and Protestants. Such divisions have created havoc in places like Ireland and Yugoslavia. But the Swiss system inspires loyalty from every ethnic and religious group.

THE SWISS EXAMPLE

Inspired by Switzerland's success, other countries have imitated its example through the years. Israel, for instance, created a citizen's militia directly modeled upon that of Switzerland and probably owes its survival to that fact. So did the fledgling United States, at the dawn of the American Republic. Patrick Henry declared:

> Compare the peasants of Switzerland with those of any other mighty nation: You will find them far more happy—for one civil war among them, there have been five or six among other nations. Their attachment to their country, and to freedom—their resolute intrepidity in their defense; the consequent

security and happiness which they have enjoyed, and the respect and awe which these things produced in their bordering nations, have signalized them republicans. . . . Let us follow their example, and be equally happy.

In his 1787 *A Defense of the Constitutions*, John Adams praised the Swiss militia, noting that "every male of sixteen is enrolled in the militia, and obligated to provide himself an uniform, a musket, powder and balls; and no peasant is allowed to marry without producing his arms and uniform."

George Mason, a delegate to the Constitutional Convention, wrote that in Switzerland, "Every Husbandman will be quickly converted into a Soldier. . . . It is this which preserves the Freedom and Independence of the Swiss Cantons, in the midst of the most powerful Nations."[28]

Sister Republics

Arguments such as these helped persuade the delegates to add the Second Amendment to the Bill of Rights, ensuring that the government would never deny to "the People" the right to keep and bear arms. They also resulted in the passage of the 1792 Militia Act, requiring every able-bodied male citizen of the United States to arm himself for militia duty.

Early on, the Swiss recognized in the fledgling United States a kindred nation. A Swiss politician named Johann R. Valltravers wrote to Benjamin Franklin in 1778, "Let us be united, as two Sister-Republicks." According to Halbrook, the term "Sister Republics" was commonly used during the nineteenth century to compare Switzerland with the United States. But as America's commitment to its militia system waned during the twentieth century, so did our gratitude toward the friendly republic across the seas and our memory of the example she once provided.[29]

A GLIMPSE OF THINGS TO COME

WRITER AND NOVELIST Tom Bradley makes his living teaching English at a Japanese university. In a January 2, 2001, article for FrontPageMagazine.com, he described the activities of a student organization on campus calling themselves "cheerleaders." Bradley writes:

> At my place of employment, they recruit underclassmen by literal arm-twisting, to the silence of the dean of students. I think he approves secretly of this return to militarism among the otherwise politically flaccid youth of Nippon.
>
> The cheerleaders spend their time frenziedly rallied under giant rising sun flags and blood-colored banners emblazoned with reversed and righted swastikas. To the accompaniment of a mammoth bass drum . . . they march outside my classroom windows and chant jingoistic songs from the thirties and forties. . . .

After these rallies, Bradley finds that his students have often yelled themselves so hoarse that they cannot participate in his conversation class. "The dean of students urges me to respect this, because all night they've been 'doing their best and trying hard and displaying enthusiasm.' When I ask, 'Trying their best to accomplish what?' all I get is an inscrutably averted gaze."

BIG-NOSES OUT

In their parades and rallies, the cheerleaders often display portraits of the late Emperor Hirohito, under whose guidance Japan attempted to conquer half the world sixty years ago. They brandish banners bearing such slogans as: "Miscegenation for America, Purity for *Dai Nippon*!"; "Big-Noses Out!";

"No HIV in our Fatherland!"; and even, "Hair Grows on Dogs' Legs, Not People's!" Just in case any readers fail to take the hint, all of these slogans are directed against Westerners.

Bradley notes that as these marchers enter the university, the old porter at the front gate bows low before them. "They are treated with all the fear and deference due to a sacerdotal caste," he observes.[30]

Feeling Safer

Michael Lev of the *Chicago Tribune* writes that he "feels a bit safer" in Japan. And perhaps he is safer. But that safety comes at a high price.

"If weapons are a token of power," say the Swiss, "then in a democracy they belong in the hands of the people." The Japanese people long ago surrendered their tokens of power. And they have paid for it in blood. During World War II, more than 337,000 Japanese civilians died in their own cities from aerial bombing, as a result of their leaders' reckless ambitions.[31]

The old porter at the gate of Tom Bradley's university no doubt remembers that time. As he bows low before the "cheerleaders," their chants must remind him of another generation of angry young men who once marched through Japan's streets brandishing portraits of Hirohito.

Whatever he thinks, he keeps his silence. Like the Japanese people themselves, he waits, hoping and praying that his leaders will make wise choices, but having no real power to influence the outcome one way or the other.

REMEMBER THE PAST

"Those who cannot remember the past are condemned to repeat it," wrote George Santayana. Gun controllers are fond of pointing to "other developed countries" as a model for the United States to imitate. But in most of those "developed" countries, the eyes of the elderly are dark with painful memories of invasion, dictatorship, bombings, and genocide.

In Europe, only Switzerland and Sweden escaped the curse, Switzerland because of its arms and Sweden because of its isolation. Every other nation in Europe, without exception, has known war, dictatorship, and terror in living memory. Recent events in Russia, the Caucasus, and the Balkans make plain that the threat of violence hangs just as ominously over Europe today as it ever did in the past.

An Island of Liberty

In 1938, as war clouds brewed over Europe, an article in the *New York Times* stated:

> Switzerland, an island of liberty and harmony in a sea of dictatorship and discord, has been a citadel of peace through stormy centuries. . . . It is a land of hard work and frugal habits, of justice and cleanness and tolerance, of the very essence of live-and-let-live. There one finds no extremes of wealth or poverty, no billionaires, no paupers.[32]

Hitler did not share this happy view of his Swiss neighbors. To him, Switzerland was an annoying pocket of defiance. It was always his plan to conquer it. In *Mein Kampf,* Hitler wrote, "Common blood must belong to a common Reich." Nazi maps published before the war show German-speaking Switzerland as a province of Greater Germany.[33] But Hitler's dream never came to pass. The stubbornness of the Swiss in clinging to their independence thwarted and infuriated him to the end.

Living in the Past?

Even as the Nazis plotted Switzerland's destruction, they murmured soothing words about their good intentions. Nazi military strategist Ewald Banse poked fun at the Swiss for their "childish" fear of Germany. "It is based upon the belief, doubtless justified in the Middle Ages but long since obsolete, that liberty and equality—those most sacred of human possessions—are at stake," he wrote.[34]

The Swiss were living in the past, said Banse. Centuries ago, their militia might have served a purpose, when hostile kings and emperors surrounded them. But no such threat existed in the new, modern Europe of Hitler and Mussolini.

The New Europe

Of course, Banse knew perfectly well that Switzerland was in grave danger of invasion. Indeed, he was one of the chief advocates of such an invasion. "Quite naturally we count you Swiss as offshoots of the German nation . . . ," he wrote. "Patience: one day we will group ourselves around a single banner, and whosoever shall wish to separate us, we will exterminate!"[35]

As the Nazi juggernaut rolled over one country after another, the Swiss grew somber, waiting for their turn. Writing from Geneva in 1940, American journalist William Shirer observed, "Everyone here is full of talk about the 'new Europe,' a theme that brings shudders to most people. . . . And now that France has completely collapsed and the Germans and Italians surround Switzerland, a military struggle in self-defense is hopeless."[36] But Shirer was overly pessimistic. The expected invasion never came. Many times the Germans considered it. But the cost of facing the Swiss "porcupine" always forced them to back down.

The New World Order

As in 1940, talk of a "new Europe" is once again on everyone's lips. The continent is forming into a single superstate with a common currency, common laws, and a common purpose. Just as in 1940, Switzerland is the odd man out, an annoying little country that insists on living in the past and doing things its own way.

Today, the European Community is pressing Switzerland hard to abandon its 800-year traditions. "Switzerland obstructs the final integration of Europe," writes Jonathan Steinberg. ". . . Brussels [the capital of the new Europe] sees Switzerland as tedious and unreliable."

Too Much Democracy

What makes the Swiss so "tedious and unreliable" is their democracy. In other European countries, people might protest Brussels' edicts, but they have no real power to resist them. Not so in Switzerland. Steinberg writes:

> Its government can never promise to fulfill treaties because the citizens say, "No." Direct democracy—that thicket of initiatives, referenda, town meetings, elected bodies . . . which makes Switzerland utterly unlike anywhere else—looks incompatible with the *acquis communautaire*, the fourteen hundred or so regulations and directives, which membership of the European Union demands.

Steinberg's observation is revealing. If the ability of a free people to say "no" is incompatible with membership in the New Europe, what does that tell us about the New Europe?

Whither the Militia?

Like the Nazi strategist Ewald Banse, Europe's new overlords argue that the Swiss are living in the past. It's time for them to let down their guard. Even some Swiss—particularly those on the Left—are beginning to take up the chant. Steinberg describes the new thinking thus: "For the first time in seven centuries, Switzerland is surrounded by 'friends.' Beyond every frontier the Swiss see peaceful, capitalist democracies not unlike their own. . . . The Swiss maintain the second largest land army in Europe. . . . To fight whom?"[37]

According to the new thinking, today's world is supposedly more peaceful than the world of sixty years ago, when Switzerland's militia saved it from ruin. Yet even now, war clouds are brewing over the Balkans, the Caucasus, Russia, and the Middle East. And one of the things that those "peaceful, capitalist democracies" want most desperately from Switzerland is cannon fodder for their wars. The Swiss are urged to break their tradition of neutrality and supply troops for NATO and UN-sponsored adventures such as those that took place in Kuwait and Yugoslavia. So far, the Swiss have remained stubborn on this point. "Its citizenry have rejected government proposals to join the United Nations and to send 'blue berets' for UN service," notes Steinberg.[38]

NO ACCIDENT

Time will tell whether our 800-year-old "Sister Republick" will withstand the pressure of its neighbors. For now, it remains an "island of liberty" in a Europe that is far less free than most Americans realize. On March 4, 2001, the Swiss voted decisively against seeking membership in the European Union.

It cannot be by accident that the United Nations omitted Switzerland from its 1997 study. As the most heavily armed nation in the world per capita, its very existence disproves the notion that guns in private hands lead inevitably to violence. As we will see in the sections ahead, some little-known events in other parts of the "developed" world debunk that notion even more decisively.

ASSUMPTION 3

Lax U.S. Gun Laws Encourage Violence

On Mother's Day, May 15, 2000, an army of women descended on Washington, D.C., to demand stricter gun laws. The so-called Million Mom March was emceed by left-wing talk-show host Rosie O'Donnell, probably the most outspoken antigun crusader in America.

The day before the march, Cokie Roberts of *ABC News* questioned O'Donnell about her views. "As you know, there's lots of controversy about gun legislation," said Roberts. "Here in Washington, we have about the toughest gun laws that there are in the country, and yet we have shootings all the time. . . . What good do they do?"

O'Donnell replied: "Well, there are 200 million guns in America and 20,000 gun laws. So the guns are winning." One must assume that O'Donnell's reply was tongue-in-cheek. It does not seem likely that she seriously advocates raising the number of gun laws to match the number of guns in circulation. Still, her jest reflected the attitude of most antigun crusaders, for whom more and stricter gun laws seem the obvious answer to violence in America.[1]

DO AS I SAY, NOT AS I DO

IN THAT SAME interview, Roberts asked O'Donnell her opinion on concealed-carry laws, which permit citizens to pack firearms in self-defense. "There is some evidence that those laws do reduce crime. But you would be against them?" asked Roberts.

"Of course I'm against them . . . ," O'Donnell responded. "This is not the wild west." O'Donnell argued that such laws "do more harm than good."

Only days after the march, however, a stunned public learned of a hidden side to O'Donnell's stand on guns. While she denounces the carrying of firearms for the general public, she apparently thinks it's okay when the safety of her own family is at stake. On March 25, the *Associated Press* reported that the full-time bodyguard assigned to accompany O'Donnell's four-year-old son to kindergarten had applied for a permit to carry a concealed weapon.

A SPECIAL CASE?

At first glance, it would seem an odd request. As *Los Angeles Daily News* columnist Chris Weinkopf pointed out, Greenwich, Connecticut, where O'Donnell lives, is "a town where houses often cost more than $1 million, where no teen is without his own SUV, and where school violence is generally limited to the lacrosse field." But O'Donnell argued that she faced special dangers, having received death and kidnapping threats as a result of her antigun stand.

"She's a high-profile person and there are many high-profile people who use security," explained O'Donnell spokeswoman Jennifer Glaisek.[2]

Hysteria

High-profile or not, O'Donnell suddenly found herself targeted by the very antigun hysteria that she had helped enflame among America's soccer moms. Local parents panicked at the thought of a gun on school property. The principal of Parkway School in Greenwich was compelled to send out a letter reassuring parents that O'Donnell's bodyguard would not bring his gun to school.

O'Donnell denied that such was ever her intention in the first place. The weapons permit was required by her bodyguard's security firm, she explained, and was not her idea at all. Yet the *New York Post* reported that the Parkway School principal had specifically asked Greenwich schools superintendent Roger Lulow for clearance to allow an armed guard to accompany O'Donnell's son to school.[3]

While denying that the gun was her idea, O'Donnell also attempted to justify it. "I don't personally own a gun," she said. "But if you are qualified, licensed, and registered, I have no problem."[4]

Not So Special

In an op-ed piece in the *Los Angeles Times*, Yale Law School professor John R. Lott Jr. observed: "O'Donnell's response that she still does not 'personally own a gun' misses the whole point. Of course, she does not need her own gun when her bodyguards have their guns with them."

Most people cannot afford a bodyguard. Yet the dangers they face are no less real than those confronting Rosie O'Donnell and her son. As Chris Weinkopf pointed out in the *Los Angeles Daily News*, "other moms, those who don't live in communities like Greenwich, or walk around with personal bodyguards, face their own set of dangers. They need to worry about rape, carjacking, and armed robbery—crimes that generally do not afflict the well-guarded celebrity set."[5]

Elitism

Public reaction to O'Donnell's double standard was sharp and widespread. "This is hypocrisy and elitism at its worst," declared Brad Bennett of Arlington, Virginia, in a typical letter to the *Washington Post*. "When it comes to Ms. O'Donnell's loved ones, a handgun is an essential tool of personal protection . . . and is perfectly safe when kept around children and toted into school zones.

"Those of us who cannot afford to hire bodyguards, though, should turn in our guns and depend on the police to protect our families. Perhaps the Second Amendment should be revised to read, 'The right of the elite to hire persons to keep and bear arms, shall not be infringed.'"[6]

The Deterrence Effect

It was at this point that things really got interesting. Assailed for her hypocrisy, O'Donnell had tried to defuse the situation by making clear that her bodyguard would not bring his weapon to school. Yet no sooner had she made this statement than she realized it was a mistake. The *Greenwich Time* reported that O'Donnell was worried that "publicity about her son's attendance at a local school—coupled with the information that the guard would be unarmed—could make him vulnerable to harm."[7]

Evidently, it had dawned on O'Donnell that bad guys might think twice about harming her son if they knew an armed guard was present. But if they knew for sure that the guard was unarmed, they might be encouraged to strike.

Gun rights advocates often joke that people who support gun control should demonstrate their sincerity by posting a sign in front of their houses stating, "We have no guns here." Of course, such a sign would be an open invitation to burglars, rapists, and murderers. The mere possibility that a household might be armed serves as a deterrent against criminals. At least, so the progun crowd has always maintained. Whatever she might have said on the podium of the Million Mom March, O'Donnell's statement to the *Greenwich Time* revealed the surprising extent to which she understood and agreed with this logic.

ROSIE IS RIGHT!

O'DONNELL MIGHT be wrong about a lot of things, but on the question of deterrence, she is correct. In his book *More Guns, Less Crime*, John Lott points out that most criminals in America choose empty houses to burglarize. They avoid late-night break-ins because, as many convicts have explained to researchers, "that's the way to get shot."[8]

Criminals in America are keenly aware that about half of all homes contain firearms. Consequently, they treat occupied houses with respect. Hot burglaries—in which the criminal enters while people are home—account for only 13 percent of all U.S. burglaries.

But in countries with strict gun control, such as England and Canada, criminals know that their victims are unarmed. They enter houses at will, without worrying whether anyone is home. The hot burglary rate in those countries is nearly 50 percent.[9]

A Close Call

Years ago, I had a close call on the subway platform at 145th Street in Harlem. Through a series of mishaps, I ended up having to change trains at that dangerous station, while coming downtown from the Bronx. To make matters worse, I was accompanied by an out-of-town friend who was on leave from the Navy. He was in full uniform and had all his luggage with him. We stood out like sore thumbs. Despite my warnings, he pulled out an expensive camera and started taking pictures.

Within seconds, two very large and husky African American fellows sidled up to us, their faces beaming with amusement. They pretended to make small talk with my companion, while eyeing the camera and luggage. In his innocent, small-town Southern way, my friend returned their greetings, apparently unaware of the danger we were facing.

All I could do was pray, which I did, quite literally. "Please get me out of this," I said silently.

Suddenly, one of the interlopers made a move toward one of my friend's suitcases. Not knowing what else to do, I quickly stepped in his way, planting myself directly between him and the suitcase and looking up at him (and I do mean *up*—he was considerably taller than me). Still praying, I waited for the inevitable attack.

To my surprise, the man stopped in his tracks. A look of shock and dismay crossed his face. He looked down at my hands, then back up at my face several times. After exchanging worried looks, the two men backed away slowly, each one placing a hand ostentatiously in his jacket pocket, as if to demonstrate—or at least to give the illusion—that he was armed. As they turned to leave, one of them said over his shoulder, "You don't know how lucky you are."

Only then did I realize what had happened. When I stepped in front of the suitcase, I had unconsciously placed both hands in my jacket pockets—a move that they evidently found threatening. Rather than run the risk that I might have a gun in my pocket, they had decided to go bother someone else.

Such a ploy would only work in America. In countries with strict gun control, criminals would not be so quick to assume that their intended victim was armed.

The Substitution Effect

"This is not the wild west," said Rosie O'Donnell, when asked how she felt about concealed-carry laws. Gun controllers typically argue that granting citizens the right to carry weapons would result in a return to frontier conditions. In fact, when states pass concealed-carry laws, typically only about 1 to 4 percent of the population actually obtains a permit. Yet experience has shown that even that small percentage makes a huge difference in controlling crime.

In a 1995 murder in Cincinnati, a robber named Darnell "Bubba" Lowery admitted to police that he and his partner had originally planned to hold up a cab driver or drug dealer. But they decided against it because they knew cabbies and drug dealers often carry guns. Instead, they approached a man they saw walking across a parking lot with a musical instrument. After robbing him, they shot him dead.[10]

In *More Guns, Less Crime*, John Lott explains:

> To an economist such as myself, the notion of deterrence—which causes criminals to avoid cab drivers, "dope boys," or homes where the residents are in—is not too surprising. We see the same basic relationships in all other areas of life: when the price of apples rises relative to that of oranges, people buy fewer apples and more oranges . . . just as grocery shoppers switch to cheaper types of produce, criminals switch to attacking more vulnerable prey. Economists call this, appropriately enough, "the substitution effect."[11]

Thus all it takes is for a few cabbies and drug dealers to carry guns, and all the other cabbies and drug dealers will benefit. The same rule applies to society in general. If only a few citizens carry concealed weapons, criminals must always think twice before attacking a person, since they never know who may or may not be armed.

Rosie O'Donnell lost the benefit of the substitution effect when she was forced to announce to the world that her son's bodyguard was unarmed. Whether or not the bodyguard actually carried a gun, the knowledge that celebrity bodyguards often do would probably have been sufficient to deter many attackers and cause them to "substitute" some other, easier victim. It is interesting how clearly O'Donnell grasped this principle when the life of her own son was at stake.

A COURAGEOUS VOICE

JOHN LOTT, who has been cited several times in this book, is one of the most important voices advocating gun rights in America today. He seems an unlikely champion for such a cause. A mild-mannered Yale economist, Lott remarked to the *Las Vegas Review-Journal* in September 2000 that "Nobody in my family as far back as I can find out had ever owned a firearm. Until about four years ago, my wife wouldn't have a firearm in the house, wouldn't even allow our children to play with toy guns."

But then Lott embarked on a course of research that was to change his life. He undertook a study of eighteen years' worth of crime statistics from around the United States. The results were clear. Clear enough to convince even Lott's wife.

"We have real guns in the house now," he says. "The change came about because my wife is also an economist, probably my harshest critic, in fact, and she evaluated the data herself. And she reached the same conclusions I did."[12]

Lott concluded:

> National crime rates have been falling at the same time as gun ownership has been rising. Likewise, states experiencing the greatest reductions in crime are also the ones with the fastest growing percentages of gun ownership."[13]

On average, Lott found that violent crime dropped by 4 percent for each 1 percent increase in gun ownership. The most dramatic improvement came in states that allowed citizens to carry concealed handguns. States enacting such laws between 1977 and 1994 experienced an average 10 percent reduction in murders and a 4.4 percent drop in overall violent crime during that period.[14]

Bulletproof

Cokie Roberts was probably referring to Lott's research when she told Rosie O'Donnell that "some evidence" showed that concealed-carry laws reduce crime. However, Lott's findings represent far more than just "some evidence." Presented in his bestselling 1998 book *More Guns, Less Crime*, Lott's study is the most thoroughgoing analysis ever conducted of the relationship between guns and crime in America. His statistics are bulletproof.

"How much confidence do I have in these results?" he wrote. "The largest previous study on gun control produced findings similar to those reported here but examined only 170 cities within a single year. This book has examined over 54,000 observations (across 3,000 counties for eighteen years) and has controlled for a range of other factors never accounted for in previous crime studies."[15]

Why Don't More People Know?

Lott's findings first appeared in a 1997 scholarly paper. Yet to this day, most Americans have no idea that the gun controllers' favorite claim—that more guns lead to more crime—has been so thoroughly debunked. On the contrary, antigun crusaders continue to claim just the opposite, with little or no correction from the media.

As for Lott himself, he was forced to defend his good name against a vicious smear campaign, orchestrated by powerful and well-funded antigun interests. "I was stunned . . . ," he later remarked. "I had no way of anticipating it."[16]

Lott had previously published more than seventy articles in academic journals. But he had never before ventured into the politically charged territory of guns and crime. He soon discovered that, when it came to the subject of firearms, the gentlemanly rules governing academic debate did not apply.

"We Can Get Good Media Whenever We Want"

Contrary to ordinary academic etiquette, antigun scholars refused to debate Lott or critique his paper until after it leaked out in the press. Only when they realized that the cat was out of the bag did they respond.

Before publishing his paper in the *Journal of Legal Studies*, Lott presented it at a conference of the Cato Institute in Washington. He attempted to get antigun scholars to preview his study and comment on it at the conference. Out of twenty-two antigun scholars he asked, twenty-one turned him down flat.

Susan Glick of the Violence Policy Center was one of those who refused. She told Lott bluntly that she didn't want to "help give any publicity to the paper." Lott tried to entice Glick by pointing out that C-SPAN would likely cover the event, providing a forum for Glick to promote her antigun message. But this did not impress her. "We can get good media whenever we want," Glick retorted.

Would she at least take a look at the paper, Lott asked, and perhaps make some private comments on it? "Forget it," she told him. "There is no way that I am going to look at it. Don't send it."[17]

Fighting Dirty

Only when the press began showing an interest in Lott's work did the gun controllers change their tactics. Instead of ignoring Lott, they set out to discredit him.

Following an August 2 article in *USA Today*, reporters started calling Susan Glick for reactions. She had still not seen a copy of Lott's study but nevertheless told an *ABC News* reporter that it was "flawed." Some critics falsely stated that Lott had published his paper in a "student-edited journal." In fact, he had published it in the prestigious *Journal of Legal Studies*. Then-Congressman Charles Schumer of New York even accused Lott of being a paid stooge of the gun industry.[18]

"The groups that made the charges knew they were false before they made them," Lott commented in 1998, "but they're still making those charges and they're still false."[19]

To date, no scholar has successfully refuted Lott's findings, though many have tried. But the rough treatment he received from the antigun camp has served its purpose. It stands as a grim warning to other scholars of what may happen to them if they dare to step out of line and publish research that is damaging to the antigun cause.

ASSUMPTION 4

Countries with Fewer Guns and Stricter Gun Laws Have Less Violence

"I FEEL VERY comfortable in England. I feel safer."

So said pop icon Madonna in November 2000, as she announced her plans to marry film director Guy Ritchie and take up residence in his native England. "She feels more secure in this country," reported *The Sun*, "and regularly goes out for walks alone—something she would never do in Los Angeles."[1]

Nine days later, Madonna was no longer feeling so safe. As happens so often in England, Canada, and other countries with strict gun control, Madonna became the victim of a "hot" burglary—a break-in that takes place while the owners are still home. While Madonna, her fiancé, and her two children slept, thieves broke into the Edwardian mansion she and Ritchie were renting in London's fashionable Notting Hill district. The bandits made off with three laptop computers, Ritchie's Range Rover, and other booty. Madonna was reportedly "very shaken" by the incident.[2]

How did the intruders get in? The house had been protected by a five-foot wall with iron railings, as well as state-of-the-art alarm and security systems. But, as one security expert explained, "Professional burglars know how to disarm most security systems. If they put their minds to it, they'll always find a way in."[3]

MORE CRIME IN BRITAIN

LIKE MOST AMERICANS, Madonna had been misled by press reports into thinking that crime is lower in England. Precisely the opposite is true. A 1998 study by the U.S. Department of Justice found that the rate of muggings in England had surpassed that in the United States by 40 percent. Assault and burglary rates were found to be almost 100 percent higher in England than in the United States.[4]

Experts have been wracking their brains in search of an explanation. But for those who study the issue dispassionately, the conclusion seems inescapable that Britain's draconian gun laws—which make it all but impossible for law-abiding citizens to defend themselves—may have a great deal to do with it.

The British "Sword Hunt"

Like the Japanese tyrant Hideyoshi, the British government has a history of using deception to disarm its citizens. When the twentieth century dawned, virtually no limits were set on the number or type of firearms Englishmen could buy. Crime was extremely low. However, the government was worried about the growing power of anarchist and communist revolutionaries.

After World War I, many countries suffered strikes, revolutions, and violent labor disorders. Russia's Bolshevik Revolution seemed to be infecting workers in every part of the world. At a cabinet meeting on January 17, 1919, the British imperial general staff warned of "Red Revolution and blood and war at home and abroad."

"It is not inconceivable," said minister of transport Sir Eric Geddes, "that a dramatic and successful coup d'etat in some large center of population might win the support of the unthinking mass of labor."

What to do? Britain's rulers had long kept the rebellious Irish in check with a strict gun licensing system. They now decided to impose similar restrictions on their own people. The masses would be disarmed, while provisions would be made to arm "friends of the Government"—such as stockbrokers, clerks, and university men—in the event of revolution.

However, Britain's rulers did not want the public to know the real reason for their action. Just as Hideyoshi disguised his "sword hunt" as a religious devotion, the British government presented its 1920 Firearms Act as an anticrime measure. Gun crime was negligible in Britain at the time. Yet the stated purpose of the bill was "to prevent criminals and persons of that description from being able to have revolvers and to use them." The new law required police permits for the purchase of rifles and pistols. Such permits were granted to only those whom the police determined had a "good reason" for owning a firearm.[5]

Creeping Regulation

Over the next seventy-six years, British gun laws grew stricter by slow increments. When the 1920 Firearms Act was passed, an Englishman could cite self-defense as one "good reason" for owning a gun. But self-defense was later disqualified. Guns were only permitted for sporting purposes. A shotgun licensing requirement was added in 1967.[6]

Even this was not enough for the gun controllers. In 1996, a madman named Thomas Hamilton massacred with an assault rifle sixteen kindergarteners and a schoolteacher in Dunblane, Scotland. The cry went out for a wholesale gun ban. Under the Firearms Act of 1997, all handguns and most rifles were outlawed and confiscated.

"Ramraiding" and "Rolex Robbers"

What happened next is something most Americans know nothing about because the press has not reported it in this country. A terrifying crime wave swept England. Stripped of the ability to defend themselves, Britons were left helpless against criminal attacks. And the criminals knew it. Their attacks grew bolder, as well as more frequent.

Between April and September 2000, street crime in London rose 32 percent over the same period in 1999. A new breed of so-called "Rolex Robbers" targeted the rich and famous with bold, daylight attacks on crowded streets, often taking watches first—hence the nickname. Among their victims were multimillionairess Vivien Duffield, Prime Minister Tony Blair's daughter Sarah Blair, supermodel Caprice, actress Britt Ekland, and British Airways chairman Lord Marshall, who was robbed while his car was stuck in traffic.[7]

Another new type of crime that arose was "ramraiding." This involved ramming a vehicle right through a storefront, after which the criminals would dismount and pick through the wreckage at their leisure. Storeowners in the United States would end such an attack with a single shotgun blast, which is probably why such tactics are not used here. But British shopkeepers could only stand by helplessly and let it happen. "Many retailers have actually gone out of business because of the repeated attacks on their premises," according to a commercial security report entitled "New Wave in Retail Crime."[8]

When Guns Are Outlawed, Only Outlaws Have Guns

A January 13, 2000, article in the *Sunday Times* of London reported an epidemic of gun crimes in London, Birmingham, and Manchester, fueled by "a steady flow of smuggled guns from eastern Europe." A Parliamentary study found that young criminals between the ages of fifteen and twenty-five "own or have access to guns ranging from Beretta sub-machineguns to Luger pistols, which can be bought from underworld dealers for as little as £200."

Detective Superintendent Keith Hudson of the national crime squad observed, "There is a move from the pistol and the shotgun to automatic weapons." Indeed, automatic weapons were "fast becoming fashion accessories among young drug dealers," according to British detectives. Unarmed police were intimidated by the prospect of "confronting teenagers on mountain bikes brandishing automatic weapons."

According to the *Sunday Times*, "Anti-gun campaigners hoped the handgun ban after Dunblane . . . would reduce firearm crime. The latest figures, however, show crime involving weapons is on the increase. . . ." The Home Office reported a 10 percent rise in gun crime in 1998.[9] And in 1999–2000, crimes using handguns hit a seven-year high in Britain.[10]

New Opportunities, New Tactics

In England, it is illegal to use a weapon to defend yourself or your home. If you do, you are likely to go to jail. Britons are supposed to sit tight and wait for the police to come rescue them.

Of course, the chance of being rescued by a cop is negligible, even under the best of circumstances. The police do not usually show up until after a crime is over. Thanks to budget cuts in England, police in many parts of the country are now even scarcer than usual. The criminals have adapted their tactics to meet the new opportunities.

State of Siege

"We once had twelve old-fashioned bobbies living in our village, and it was always well policed," wrote Kentish farmer Jon Pritchett in an August 25, 1999, opinion piece in the London *Daily Mail.* "Now there are two policemen covering the area in patrol cars. It is meant to be cheaper and more efficient, but the reality is that it takes them forever to get to the scene of a crime."

Consequently, farmers in Pritchett's area live in a veritable state of siege. Most have invested in expensive alarm systems.

But burglars simply ignore the alarms. They know, in advance, approximately how long it will take the police to show up. And they know that no matter how many people are awakened by the alarm, the homeowners are either unarmed or forbidden by law to use their arms against criminals. So crooks are free to do their work openly, with little fear of interruption.

A Vulnerable "Fortress"

One of Pritchett's neighbors had a house "like a fortress," wired from end to end with alarms and floodlights. One night, the alarm went off. Pritchett's neighbor went outside and found a raiding party of seven men in ski masks ransacking his garage. "They were happily going about their business although the place was illuminated like Blackpool promenade," writes Pritchett.

"Stay inside or we'll do you," one of the men threatened. The neighbor did as he was told. By the time the police arrived, forty minutes later, the burglars were long gone.

"Stomach-Churning Fear"

Pritchett himself had an even worse experience. One winter night, his bedroom alarm went off. Thieves had broken into his warehouse, where he stored wine from his vineyard. Grabbing a shotgun, Pritchett went out to confront them. "In the pitch darkness I accidentally peppered them with my 12-bore shotgun," he writes.

When the police arrived, they arrested Pritchett and charged him with two counts of causing grievous bodily harm and one of using a firearm with intent to endanger life. "I was stripped, body-searched, fingerprinted, DNA-tested and held in a filthy cell in Sevenoaks police station," he writes. "I have never seen anything quite as disgusting as the toilet, which I—an innocent victim of an attempted robbery—was expected to use."

The charge of intent to endanger life was later dropped, and Pritchett was found not guilty of causing grievous bodily harm. "But I—a respectable farmer and businessman in my late 50s—had lived in stomach-churning fear for six months," he writes. "I knew I could easily have gone down for a long stretch merely for defending my wife and my property." The burglars got off with probation, though both had long records of criminal violence.

Pritchett says that he and his wife now live in constant fear. Traumatized by his brush with the law, Pritchett has developed a bad stutter and finds that he breaks down when trying to tell his story. "We feel a dignified and secure old age has been denied us in Britain . . . ," he writes. The couple plans to move to Australia.

NO ESCAPE

I DO NOT KNOW whether the Pritchetts ever followed through on their plan to emigrate. If they did, they must have come in for a rude shock. Australia, too, is in the grip of an unprecedented and catastrophic crime wave.

When a madman slaughtered thirty-five people at a Tasmanian resort in 1996, the Australian government responded by banning most firearms. More than 640,000 guns were seized from law-abiding citizens.

The result was a sharp increase in violent crime. In the two years following the gun ban, armed robberies rose by 73 percent, unarmed robberies by 28 percent, kidnappings by 38 percent, assaults by 17 percent, and manslaughter by 29 percent, according to figures that appeared on the Web site of the Australian Bureau of Statistics in January 2000.[11]

Blowing Smoke

Since those statistics were published, a great deal of smoke has been blown regarding the Australian crime rate. For instance, the Web site of Handgun Control's Center to Prevent Handgun Violence has published claims that crimes involving firearms in Australia were down to their lowest point in four years in 1998.

"The next time a credulous friend or acquaintance tells you that Australia actually suffered more crime when they got tougher on guns . . . offer him a Foster's, and tell him the facts," says the site.[12]

Puzzled by this report, I returned to the Web site of the Australian Bureau of Statistics on May 10, 2001. Crime figures for 1996 were no longer shown, and figures for 1999 had been added since the last time I visited. The figures still showed a dramatic net increase in crime. For the three-year period from 1997 to 1999, murders were up by 6.5 percent, attempted murders by 12.5 percent, assaults by 7.3 percent, kidnappings by 35.8 percent, armed robberies by 4.3 percent, and unarmed robberies by 7.4 percent.[13]

More startlingly, a recent survey ranked Australia number one in violent crime, among industrialized nations. England ranked second on the list.

According to the International Crime Victims Survey, released by Leiden University in Holland in February 2001, "Twenty-six percent of English citizens—roughly one quarter of the population—have been victimized by violent crime," reports Jon Dougherty in WorldNetDaily.com. "Australia led the list with more than 30 percent of its population victimized. The United States didn't even make the 'top 10' list of industrialized nations whose citizens were victimized by crime."[14]

SCRAMBLING FOR EXPLANATIONS

CRIMINOLOGISTS AND social scientists the world over have been scrambling for an explanation—any explanation—for the upsurge in violent crime in England and Australia. American sociologist Charles Murray warns of the rise of an "underclass" of "violent, unsocialized people" in Britain, many of whom "are not being raised by two mature, married adults." Others blame high unemployment.[15] Still others point bluntly to Britain's rising number of black immigrants. Jamaican gangs account for much of the increase in gun crime.[16]

Yet few seem willing to look squarely at the most obvious cause: By disarming honest citizens, these countries have emboldened the criminals, who now go about their business without fear.

MYTH 2

PULLING A GUN ON A CRIMINAL ENDANGERS YOU MORE THAN THE CRIMINAL

THE MOVIE *Predator II* depicts a futuristic, twenty-first-century metropolis in which brigands rule the streets. In one scene, a gang of urban marauders approaches a well-dressed, middle-class man on the subway.

Trembling with fear, the man pulls out a pistol and points it directly at the face of one of his tormentors. But the would-be vigilante is so frightened, he cannot hold the gun steady. The thug laughs out loud and takes the pistol from the man. Only the sudden intervention of some plainclothes cops who happen to be in the car saves the day.

Hollywood films abound with such scenes. Armed citizens who attempt to "take the law into their own hands" are portrayed as fools, incompetents, and cowards. Criminals, on the other hand, are portrayed as supermen, without fear, who can stare right down the barrel of a loaded gun and laugh.

The news media support these stereotypes. When ordinary citizens defend themselves successfully with firearms, the news is hushed up. Not so when an armed, off-duty cop happens to stop a crime in progress. Such stories are given wide play. The silent message behind such selective news editing is obvious: Let the professionals do the crime-fighting.

THE INCOMPETENT CITIZEN

IN HIS BOOK *Inside the NRA*, columnist Jack Anderson describes his 1989 mugging only seven blocks from the White House. A young man hit him on the head with a pipe, then fled as passersby ran to Anderson's assistance. "In a fraction of a second," writes Anderson, "I understood the deep fear of the average American that he or she could at any moment become the victim of senseless, violent crime at the hands of a stranger."

However, his epiphany was incomplete. The pipe-wielding mugger may have bruised Anderson's skull, but he made no dent in the liberal columnist's antigun prejudice. "If I'd had a .44 caliber Magnum automatic in a shoulder holster, it would have done me no good," he concludes. Had he fired on his attacker, says Anderson, "I would just as likely have hit some innocent person on the street—more likely, in fact, because there were more of them."[1]

Anderson goes on to cite "statistics"—whose source he does not name—that "45 percent of all people who try to defend themselves with guns become gun victims instead."[2] Like the creators of *Predator II*, Anderson portrays ordinary citizens as incompetent fools, when it comes to firearms. It is better to let yourself be robbed, mugged, raped—or even killed, he implies—than to risk your life or the lives of others by fighting back.

THE FACTS

JACK ANDERSON'S claim that "45 percent of all people who try to defend themselves with guns become gun victims instead" is flatly contradicted by the best available research.

According to Florida State University criminologist Gary Kleck, U.S. citizens use guns to defend themselves from criminals about 1 million times each year. In 98 percent of those cases, no shots are fired. The criminal flees at the mere sight of the gun. Citizens actually have to shoot their attackers in only 2 percent of the cases.[3] In only 1 percent of defensive gun uses do attackers manage to take the gun away from the victim.[4]

In his characteristically meticulous fashion, John Lott offers a wider range of estimates of defensive gun uses. Based on a study of fifteen national polls by organizations such as the *Los Angeles Times*, Gallup, and Peter Hart Research Associates, Lott deduces that the number of defensive gun uses may be as high as 3.6 million per year or as low as 760,000. Either way, the data suggest that such incidents are extremely common.[5]

A LESSON IN MEDIA MANIPULATION

THANKS TO THE saturation coverage it received in the media, most readers probably have a clear recollection of the death of Japanese exchange student Yoshihiro Hattori, shot by Louisiana homeowner Rodney Peairs on Halloween night, 1992. The Hattori story became an international *cause célèbre* and was later made into a documentary film called *The Shot Heard Round the World.*

Hattori approached Peairs's house, thinking it was the address of a Halloween party. Spooked by what he described as Hattori's "bizarre" behavior and by the student's failure to stop when commanded, Peairs shot him dead. Both families paid a terrible price. The Hattoris lost a son. Rodney Peairs lost his job and his house and was slapped with a $653,077 judgment, of which his insurance company would pay only $100,000. It was a tragedy for all concerned.[6]

But why was it such big news?

Hattori's death was an accident, a case of mistaken identity. Peairs thought he was defending his home from a dangerous criminal. However much one might fault Peairs for his recklessness, the killing was still an accident. Why did it make headlines, while thousands of other accidents—such as those caused by reckless driving—do not?

The answer, of course, is that the media treated the Hattori story as more than a simple accident. It was presented as an object lesson in gun control. Over and over, wherever the story was told, the lesson was hammered in: This is the sort of thing that happens when ordinary citizens, such as Rodney Peairs, are allowed to own guns.

MISTAKEN SHOOTINGS

WHAT THE MEDIA failed to point out is that cases such as that of Yoshihiro Hattori are rare. Only about thirty innocent people per year are killed in the United States by armed citizens who mistake them for intruders.[7]

Gun controllers might argue that thirty victims is thirty too many. Of course, they are right. But how would we go about avoiding such accidental shootings? Leaving all crime fighting to the police would not solve the problem. Indeed, the data show conclusively that police are far more likely to shoot the wrong person than private citizens are.

Whereas armed citizens shoot the wrong person 2 percent of the time, police officers do so 11 percent of the time.[8]

In "Shall Issue: The New Wave of Concealed Handgun Permit Laws," Cramer and Kopel suggest some possible reasons for this disparity. Civilians can often pick and choose whether to intervene in an ongoing crime. They can avoid situations that seem confusing or daunting. Police, on the other hand, must step in every time and take action. Consequently, they are more likely to make mistakes.[9]

Attorney Jeffrey Snyder adds this observation:

> Rape, robbery, and attempted murder are not typically actions rife with ambiguity or subtlety, requiring special powers of observation and great book-learning to discern. When a man pulls a knife on a woman and says, "You're coming with me," her judgment that a crime is being committed is not likely to be in error. There is little chance that she is going to shoot the wrong person. It is the police, because they are rarely at the scene of the crime when it occurs, who are more likely to find themselves in circumstances where guilt and innocence are not so clear-cut, and in which the probability for mistakes is higher.[10]

IT WORKS

WHATEVER THE REASON, armed resistance by private citizens works. Most criminals are not the fearless supermen portrayed in films such as *Predator II.* Most are not skilled martial artists capable of plucking a loaded gun from a determined adversary's hands. By and large, they are cowards who prey on women and old people, seeking to avoid a fair fight at all costs. That is why, in 98 percent of the reported cases, criminals flee the moment they realize their intended victim is armed.

John Lott offers these real-life examples:

- A man tried to kick down the door of a seventy-year-old woman. She opened a window and pointed a gun at him. He turned and fled, running right into a wall in his panic.
- John Haxby, a TV newsman for a CBS affiliate in Omaha, was riding with his brother in a car. As they stopped at a light, a man with a butcher knife opened the passenger door. He moved toward Haxby, then

suddenly stopped and fled. Haxby turned to see a pistol in his brother's hand.

- While a New Jersey woman sat in a car, two men tried to open the doors, one on either side of the car. She pulled out her gun and yelled. Both men backed away instantly at the sight of the gun and ran for their lives.[11]

"ACTIVE COMPLIANCE"

ACCORDING TO University of California Berkeley criminologist Franklin Zimring, the best way to survive a robbery is through "active compliance." In other words, do exactly what the criminal says, as quickly as possible.[12]

The statistics suggest otherwise. After examining data from the Department of Justice National Crime Victimization Survey from 1979 through 1987, Gary Kleck found that the best way to survive a criminal attack was to resist—with a gun.

Women were 2.5 times more likely to suffer serious injury if they offered no resistance than if they resisted with a gun. Having a gun made the crucial difference. Women who resisted without a gun were four times more likely to be seriously hurt than those who resisted with a gun. "In other words," writes John Lott, "the best advice is to resist with a gun, but if no gun is available, it is better to offer no resistance than to fight."

In the case of men—no doubt, because of their greater physical strength—having a gun made considerably less difference in the success rate of their resistance and in the likelihood of their being injured. But it still proved advantageous. Men who offered no resistance turned out to be 1.4 times more likely to be seriously hurt than those who resisted with a gun. Men who resisted without a gun were 1.5 times more likely to be injured than those resisting with a gun.[13]

The Wichita Horror

Kleck's study is compelling, but these dry statistics tell only part of the story. There is another reason for people to think twice before engaging in "active compliance." Victims who choose passivity risk far more than mere injury or death.

On December 14, 2000, a young schoolteacher—identified in the press only as "H. G."—went to visit her boyfriend Jason Befort, 26, at his townhouse in northeast Wichita, where he lived with two other men. As Jason and H. G. lay in bed, the porch light came on and they heard one of the roommates Aaron Sander, 29, talking to someone.

The next thing they knew, "the bedroom door burst open," the woman later recalled in court. "A tall black man was standing in the doorway. He ripped the covers off of me, and I don't remember what he said. Right after that, Aaron was brought in by another black male. He was kind of just thrown onto the bed."

The two men pointed guns at their prisoners and demanded to know who else was in the house. When all occupants—three men and two women, all single, white professionals in their twenties—had been rounded up, the intruders demanded that they strip naked.

The Horror Unfolds

It has been alleged that the intruders were Jonathan and Reginald Carr, two brothers, ages twenty and twenty-three. They ransacked the house for booty. At one point, they found an engagement ring. "That's for you," said Jason Befort to his girlfriend H. G. "I was going to ask you to marry me."

Befort's girlfriend has reported that during the course of the night, she and the other woman, Heather Miller, 27, were repeatedly raped. She also said that the bandits forced the prisoners to perform sex acts on each other.

The intruders then asked for the car keys and began driving the prisoners one by one to the ATM to make withdrawals, leaving the others back at the house, under guard, locked in a closet. At one point, two of the men were in the closet together.

Befort's fianceé recalls, "Aaron asked Brad [Heyka, 27] if we should try to do anything, if they were going to kill us. Brad didn't respond."

Finally, the thieves drove their prisoners to an empty soccer field and told them to get out. "I turned to Heather and said, 'They're going to shoot us,'" remembers the schoolteacher.

She was right. All five prisoners were made to kneel in the snow. The bandits shot them, one-by-one, execution-style, in the back of the head, then ran over the bodies with their truck.

Only Jason Befort's fianceé survived to tell the tale. Naked, bleeding, and shot in the head, she managed to walk more than a mile through the snow to get help.[14]

A Massive Cover-Up

Those five young people in Wichita, Kansas, chose "active compliance." They did exactly as they were told. Perhaps if more people understood the sorts of things that can happen when you choose this course, they might weigh other options more seriously.

Unfortunately, the general public usually does not find out about crimes such as the Wichita Horror. They are reported only in local papers and often with the most horrifying details edited out. When it first occurred, only the *Wichita Eagle* paid attention to the alleged crimes of the Carr brothers. Our Web site, FrontPageMagazine.com, discovered the story about a month later and published it on the Internet, whereupon it rapidly became a *cause célèbre*—but only on the Internet and in conservative papers such as the *Washington Times*. You will not see Tom Brokaw, Dan Rather, or Peter Jennings talking about this crime.

OUR CENSORED NEWS

THE REASON such crimes are covered up probably has a lot to do with race. As previously mentioned, news organizations routinely ignore most crimes that occur within minority communities. Any newspaper or TV station that tried to report every black-on-black murder, in all its gory details, would be accused of "racism." They would be charged with presenting minorities in a negative light.

Covering interracial crimes—crimes between people of different races—can also be politically risky for journalists. As mentioned in the last chapter, in approximately 90 percent of all interracial attacks, white people are the victims and black people the perpetrators.[15] If these crimes were all given equal weight in the press, once again, journalists would be accused of "racism" for portraying African Americans as the villains in so many cases.

The safest sort of crime story for a journalist nowadays—and the type of story most likely to win him praise or awards—deals with a relatively rare sort of crime, one in which a white person attacks a black person (or some other protected "minority"), as in the beating death of gay student Matthew Shepard or the dragging death of James Byrd, a black man killed by white bigots in Texas.

UNTOLD STORIES

FOCUSING ON "hate crimes" committed by white people might be good for a journalist's career. But it gives the public a very inaccurate view of what is actually happening on the street. We journalists are often accused of focusing on bad news. But, in some ways, the news we present is not as bad as it needs to be. Sometimes people need to hear the worst in order to wake up to real dangers. Many of the "racially sensitive" crime stories that journalists censor happen to be exactly the sort of stories that people of *all* races need to hear, in order to be aware of the dangers inherent in "active compliance."

For instance, on July 21, 1997, three white Michigan teenagers, in search of adventure, decided to jump a train. Unfortunately, they got off in the wrong neighborhood. A gang of armed black youths surrounded them. They killed Michael Carter, fourteen, and shot Dustin Kaiser, fifteen, in the head (miraculously, Kaiser survived). The third victim, a fourteen-year-old girl, was pistol-whipped and forced to perform oral sex on the gang, after which she was shot point-blank in the face. The six gang members were later captured and prosecuted.The outrage was reported locally but did not receive national attention.[16]

Then consider the case of Terrell Rahim Yarbrough and Nathan D. Herring. On May 31, 1999, they kidnapped Brian Muha and Aaron Land, two white college students at Franciscan University in Ohio. According to the suspects' own statements, the students were beaten, robbed, and—in what is fast becoming a familiar scenario—forced to perform oral sex on each other, before they were shot with a .44 revolver. Yarbrough and Herring were convicted and sentenced to death. Their case has been largely ignored by the mass media.[17]

DEATH BEFORE DISHONOR

IN EACH OF these cases, "active compliance" resulted in suffering and indignity far beyond mere injury or death. Since the victims were unarmed, it is hard to say what might have resulted had they attempted to fight back. Perhaps they would have died anyway. But they would have died with their dignity intact. And their struggle might at least have given the bandits something to think about next time.

In past generations, girls and boys alike were taught to prefer death to dishonor. Rape was called "a fate worse than death." Girls were expected to defend their chastity, even at the risk of their lives. How far we have come from our forefathers' thinking. In the 1970s, feminists actually began suggesting that women ask their rapists to please use a condom.

During World War II, parents who lost a son at the front would display a gold star on a white flag, for each child lost. A "Gold Star Mother" was honored in her community. She displayed the star proudly as a token of her sacrifice for the greater cause.

Society changed during the 1960s. The antiwar spirit that swept America during the Vietnam conflict wiped out any notion that death could be honorable. "Make love, not war," said the hippies and protesters. Nothing was worth dying for. All that mattered was staying alive.

Not Worth Fighting

On July 14, 2000, a woman named Glenda Renee Hull entered a 7-Eleven store in Martinsburg, West Virginia, brandishing a rifle and demanding money. Store clerk Antonio Feliciano jumped her and held her down until the sheriff's deputies arrived. In another time, Feliciano would have been hailed as a hero. But in this age of "active compliance," he was fired for his action.

"No asset in a 7-Eleven store is worth defending with an employee's life," said company officials in a statement explaining Feliciano's firing. The 7-Eleven chain requires employees to hand over the money quietly during robberies.

Feliciano remarked that company regulations had not been his top concern during the crisis. "I just wanted to be sure that I was coming home that night," he said.[18]

A NATION OF COWARDS

DID THOSE 7-Eleven officials have a point? Is it right to risk your life or to take someone else's life, simply to prevent money from being stolen? Attorney Jeffrey Snyder says it is. In his now-famous 1993 paper, "A Nation of Cowards," he explains why:

> Crime is . . . a commandeering of the victim's person and liberty. . . . It is, in fact, an act of enslavement. Your wallet, your purse, or your car may not be worth your life, but your dignity is; and if it is not worth fighting for, it can hardly be said to exist.

Snyder went further. He concluded that "Crime is rampant because the law-abiding, each of us, condone it, excuse it, permit it, submit to it. We permit and encourage it because we do not fight back immediately, then and there, where it happens. . . . The defect is there, in our character. We are a nation of cowards and shirkers."[19]

A SAFE DISTANCE

FEW WOULD DENY that the Jews in Nazi-occupied Europe had the right—even the obligation—to take up arms against their oppressors. After all, their lives were at stake. Yet at the time, most Jews had no way of knowing, up until the moment they were killed, that death would be the final result of their "active compliance" with the SS. Most hoped they would survive if they just quietly did as they were told. And, indeed, many did manage to escape with their lives, even after years of imprisonment in death camps such as Auschwitz and Treblinka.

But those we call heroes were the ones who fought back, in suicidal gestures such as the Warsaw Ghetto Uprising. Their resistance may have ended in death, but at least they died fighting. From the safe distance of sixty years, we admire their conduct. Yet we do not seek to emulate it in our own lives.

THE DEATH WISH QUESTION

In the 1974 film *Death Wish*, a Manhattan architect played by Charles Bronson comes face-to-face with the emptiness of his liberal ideas when intruders kill his wife and rape his daughter, leaving her a mental vegetable. He becomes a vigilante, prowling the streets and subways of New York, gunning down anyone who attempts to mug him.

In one scene, the Bronson character and his son-in-law, Jack, debate the ethics of taking the law into one's own hands.

"We're not pioneers anymore," his son-in-law objects.

"What are we, Jack?" Bronson responds. "If we're not pioneers, what have we become? What do you call people who, when they're faced with a condition of fear, do nothing about it—they just run and hide?"

"Civilized?" Jack suggests.

Bronson shakes his head. "No."

What Are We?

The question Bronson asked in that 1974 film haunts our society still. What are we? What have we become? What do you call people who sit and do nothing while their loved ones are raped and butchered? What do you call people who fear death so deeply that they will accept any dishonor in its stead?

Those who push for gun control say that Americans no longer need guns to defend themselves. After all, we are no longer threatened by Indian raids. And we're not facing a Nazi extermination effort, such as the Jews faced in World War II.

But their complacency is unjustified. Those five young people in Wichita, Kansas, are just as dead as if they had been scalped by Indians on the frontier or machine-gunned at Babi Yar. What difference did it make if the intruders were marauding Indians or marauding street thugs? The result was the same.

Like the Jews in World War II, the Wichita victims faced a choice. They could fight or obey. Until the very end, they placed their hope in obedience. And, like the Jews in Nazi Europe, their "active compliance" led them to catastrophe.

JUDGE NOT

WHEN WE FIRST published the story of the Wichita Horror on FrontPageMagazine.com, a number of readers posted comments on our message board, asking why the victims had not fought back. It is not my purpose to raise that question here. The dead must rest in peace.

We can no more judge the actions of the Wichita Five than we can judge the 34,000 Jews who perished at Babi Yar in 1941. Whatever choices they made seemed right to them at the time. None of us can say what we would have done in their place, because we were not there.

I earlier quoted Abram L. Sachar in *The Redemption of the Unwanted*, who wrote of the slaughter at Babi Yar, "This, the most appalling massacre of the war, is often alluded to as a prime example of utter Jewish helplessness in the face of disaster. But even the few desperate attempts, almost completely futile, to strike back served as a reminder that *the difference between resistance and submission depended very largely upon who was in possession of the arms* that back up the will to do or die" (emphasis added).

So it was with the Wichita Five, none of whom possessed the arms they needed to "back up the will to do or die."

The question of resistance is both moral and practical. The moral dimension can be resolved only in the privacy of our hearts. The practical question can be determined only in the moment of crisis, depending on the situation one faces.

I offer this chapter not as a facile prescription for action but as a spur to soul-searching. It is worth pointing out that the one time in my life that I was held up at gunpoint, I handed over my wallet instantly. I do not know, any more than do my readers, what I would have done at Babi Yar or in that deserted soccer field in Wichita. Until the crisis is upon us, the question yawns unanswered like a black and empty abyss.

MYTH 3

GUNS POSE A SPECIAL THREAT TO CHILDREN

ON JUNE 8, 2000, a test audience in Los Angeles attended a screening of SONY's soon-to-be-released Revolutionary War epic *The Patriot*, starring Mel Gibson. As the film rolled, a gasp of shock rose from the audience.

On screen, the Mel Gibson character had armed his sons—ages ten and thirteen—with muskets and led them into the woods to ambush the British. Cyber-journalist Matt Drudge reports that some viewers reacted with horror when the camera zoomed in on the kids blasting away at British redcoats.[1]

The spectacle of children firing guns was evidently too much for them. Perhaps it evoked memories of Columbine and other well-publicized school shootings.

A CHANGING CULTURE

Nothing is new or unusual about boys wielding firearms in Hollywood films. In *Dances with Wolves*, for instance, there is a scene in which Kevin Costner's love interest suddenly recalls the Indian raid in which her family was killed. Her last memory is of her neighbor's son—a prepubescent boy—telling her to run for her life, as he readies his rifle to fire at the Indians.

No one gasped when they saw that scene. It was not considered worthy of remark.

But that was in 1990. America has changed since then. What seemed normal and wholesome yesterday has become diabolical, in some people's minds. The gun-ban lobby can take much of the credit for this. It has made great strides in convincing Americans—and particularly American women—that kids and guns don't mix.

FOR THE CHILDREN

"I've been a child advocate my entire career," said Rosie O'Donnell to ABC's Cokie Roberts before the Million Mom March. ". . . as a child advocate, gun control is a major issue for me. When everyone was all upset about Columbine, I, too, felt spiritually called to the table to speak for the 4,000 children that are killed every year by gunshot wounds."[2]

Statements of this sort drive the gun-ban lobby. Child safety is presented as the paramount concern. Anyone who opposes gun control is cast as a child killer.

Even the staunchest gun rights advocates shrink before this emotional argument. In their hearts, they know it is flawed. After all, children in Switzerland live intimately with fully automatic assault rifles in their homes and are encouraged to pursue shooting from an early age, for both sport and military readiness. Only a generation ago, American boys were also encouraged to shoot, early in life. Many received their first rifles before they turned twelve.

But 4,000 children killed per year is a high number. Few want to cast themselves as insensitive to such carnage. Before we can explore the relationship between guns and children with any objectivity, we must first take a closer look at Rosie O'Donnell's statistics.

IS THERE A GUN SAFETY CRISIS?

STATISTICIANS FIRST BEGAN recording the number of gun accidents in America in 1903. At that time, there were far fewer guns. Yet not only was the per capita rate of fatal accidental shootings higher than today, but also the actual number of such incidents exceeded today's. "The number of fatal gun accidents is at its lowest level since 1903," wrote David Kopel in April 2000. One can only conclude that Americans today are using guns more competently and safely than they did a century ago.

But what about those 4,000 children killed each year by gunshot wounds—approximately 11 per day? Some antigun crusaders cite even higher figures of 13, 15, or even 17 children killed per day. The impression they give is of a nation swept by an epidemic of shootings, both deliberate and accidental.

What would account for such extraordinary carnage? Who is killing these children and under what circumstances? Kopel observes:

> The claims are true only if you count a 19-year-old drug dealer who is shot by a competitor, or an 18-year-old armed robber who is shot by a policeman, as "a child killed by a gun." As for actual children (14 years and under), the daily death rate is 2.6. For children ten and under, it's 0.4 per day—far lower than the number of children who are killed by automobiles, drowning, or many other causes.[3]

When citing gun death figures, antigun activists typically categorize people up to twenty years of age as "children." This allows them to include the astronomical death toll among black and Hispanic young men involved in drug trafficking.

The carnage in our inner cities is certainly a problem. But is it a child safety problem? In view of the fact that our armed forces routinely put eighteen- to twenty-year-olds into combat, it would seem that Rosie O'Donnell's definition of a "child" is somewhat broader than the ordinary one.

Apples and Oranges

According to John Lott, the number of children—age fourteen and under—who died from gunshot wounds in 1995 was 200. In that same year, 2,900 children died in car crashes, 950 drowned, and 1,000 died of burns. "More children die in bicycle accidents each year than die from all types of firearm accidents," observes Lott.[4]

Some might argue that Lott is comparing apples to oranges. Car crashes are tragic but unavoidable, they might say. Everyone has to drive a car, whereas no one really needs a gun.

Let us ignore, for the sake of argument, the contention of eco-extremists such as Al Gore that society really doesn't need cars at all. Let us also ignore, for a moment, the traditional American belief that guns are crucial for liberty—whereas cars are not.

Let us focus instead exclusively on bicycle and drowning deaths.

A Parent's Choice

I have met parents who—because of their fears—have never allowed their children to take swimming lessons or to frolic in the surf at the seashore. Better safe than sorry is their motto. Teaching children to swim will only encourage them to take risks. And letting them play in the sea exposes them to sudden death from trick currents.

Most parents, however, are willing to accept a certain level of risk for their children. Most encourage their kids to swim.

And almost all parents allow their children to ride bicycles. But why do they do it?

Swimming is not essential to life. It might save you in a flood or a boating accident, but how likely is that to happen? As for cycling, it is entirely frivolous. There is no place that children need to go that they cannot reach more safely by walking or taking public transport. So why endanger them needlessly by encouraging them to ride a bike?

The reason is that swimming and cycling are part of our culture. We assume that children have a right to enjoy these sports—despite the dangers involved—simply because we enjoyed them ourselves as children, and because our parents and grandparents enjoyed them before us.

THE CULTURE WAR

GUNS ARE ALSO part of our culture. We have traditionally encouraged children—especially young boys—to shoot because that is what our parents did and our grandparents before them. But the gun-ban lobby is trying to change that. The culture war is raging in every home and school. It is a radical experiment in social engineering on a scale not attempted since the days of Prohibition.

Like the current antigun crusaders, Prohibitionists argued that violence was out of control. They pointed to a direct statistical link between violence and alcohol consumption. They also argued that alcohol posed a special threat to the young. No one could refute their logic. And so we ended up with the Volstead Act of 1919, banning the sale of alcoholic beverages in the United States.

Millions of Americans were instantaneously transformed into criminals by a stroke of the pen. An activity that we had always viewed as normal had suddenly become illegal. Honest distillers became "bootleggers." Importers became "rum-runners." Saloons became "speakeasies." And your innocent after-dinner brandy became "hooch" or contraband.

The New Prohibition

Prohibition was a disaster. But a similar experiment is being attempted in America today. A once-respectable activity—owning and shooting a gun—is now stigmatized and demonized. Though guns are literally less dangerous to children than bicycles, the new Prohibitionists have managed to imbue firearms with such a powerful aura of evil that even toy guns are now viewed with suspicion.

Some months ago, I attended a child's birthday party. While we grownups sat jawboning around the dining-room table, a ruckus broke out. A little girl of about five ran from the kitchen, chasing the birthday boy. She wielded a plastic AK-47 assault rifle that sparked and sputtered as she fired at the boy.

"Now, now, play nice," said our host, the boy's father, casting nervous glances at the other adults, as he pried the toy gun from the girl's hands.

Presumably, our host had no aversion to toy guns, or it would not have been lying around his house. But he seemed uneasy about letting the other grownups see it. Perhaps he feared being denounced as a promoter of future Columbine shootings.

A "Fad"

At the same party, a woman had been employed to paint the children's faces. I noticed that all the little girls were adorned with intricate floral designs, whereas the boys were not painted at all. I asked why not.

"The boys aren't interested," one of the mothers explained. One boy had asked for a gun to be painted on his face. The face painter had said no. After that, the boys lost interest.

"You should have told them it was war paint," I suggested. "That would have gotten their attention."

The women at the table exchanged glances. I sensed that they agreed with me but were hesitant to say so. Finally, one of them, a Romanian immigrant, explained, "You can't have anything related to war. It's a fad with all the parents now. No war."

By chance, most of the women sitting at the table happened to be Eastern European immigrants. Having spent considerable time, since the 1970s, working, studying and traveling in the Soviet Union, I had a hunch that their private thoughts about this "fad" probably differed from those of the average American soccer mom. So I said something that I probably would not have said at a party filled with native-born Americans.

"Well, if there's ever a war someday," I said, "nobody's going to know how to fight."

There was instant agreement around the table. These women knew that it was pointless, silly, and even unwise to discourage little boys from playing war. However, being Eastern European, they also knew how to lie low and keep their mouths shut when their opinions differed from the Party Line. In whatever play groups and school functions they frequented, their important perspective on this issue no doubt went unspoken and unheard.

A More "Innocent" Age

When I was a boy, one of my favorite toys was a plastic Thompson submachine gun that sparked and sputtered just like the little girl's AK-47. My playmates and I also wielded realistic-looking plastic trench knives, Colt .45 automatic pistols, six-shooters, tomahawks, bows and arrows, and so forth.

We did not have ultraviolent video games such as Doom, but our imaginations supplied comparable levels of gore. Inspired by Western movies, we often pretended, during our cowboy-and-Indian games, to be inflicting gruesome tortures on each other. We might pretend to be scalping someone alive. Or we might go through the motions of pretending to bury a prisoner up to his neck in an anthill, while he, in turn, pretended to scream in agony as hundreds of imaginary ants burrowed into his eyeballs.

AGGRESSION IS NATURAL

DID THIS sort of play harm us? The Mia Farrows of this world would say yes. "I don't let my kids play with toy guns, even with squirt guns," Farrow told Larry King in a June 2, 1999, interview.[5]

The Mia Farrow types believe that play violence conditions children to be wife-beaters, serial killers, and schoolyard snipers. But does it?

On this subject, the politically correct crowd contradicts itself. Most of the time, the hand-wringers of the Left claim that Mother Nature knows best. They say that global warming, soil depletion, mass extinction of animal species, and other infelicities of modern life are caused by man's arrogance in trying to bend nature to his will. Even sexual restraint is discouraged, on the grounds that carnal desires are "natural."

But when the topic turns to aggression and violence, the Mia Farrows and the Rosie O'Donnells sing a different tune. It doesn't matter if aggression is natural, they say. It must be suppressed.

Play Violence

Scientists have long noted that when young animals play, they mimic violent behavior. Kittens bite, stalk, scratch, and pounce on a ball of string, reproducing the motions of attacking and killing a small animal. Young deer chase each other, practicing the charges, feints, leaps, and quick turns that will one day help them elude and fight off predators.

Humans are the same. Children playing hide-and-seek will scream in mock terror when their hiding place is discovered, exactly as they would scream in real life if found by a stalking predator or foe.

Scientists say that all this chasing and fighting stimulates the nervous system, building up important neural connections in a young animal's brain. Mock fights also teach animals to interact with others of their species.

"Through play bouts, an animal's aggressive tendencies are socialized," says Dr. Stephen J. Suomi, an expert in primate play, who is chief of the Laboratory of Comparative Ethology at the National Institute of Child Health and Human Development in Bethesda, Maryland. "The animal learns when to submit and when to pursue, and it will learn how to lose a fight gracefully."[6]

Indeed, Suomi observes that monkeys who play less when young tend to be awkward and ill-at-ease in their mating and socializing as adults.

Defying Mother Nature

As beneficial as play fighting seems to be for young animals and humans, the Mia Farrow crowd wants it stopped. They would reject millions of years of evolution for the sake of their pacifist notions.

What will be the long-term effects of suppressing children's aggression? Nobody knows. But with more and more parents and teachers embracing a "zero-tolerance" policy toward play violence, it appears we are going to find out.

ZERO TOLERANCE

IN MARCH 2000, four kindergarteners in Sayreville, New Jersey, were suspended from school for three days. Their offense? They had been playing cops and robbers on the school playground, pretending to shoot each other with "finger guns." School officials explained that other children became frightened by the game.[7]

In January 2001, an eight-year-old first-grader in Jonesboro, Arkansas, was suspended for three days for pointing a breaded chicken finger at a friend and saying, "Pow, pow, pow." The boy later explained, "The teacher thought I was pointing it at her, but I was pointing it at my friend."[8]

Other victims of school "zero-tolerance" policies have included a third-grader in Green Bay, Wisconsin, suspended for having a key chain with a small gun replica attached and an eleven-year-old girl suspended in the Atlanta suburbs because the chain attached to her Tweety Bird wallet was judged to be too long by school administrators and thus potentially useful as a weapon.[9]

WITCH HUNT

These "zero-tolerance" policies obviously go far beyond the goal of simply keeping guns and violence out of schools. They attempt to wipe out every trace of aggression from children's thoughts and play. The fanaticism with which such policies are pursued reminds one of the Salem Witch Hunts.

Take Santa Fe sculptor Linda Strong. Back in 1979, she created a bronze fountain, depicting her son and daughter engaged in a water fight, the daughter with a hose, the son with a water pistol. Entitled *The Children's Fountain*, it was placed in a city park. When the fountain was turned on, streams of water squirted from hose and pistol.

Twenty years went by with no problem. Then the gun-ban movement arrived. Suddenly, the image of a little boy pointing a gun—even a water pistol—was too much for some local activists. The city was besieged with complaints. When no action was taken, vandals defaced the statue. Strong was forced to modify it, to head off further vandalism. She cut off the water pistol and replaced it with a hose.[10]

Where Does It End?

Strong's modification may not be enough, however. Even squirting another child with a hose could be viewed as "violent" by some of the antiaggression ideologues who now set policy in our nation's public schools.

Many school districts are phasing out dodge ball—a venerable playground activity in which two teams try to hit each other with big rubber balls. "Activities requiring human targets" are inappropriate, explains the Cecil County, Maryland, school board.[11]

A child's interest in the armed forces can also result in disciplinary action nowadays. Nevis, Minnesota, high school senior Samantha Jones was planning on joining the army after graduation. She had her yearbook portrait taken sitting on a 155-mm howitzer outside the local Veterans of Foreign Wars post. Her school refused to publish the photo, saying that it violated the rule against displaying images of weapons, whether on shirts, hats, or other media. "Whether it's in military, recreational, or sporting form, anything shaped like a gun or knife is banned," explained Superintendent Dick Magaard.[12]

"GUNS ARE DEMONS"

IMAGINE IF you went to your doctor with an infection, and instead of giving you antibiotics, he began dancing around the room, chanting and shaking rattles over you. Not only would his behavior be eccentric, but it would also be unhelpful. Science has developed far more effective procedures for dealing with troublesome microorganisms.

Similarly, our society long ago developed methods for teaching children to use firearms safely and responsibly. These methods work. Yet today's antigun hysterics ignore them. They seek to banish violence through strange and exotic methods—such as "zero tolerance" policies—equivalent to the ministrations of a witch doctor.

A strong element of superstition pervades the attitudes of many gun controllers. Years ago, I remember watching a TV drama called "The Gun." It traced the life of a handgun from one owner to the next. Each person who came into possession of the weapon fell under a kind of curse, winding up in some deadly tragedy, as if the gun itself had demonic power to infect people with madness, violence, and ill fortune.

Many antigun crusaders appear to view guns in just this way, as literal conveyors of spiritual evil. "Demons exist in the world today and guns are demons . . . ," said Father Marshall Gourley of Our Lady of Guadalupe Church in Denver. "We look at different possibilities of casting out those demons."[13]

GUN SAFETY

THE EFFECT OF today's zero-tolerance policies can only be to instill in children a superstitious fear and awe of weapons. Yet experience has shown that just the opposite approach is needed. Children who are familiar with firearms and trained in basic safety rules are less likely to play with them inappropriately.

For instance, the National Rifle Association offers the Eddie Eagle Gun Safety Program for children, used by the FBI and taught by police officers in many schools. Among other things, the course teaches young children that if you find a gun, you should "STOP, DON'T TOUCH, LEAVE THE AREA, AND TELL AN ADULT."

Handgun Control Inc., has mocked the program as ludicrous. "This is an organization that believes children can be left unattended with guns so long as they're told not to touch them," it said in one press release.

Yet the course is undeniably effective. Some years ago, *ABC News* videotaped an experiment in which two groups of preschool children were left alone in a room with an unloaded gun. Both groups of children quickly discovered the weapon. The first group, which had taken the Eddie Eagle course, left it alone. The children in the second group—which had not taken the course—immediately picked it up and began pointing it at each other and pulling the trigger.[14]

THE REAL QUESTION

OF COURSE, gun controllers would argue that such training is only necessary because we have a "gun problem" in the first place. In a gun-free world, there would be no danger of kids stumbling accidentally upon a gun. And so they would not have to be trained for that possibility.

They are correct. And this brings us to the real question behind the gun control debate. Most observant people have figured out by now that all the fuss over trigger locks, safe storage laws, gun-show "loopholes," licensing procedures, and so forth is just a smokescreen. The gun controllers' ultimate aim is plainly to institute a total or near-total gun ban, such as exists in Japan. Many have admitted as much, in their more candid moments. Indeed, today's "zero-tolerance" policies in schools demonstrate that not only weapons, but all forms of aggressive thought and emotion, have been targeted for complete elimination.

The real question we need to be asking is whether we, as a people, believe that a world without weapons or aggression would be a better or worse place. Those imbued with the pacifist notions of the '60s may feel that such a question does not even need to be asked. But let us ask it anyway, and see where it leads us.

Demolition Man

The 1993 film *Demolition Man* portrays Sylvester Stallone as a tough cop in a nightmarish future society wracked by out-of-control urban violence. Stallone proves to be a little too tough for his superiors. As punishment for his excessive use of force, he is placed in suspended animation.

Decades later, the Stallone character wakes up in a new world. Violence and aggression have vanished. Crime is unknown. Guns exist only in museums. Everyone speaks in the soft, touchy-feely tones of a Mr. Rogers or a therapy group leader. If anyone inadvertently uses a four-letter word, an alarm sounds and he is fined. It is a pacifist's paradise. The only problem is that freedom has vanished along with aggression. A sinister cult leader rules the world, and no one would dare be so impolite or aggressive as to disobey him.

To make a long story short, Stallone saves the day through the application of a little old-fashioned rudeness, barbarism, and, yes, firepower. In the process, he arouses the ardor of a lady cop, played by Sandra Bullock, who has never before met a real man.

A Glimpse in the Mirror

Demolition Man is one of the cleverest, funniest, wisest, and most entertaining science fiction films I have ever seen. It is certainly among Stallone's best. Yet it was skewered by many critics. I suspect they disliked the film's message. In the sheeplike subservience of the futuristic people it portrayed, I suspect those critics saw a little too much of themselves.

Demolition Man is a fantasy, but it warns of a real danger. There will always be wolves in the world. Transforming ourselves into sheep will not make the wolves go away. It will only provide them with an easier meal.

A TELLING INCIDENT

Several years ago, I was waiting in line at Kinko's late one evening when a ruckus broke out among the copying machines. A young man, possibly an NYU student, came running up to the counter saying that some of his materials were being stolen. Everyone turned to look where he was pointing. An African American man of about the same age and height as the other fellow—who was white—was striding out the door. He hurled some abusive words at the complainant as he left.

"Look, he's leaving with my stuff!" said the complainant, wringing his hands in frustration.

Behind the counter were three or four young men in their early twenties, all white, all sporting some combination of bizarre haircuts, earrings, pierced noses, and other countercultural appurtenances. All stared blankly at the customer who was complaining. No one made a move to help.

The only person who acted was the manager, a chubby, bespectacled young woman no taller than five feet. At first, she looked around at the male employees, as if expecting them to do something. Then, with a sigh of frustration, she came out from behind the counter and rushed out the door herself—alone—to confront the alleged thief.

Something Wrong

Admittedly, it was a confusing situation. The manager returned only moments later, empty-handed, and took the irate customer aside to speak with him. I have no idea what they discussed. For all I know, the whole incident may have turned out to have been some sort of interpersonal dispute, with complexities unknown to bystanders such as myself.

Still, something about the glazed passivity of those male employees bothered me. At the very least, they should have approached the alleged thief and politely asked him to help clarify the situation. Instead, they stood like mannequins and allowed a five-foot-tall woman to take all the risk.

Times Are Changing

Perhaps I'm getting old. I can remember when young men would have been ashamed to behave that way.

At age nineteen, I worked as a short-order cook at an eatery just off the Syracuse University campus. In those days, in the late 1970s, this establishment boasted an eclectic clientele of students, hippies, bikers, and other "townies." Late at night, as the beer and wine flowed, it transformed from campus hangout into barroom.

One night, around closing time, a gang of townies—Italian Americans from the North Side—started a brawl. They pushed the manager to the floor and began stomping him mercilessly. We employees jumped in at once.

It was a frightening experience. Chairs and heavy glass beer pitchers flew through the air. One of our regulars—a hard-boiled Vietnam vet with a beard like Jeremiah Johnson—

entered the fray on our side and ended up in the emergency room with a deep gash on his forehead. Not being an experienced streetfighter, I'm afraid I took more punishment than I delivered that night. But I gave it my all.

Afterward, when I had returned to the dishroom, my broken glasses dangling crookedly down my nose, Bill, the manager, came up to me and shook my hand.

"Thank you," he said. "Thanks for jumping in."

It turned out that not all the employees had jumped in. Some had just stood back and watched. A deep feeling of pride surged through me as I realized that I was among the chosen few who had proved their bravery. When Bill shook my hand, it was as if he had bestowed a Bronze Star on me. For days afterward, those of us who had participated in the fight told and retold our stories endlessly over pitchers of beer. It was a minor brawl in an insignificant bar in a city that most people have never heard of. But from the way we talked, you'd think we had all landed together on Omaha Beach.

The Greatest Motivator

In a violent situation, there are innumerable good reasons for hanging back and not getting involved, ranging from fear of injury or death to wariness of lawsuits or even arrest, should things go awry.

Yet one force can overcome these inhibitions and goad any man into action. That force is shame. It is the fear of being called a coward.

As I stood in Kinko's that night, it occurred to me that those glassy-eyed young men behind the counter with their earrings and pierced noses did not know this fear. They had probably been taught to fear accusations of "racism," "sexism," and "homophobia." But the word *coward* was not in their vocabulary.

I was in my late thirties that night at Kinko's, separated from those clerks by a generational gap of only fifteen years or so. But what a long fifteen years it had been, and how deeply America had changed in the interim.

"MOLON LABE"

IN THE YEAR 480 B.C., the Persian king Xerxes invaded Greece with an army of at least 200,000 men (ancient accounts say that he brought as many as 2 to 3 million troops, but modern historians find that unlikely). Xerxes probably would have conquered Greece had it not been for a small force of 300 Spartan warriors who blocked him at a mountain pass at Thermopylai, buying precious time for the Greeks to organize their defense.

It is said that when the Persians ordered the 300 Spartans to surrender their arms, their King Leonidas replied, "*Molon Labe*!" (Come and get them!). Leonidas and his troops were slain to the last man.

THE SPARTAN WOMEN

Bravery such as the Spartans exhibited at Thermopylai does not spring out of thin air. It must be carefully nurtured from early childhood, and deeply embedded in one's culture. The Spartan women, as wives and mothers, were just as responsible for their people's victories as the men who fought on the battlefield.

When a Spartan youth went to war, his mother would hand him his shield saying, "Come back carrying your shield or come back dead upon it."

A coward who fled in battle would typically throw his shield away so he could run faster. The Spartan women let their men know that if they did such a thing, they should just keep on running, for they would no longer be welcome in their homes.

The Path of the Warrior

Unlike today's soccer moms, the Spartan women did not look upon "safety" as their paramount concern. They felt a duty to instill in their men a warrior spirit, even if it meant losing the sons and husbands they loved. This took a special kind of courage, of a sort that American women have largely forgotten today.

We stand at a crossroads in America, and it is largely the women who will choose which way we will go. Will we continue to raise our children as warriors? Or will we abandon the warrior's path, take a roll of the dice, and see what comes next? History shows that those who turn from the warrior's path generally end up losing their freedom.

"Watch how children play," wrote the Japanese poet Takeji Muno. "When you see that, you will know whether society will progress or not."[15]

No doubt children would be marginally safer—at least from gun accidents—if all weapons were banned from our society. But the real question is, What will happen to society itself if we cease to raise children as warriors? In the concluding section of this book—entitled "The End of Manhood"—we will continue this vital discussion of guns, women, children, and warriorship.

MYTH 4

THE SECOND AMENDMENT APPLIES ONLY TO MILITIAMEN

A well-regulated militia being necessary to the security of a free State, the right of the people to keep and bear Arms shall not be infringed.

THE SECOND AMENDMENT OF THE U.S. CONSTITUTION, 1791

"SCHOLAR'S VIEWS on Arms Rights Anger Liberals," said a curious headline in the August 27, 1999, *USA Today*. The article reported that Harvard law professor Laurence Tribe had shocked and dismayed many colleagues by stating that the Second Amendment of the Constitution guarantees to each and every American a right to keep and bear arms.

Wait a minute. What's so shocking about that? Even today, most Americans take for granted that the Second Amendment ensures such a right. But it turns out that liberal law professors do not. For them, Tribe's statement was a betrayal, a concession to the enemy.

"I've gotten an avalanche of angry mail from apparent liberals who said, 'How could you?'" Tribe related. His treason cut the Left with special keenness, not only because Tribe himself is a noted liberal but also because—in the words of *USA Today*—he is "probably the most influential living American constitutional scholar." Tribe's treatise *American Constitutional*

Law is a standard text in many law schools and has been cited over fifty times in Supreme Court opinions.

NOT "WHOLLY IRRELEVANT"

FIRST PUBLISHED in 1978, earlier editions of Tribe's treatise had consigned all discussion of the Second Amendment to a footnote. But Tribe corrected that oversight in a new edition published in 1999. "As someone who takes the Constitution seriously, I thought I had a responsibility to see what the Second Amendment says, and how it fits," Tribe explained.

His study of the issue led Tribe to the conclusion that the right to keep and bear arms should not be written off as "wholly irrelevant." Indeed, he wrote, the Constitution ensured to each American a right, "admittedly of uncertain scope," to "possess and use firearms in the defense of themselves and their homes." Tribe also opined that "the federal government may not disarm individual citizens without some unusually strong justification." These modest assertions proved sufficient to send Tribe's liberal colleagues into a whirl of rage and confusion.[1]

THE ORPHAN OF THE BILL OF RIGHTS

In my view, *USA Today* missed the real story. The fact that Tribe had recognized a right to keep and bear arms was not really so stunning. The real shocker was that a man called "the most influential living American constitutional scholar" had waited twenty years before deciding to do so. For two decades, none of his colleagues seemed to notice or care about this glaring oversight in his treatise.

The Second Amendment is truly the orphan of the Bill of Rights. "One will search the 'leading' casebooks in vain for any mention of the Second Amendment," notes University of Texas law professor Sanford Levinson in the *Yale Law Journal.*

Professor Larue comments, "the second amendment is not taken seriously by most scholars."[2]

Why not?

According to Levinson, antigun sentiment may lie at the root of it. He writes: "I cannot help but suspect that the best explanation for the absence of the Second Amendment from the legal consciousness of the elite bar, including that component found in the legal academy, is derived from a mixture of sheer opposition to the idea of private ownership of guns and the perhaps subconscious fear that altogether plausible, perhaps even 'winning,' interpretations of the Second Amendment would present real hurdles to those of us supporting prohibitory regulation."[3]

A Domino Effect

The disdain with which the Second Amendment is regarded in law schools naturally affects the way it is applied in court. Dr. Michael S. Brown, a prominent gun rights activist and member of Doctors for Sensible Gun Laws, describes the situation in a June 19, 2000, article:

> I recently spoke with some attorneys who have observed 2nd Amendment issues in the courts. It seems that good defense attorneys hate to bring up the 2nd Amendment in court for very good reasons. Since the 2nd Amendment is almost completely neglected in law school, most lawyers know very little about it. If they are told anything at all, they hear only that it guarantees the right of the National Guard to be armed. Since judges attended those same law schools, this is the interpretation that they normally use. Defense attorneys who argue otherwise, along with their clients, are dealt with harshly. Therefore, only the most desperate or incompetent counselors ever use the 2nd Amendment as a defense.

This situation is self-perpetuating. Judges see the 2nd Amendment cited by underpaid public defenders representing the most undeserving clients. Each time they rule against these hapless counselors and loathsome criminals, another anti-Second Amendment decision is recorded in legal history. These poorly argued cases can then be used by government lawyers to show that legal precedent is on their side.[4]

THE LINES ARE DRAWN

IN THE INTRODUCTION, we noted the argument put forth by U.S. Justice Department attorney William B. Mateja in the case of *United States of America v. Timothy Joe Emerson.* Representing the U.S. government before a three-judge panel on June 13, 2000, Mateja argued that the Second Amendment ensured only the right of militiamen—which he defined as people serving in the National Guard—to keep and bear arms, and then only such arms as they had been issued for their military duties.

"You are saying that the Second Amendment is consistent with a position that you can take guns away from the public?" asked Judge William L. Garwood. "You can restrict ownership of rifles, pistols, and shotguns from all people? Is that the position of the United States?"

Mateja answered, "Yes."

The judge asked: "Is it the position of the United States that persons who are not in the National Guard are afforded no protections under the Second Amendment?"

"Exactly," said Mateja.[5]

Interestingly, the American Civil Liberties Union (ACLU) shares Mateja's view on gun rights. An ACLU policy statement contends that "the individual's right to keep and bear arms applies only to the preservation or efficiency of a well-regulated [state] militia. Except for lawful police and military purposes, the possession of weapons by individuals is not constitutionally protected."[6]

The Nihilist Theory

Mateja and the ACLU espouse what gun rights scholars David Kopel and Stephen Halbrook have called "the nihilist theory" of the Second Amendment—a theory that holds that "the Second Amendment means nothing at all."[7] If Mateja and the ACLU are correct, then the gun rights of individual Americans would be exactly the same with or without the Second Amendment. Either way, they would be nonexistent.

Only the National Guard would have a right to bear arms—a "collective" right, as the nihilists like to say, not an individual right. But such a "collective" right would be superfluous. It would be secure whether or not the Second Amendment existed. Soldiers are always permitted to bear arms, even in dictatorships. This is no more a "right" than the "right" to pay taxes. Saddam Hussein and Fidel Castro allow their troops to bear arms, as did Hitler, Stalin, Napoleon, and Genghis Khan.

If guaranteeing the right of National Guardsmen to bear arms is really the purpose of the Second Amendment—as the ACLU and the U.S. Justice Department allege—then it is truly a superfluous and meaningless amendment.

THE PAPER TRAIL

This leaves us at an impasse. On the one hand, most lawyers, courts, and bureaucrats seem united in the conviction that Americans have no right to keep and bear arms. On the other hand, most Americans insist that they do have such a right.

In situations where a dispute arises over the meaning of the Constitution, scholars generally turn to the writings of the

Framers in order to discern their original intent. The Second Amendment nihilists would have us believe that such an exercise would be useless, in this case. "It is doubtful that the Founding Fathers had any intent in mind with regard to the meaning of this [the Second] Amendment," concluded a 1975 report of the American Bar Association.[8]

The report implies that the Founding Fathers wrote the Second Amendment in a fit of absentmindedness. Yet this is clearly untrue. Not only did the Framers have a clear intent in mind, but they also left an unmistakable paper trail, in the form of letters, pamphlets, and articles, stating those intentions. Any honest scholar—even a liberal one, such as Laurence Tribe—who takes the trouble to read and study the available documents will quickly find that the nihilist argument falls apart.

An Anglo-Saxon Tradition

In composing the Bill of Rights, the Framers leaned heavily on English tradition and common law. One of those traditions held that every Englishman had both the right and duty to bear arms, in self-defense and for defense of the realm.

In addition to serving in war, Englishmen were expected to help keep the peace in their communities. When a serious crime was committed, they were duty-bound to answer the "hue and cry," armed and ready to pursue a fleeing fugitive. The tradition of "watch and ward" required them to take turns guarding their towns, by day and night. Riots and disorders were quelled with the help of a *posse comitatus* of armed citizens.

The tradition of an armed and vigilant citizenry has ancient roots among the English people. It goes back at least to Anglo-Saxon times, when the law of the *fyrd* bound every free man, ages sixteen to sixty, to arm himself in readiness for military service.[9] Some form of this custom appears to have existed even among the earliest Germanic ancestors of the Angles and Saxons, centuries before they settled in England.

The Roman historian Tacitus observed in the first century that, among the Germans, "No business, public or private, is transacted except in arms. But it is the rule that no one shall take up arms until the tribe has attested that he is likely to make good. When the time comes, one of the chiefs, or the father or a kinsman equips the young warrior with sword and spear in the public council. This with the Germans is our equivalent of the toga—the first public distinction of youth. They cease to rank merely as members of the household and become members of the tribe."

The Militia

Under the Normans, the difference between free men and slaves was largely defined by ownership—or nonownership—of weapons. "If any person is willing to enfranchise his slave," said the Norman law code, "let him . . . deliver him free arms, to wit, a lance and a sword; thereupon he is a free man."[10]

The word *militia* came into common use around 1590 to describe the whole population of able-bodied men, ages sixteen to sixty, who were required to bear arms. When the first British colonists arrived in America, they brought the militia with them. Only three years after the Mayflower landed, Plymouth colony enacted a law requiring "that every freeman or other inhabitant of this colony provide for himselfe and each under him able to beare armes a sufficient musket and other serviceable peece for war . . . with what speede may be."[11] As in Britain, authorities in every colony stipulated that "All men between the ages of sixteen and sixty were liable for militia service, with some exceptions for clergy, religious objectors, and

Negroes," writes Joyce Lee Malcolm in *To Keep and Bear Arms: The Origins of an Anglo-American Right*.[12]

A Bulwark of Liberty

British thinkers have long pointed to England's militia system as a bulwark of liberty. The great eighteenth-century jurist Sir William Blackstone observed that laws on parchment were only as good as the willingness of rulers to obey them. Should a tyrant arise with no respect for the law, then, warned Blackstone, "In vain would these rights be declared, ascertained, and protected by the dead letter of the laws if the constitution had provided no other method to secure their actual enjoyment."

What sorts of "other methods" did Blackstone have in mind for securing one's rights? Among them was the people's right "of having arms for their defence . . . the natural right of resistance and self preservation, when the sanctions of society and laws are found insufficient to restrain the violence of oppression."[13]

Centuries before, Aristotle had similarly observed that "those who possess and can wield arms are in a position to decide whether the constitution is to continue or not."[14] Blackstone noted approvingly that "in cases of national oppression, the nation has very justifiably risen as one man, to vindicate the original contract subsisting between the king and his people."[15] Historian Thomas Macaulay echoed Blackstone's sentiment in 1850 by calling the Englishman's right to bear arms "the security without which every other is insufficient."[16]

Scottish Whig Andrew Fletcher declared in 1698 that "The possession of arms is the distinction between a freeman and a slave."[17] Instead of a militia controlled by the crown, Fletcher called for a "well-regulated militia" under its own authority. He wrote, "Now let us consider whether we may not be able to defend ourselves by well-regulated militias against . . . invasion from abroad, as well as from the danger of slavery at home."[18]

THE MINUTE MEN

Most of us learned in school that unhappiness over British taxes was the chief cause of the American Revolution. However, a much more vexing issue to the colonists was the question Fletcher and other freedom-loving Britons had raised: Who would control the militia?

America's colonial militia was subservient to the crown and hence could be turned against its own people. As relations with the king deteriorated, patriots began stockpiling weapons and forming their own "well-regulated militias"—the famous Minute Men—answerable only to themselves. A plan was concocted in 1775 to outfit an army of 15,000 volunteers, independent of royal authority. Weapons for this army were being stored in the Massachusetts towns of Lexington and Concord. British troops set out from Boston on April 18, 1775, with orders to confiscate these weapons and arrest the ringleaders, including John Hancock and Samuel Adams. But the Minute Men met the British with gunfire, and thus began the American Revolution.[19]

THE MILITIA DEBATE

Having won their liberty, Americans now had to preserve it. Many worried that the newly formed American government might itself become tyrannical someday. Americans split into two camps over the question of how to counter this threat.

The Federalists argued that the problem would take care of itself, since the militia—consisting of all able-bodied men, ages sixteen through sixty—would overthrow any tyranny that arose. "The supreme power in America cannot enforce unjust laws by the sword," argued Noah Webster, "because the whole body of the people are armed. . . ."[20]

The anti-Federalists, however, pointed out that Congress might one day disband the general militia and replace it with a "select militia," loyal only to the government. "When a select militia is formed; the people in general may be disarmed," warned John Smilie at the Pennsylvania convention.[21]

"That Every Man Be Armed"

To prevent this from happening, the anti-Federalists demanded a Bill of Rights that would guarantee, among other things, an unalienable right to keep and bear arms. "The great object is that every man be armed . . . ," declared Patrick Henry. "Everyone who is able may have a gun." Richard Henry Lee concurred: "To preserve liberty, it is essential that the whole body of the people always possess arms, and be taught alike, especially when young, how to use them." With a population thus armed, Congress would be powerless to disband the militia.

Supporters of the Bill of Rights punctuated their point with the threat of force. One wrote that people all over his state were "repairing and cleaning their arms, and every young fellow who is able to do it, is providing himself with a rifle or musket, and ammunition." Only the passage of a Bill of Rights, he warned, would head off civil war.[22]

Private Arms

While the Bill of Rights was being debated in the House, Tench Coxe published a defense of the proposed amendments in the Philadelphia *Federal Gazette*. Unlike today's judges, lawyers, and ACLU activists, Coxe showed a clear understanding of the Second Amendment's meaning. He described it in these words:

> As civil rulers, not having their duty to the people duly before them, may attempt to tyrannize, and as the military forces which must be occasionally raised to defend our country,

> might pervert their power to the injury of their fellow citizens, the people are confirmed by the next article in their right to keep and bear their private arms.[23]

The "Insurrectionist Theory"

Today, antigun activists would accuse Tench Coxe of promoting the "insurrectionist theory" of the Second Amendment, an allegedly dangerous teaching that they say twists the Amendment's original meaning and encourages people such as Timothy McVeigh to join right-wing militias and bomb government buildings.[24]

Yet there is no question that Coxe's explanation reflected the exact thinking of the Framers and particularly of Coxe's friend James Madison, the author of the Bill of Rights. Upon receiving a copy of the article, Madison told Coxe that he was "indebted to the co-operation of your pen" for helping to explain the amendments to the public. Stephen Halbrook writes:

> Coxe's defense of the amendments was widely reprinted. A search of the literature of the time reveals that no writer disputed or contradicted Coxe's analysis that what became the Second Amendment protected the right of the people to keep and bear their "private arms." The only dispute was over whether a bill of rights was even necessary to protect such fundamental rights.[25]

"As Numerous as the Sands upon the Seashore"

Indeed, many Americans considered it downright dangerous to spell out one's rights on paper. To list them was to put limits on them, when, in fact, the rights of free men were "as numerous as the sands upon the seashore," as one writer put it.[26] Many Americans opposed the Bill of Rights on the grounds that it would give future generations of lawyers, bureaucrats, and sophists an excuse to claim that any right not specifically stipulated on that piece of paper did not exist.

James Madison took this argument seriously. He wrote, "This is one of the most plausible arguments I have ever heard urged against the admission of a bill of rights into this system, but, I conceive, that it may be guarded against."[27]

Madison's solution was to write what became the Ninth Amendment. It states: "The enumeration in the constitution, of certain rights, shall not be construed to deny or disparage others retained by the people." In other words, simply because the Bill of Rights does not mention a particular right, it should not be assumed that such right does not exist. The "natural" or God-given rights of free men take precedence over written rights. And no natural or God-given right was more widely recognized by the Founders than that of bearing arms in self-defense.

THE DEATH OF THE NINTH AMENDMENT

If the Ninth Amendment were still honored today, there would be no debate over the Second Amendment. No one would care whether it referred to an "individual" right or a "collective" one. The question would be academic. No matter what the Second Amendment said, our rights would not be limited by its stipulations.

Unfortunately, the Ninth Amendment—like the Second—is now widely ignored by our legal system. "How do courts see the Ninth Amendment today?" asks George Mason University economist and columnist Walter Williams. "It's more than a safe bet to say that courts, as well as lawyers, treat the Ninth Amendment with the deepest of contempt. In fact, I believe that if any appellant's lawyer argued Ninth Amendment protections on behalf of his client, he would be thrown out of court, if not disbarred. That's what the Ninth Amendment has come to mean today."[28]

The very fact that our society is now locked in bitter controversy over the Second Amendment shows that the fears of the Federalists were justified. We have moved from a society in which man's rights are "as numerous as the sands upon the seashore" to one in which those rights are assumed to be limited to the ten amendments of the Bill of Rights. And now even those ten amendments are under siege.

THE MILITIA TODAY

FOR THE time being, we still have a militia in America, though it has fallen into disuse. The Militia Act of 1792 decreed that "every free able bodied white male citizen" was part of the militia (the word "white" was removed in 1867). The Supreme Court later upheld this interpretation when it defined the militia as "all males physically capable of acting in concert for the common defense" (*United States v. Miller*, 1939).

The U.S. Code actually distinguishes between the organized militia (the National Guard) and the "unorganized militia," consisting of all men eligible for militia service but not formally enrolled.[29] "Women are probably also included, given the Supreme Court's sex-equality precedents," notes UCLA constitutional law instructor Eugene Volokh in the *Wall Street Journal*.[30] However militia membership may be defined, the Ninth Amendment—as noted above—makes clear that gun rights apply to all Americans, whether or not they are eligible for militia service.

"Assault Weapons"

Sadly, most of our "militiamen" no longer bother to arm themselves or to drill in units. We have surrendered that responsibility to a "select militia" of National Guardsmen, Army reservists, FBI SWAT teams, and Delta Force commandos. Just as the early patriots feared, our failure to exercise our militia rights has resulted in a rapid erosion of those rights.

In 1989, President George Bush banned the import of "assault weapons" and argued that Americans should only be allowed to own weapons suitable for "sporting purposes." Since then, the call for a general ban on "assault weapons" has grown deafening. Should it succeed, U.S. citizens will be stripped, for the first time since the Revolution, of the right to keep and bear arms suitable for military use. The militia—as our Founding Fathers conceived it—will no longer exist.

DOWNRIGHT FORCE

"GUARD WITH jealous attention the public liberty," warned Patrick Henry. "[N]othing will preserve it but downright force. Whenever you give up that force, you are ruined."[31]

Through an endless series of gun-control "compromises," Americans have come perilously close to the "ruin" that Patrick Henry predicted. Yet there is hope. The Swiss have proved that a well-trained and well-equipped militia can defend a modern state. For a generation stricken with *Private Ryan* guilt, the rebuilding of our lawful and constitutionally mandated militia would be a worthy project indeed.

MYTH 5

THE SECOND AMENDMENT IS AN OBSOLETE RELIC OF THE FRONTIER ERA

"IT'S TIME TO rethink [the Second Amendment] . . . ," says Mia Farrow.[1]

"I think [the Second Amendment] is in the Constitution so we can have muskets when the British people come over in 1800," opines talk-show host Rosie O'Donnell.[2]

"Whatever right the Second Amendment protects is not as important as it was 200 years ago . . . ," writes conservative pundit George Will.[3]

"Our forebears recognized that times would change . . . ," writes liberal columnist Jack Anderson. "They may have left us with this odd legacy known as the Second Amendment, but they understood it could become obsolete. . . ."[4]

"I say if you really insist on keeping (the second) amendment in the Constitution, then we must keep to the spirit of it, which means you can still own a gun, but it must be a musket," quips comedian Bill Maher, host of ABC's inappropriately named *Politically Incorrect* talk show.[5]

It's unanimous. The chic, the pompous, the fashionable, and the trendy have ruled on Americans' right to keep and bear arms. And they've decided we don't need it. But on what basis? Are Americans today really safer and more secure than our ancestors were two hundred years ago? Are we really less likely to need a firearm than they were?

UNPREPARED

BILL MAHER, at least, should know better. When riots broke out in Los Angeles in April 1992, he was not prepared. He had to borrow a gun from a friend for self-defense.[6] No doubt, Maher had always assumed that the police would quell any large-scale disorder before it came close to threatening him personally. But he was wrong. When the LA riots broke out, the police retreated, allowing the violence to spin out of control. Only the arrival of Federal and National Guard troops three days later put an end to the disturbance.

In the meantime, more than 50 people had been killed, 4,000 injured, 12,000 arrested, 700 buildings burned down, and more than $1 billion worth of property destroyed. Those who weathered the storm best were the brave store owners—mostly Korean—who stood guard over their property with shotguns and assault rifles.

DIAL 911 AND DIE

EARLY AMERICANS on the frontier had to fend for themselves. If a war party of marauding Indians appeared, they could not dial 911. They had to fight. Today's gun-ban lobbyists argue that the situation has changed. We don't have to worry about marauding Indians anymore, they say. So the danger is past.

Yet the average city-dweller today lives in constant peril from attackers as fierce and deadly as any Apache raider. Like the frontiersman of old, he never knows when enemies will strike. The only difference is that he is poorly equipped to defend himself. Thanks to strict gun laws, people in the most crime-ridden urban areas are often the least able to arm themselves in self-defense. Their only weapon is the telephone.

They can call the police and beg for protection. But how likely are the police to help? An organization called Jews for the Preservation of Firearms Ownership (jpfo.org) in Hartford, Wisconsin, distributes a book on that subject, entitled *Dial 911 and Die* by attorney Richard W. Stevens. It suggests some shocking answers to this question. (Interested readers can obtain a copy from JPFO at 800-869-1884.)

THE RISS CASE

STEVENS POINTS OUT that police lack the resources to protect each and every citizen from harm. In 95 percent of the cases, by the time police respond to a 911 call, the crime is already over and the perpetrator gone.[7] "Put more cops on the street," the gun-ban lobbyists suggest. But this will not solve the problem. For one thing, any cops you put on the street today will inevitably be cut the next time the budget ax falls. There is no such thing as a permanent budget.

More to the point, no matter how many officers you hire, there are built-in limits to what police can and will do for you. Police have no legal or constitutional obligation to guard or protect you from harm. Their only obligation is to enforce the law—which generally means to arrest criminals after they have committed a crime. The right of police to stand by and do nothing while citizens are attacked and even killed has been upheld many times in court.

To give but one example, a New Yorker named Linda Riss sought police protection from her vengeful boyfriend in 1959. For months, he had been warning her, "If I can't have you, no one else will have you, and when I get through with you, no one else will want you." After one particularly ominous threat,

Riss begged the police to help her, but they declined. The next day, a hired thug threw lye in her face, blinding her in one eye and scarring her for life. Riss sued the city but lost. The Court of Appeals of New York ruled that Riss had no right to police protection, and that the government could not afford to provide such protection even if it wished to do so.[8]

Catch-22

"The amount of protection that may be provided is limited by the resources of the community and by a considered legislative executive decision as to how these resources may be deployed," said the court in the Riss case. "For the courts to proclaim a new and general duty of protection . . . even to those who may be the particular seekers of protection based on specific hazards, could and would inevitably determine how the limited police resources of the community should be allocated and without predictable limits."

Judge Keating dissented, noting the cruel irony in the fact that the City of New York denied protection to Riss while at the same time forbidding her to arm herself. "What makes the city's position particularly difficult to understand is that, in conformity to the dictates of the law, Linda did not carry any weapon for self defense. Thus, by a rather bitter irony she was required to rely for protection on the City of New York, which now denies all responsibility to her" (*Riss v. City of N.Y.*, 293 N.Y. 2d 897 [1968]).

"No Right to Be Protected"

Judge Keating's dissent notwithstanding, the Court of Appeals of New York was on solid constitutional ground. As far back as 1856, the U.S. Supreme Court ruled that local police had no duty to protect any particular person (*South v. Maryland*, 59 U.S. [How.] 396, 15 L.Ed., 433 [856]).

"There is no Constitutional right to be protected by the state against being murdered by criminals or madmen," said the U.S. Court of Appeals, Seventh Circuit, in 1982. "It is monstrous if the state fails to protect its residents against such predators but it does not violate the due process clause of the Fourteenth Amendment or, we suppose, any other provision of the Constitution" (*Bowers v. DeVito*, U.S. Court of Appeals, 7th Circuit, 686F.2d 616 [1982]). (See also *Reiff v. City of Philadelphia*, 471 F.Supp. 1262 [E.D.Pa. 1979].)[9]

ASK A COP

AWARE OF their own limitations, most cops favor the idea of citizens bearing arms in self-defense. "How I wish that the information in this book were not true," comments Richard Mack, former sheriff of Graham County, Arizona, regarding *Dial 911 and Die*. "Nevertheless, this book speaks to the irrefutable truth: *police do very little to prevent violent crime*. We investigate crime after the fact. I applaud Richard Stevens for his tremendous research and his courage to tell this truth."[10]

Some readers may be surprised by Mack's statement. They have been led by the media and the antigun lobby to believe that police favor gun control and oppose people "taking the law into their own hands." But such sentiments generally come from high-profile police brass in major cities, not from rank-and-file officers. The police chiefs and public relations flacks who typically present the "police" point of view to the media take their marching orders from politicians. Their jobs depend on toeing the party line.

"STRAIGHTEN HIM OUT"

During a 1990 crime wave in New York City, an ex-cop named Stephen D'Andrilli suggested on a TV talk show that the city issue one million permits to carry handguns. Talk-show host

Dick Oliver asked New York Governor Mario Cuomo to respond to this proposal. After soundly condemning the idea, Cuomo snapped, "Why don't you ask the cops what they think of everybody packing guns?"

"It happens that Mr. Byrne, head of the Police Benevolent Association, walked by before and I asked him," replied Oliver. "He said, 'It's a good idea.'"

"Well, somebody better talk to Mr. Byrne, straighten him out," said the governor.[11]

Many high-ranking police officials have doubtless been "straightened out" behind the scenes in precisely the manner that Governor Cuomo prescribed. Yet despite all the arm-twisting, when the National Association of Chiefs of Police conducted a mail survey of 15,000 sheriffs and police chiefs in 1996, 93 percent said they approved of law-abiding citizens arming themselves for self-defense. A 1991 national reader survey by *Law Enforcement Technology* magazine revealed that 76 percent of street officers believed that handgun-carry permits should be issued to all trained, responsible adults who requested them. "If anything, the support among rank-and-file police officers for the right of individuals to carry guns for self-protection is even higher than it is among the general population," notes John Lott.[12]

WHEN COPS AREN'T ENOUGH

ORDINARY STREET CRIME is bad enough. But in large-scale disasters, such as earthquakes, hurricanes, blizzards, floods, and even electrical blackouts, looting and brigandage can break out on a scale that goes far beyond what any police department can handle. Sometimes order is not restored for days.

It can happen anywhere, at any time. In 1977, for instance, Buffalo, New York, was hit with a killer blizzard. More than thirteen feet of snow fell in forty-seven consecutive days. On January 28, with winds reaching sixty-nine miles an hour and the wind-chill factor plunging to fifty degrees below zero, more than 13,000 cars and trucks were stranded and some motorists froze to death before help could arrive.

"When the big blow finally stopped, Buffalo resembled an eerie, science-fiction movie," reported *U.S. News & World Report*. "It was as if a radioactive cloud had descended on the city and brought life to an abrupt standstill."[13]

Sensing the city's helplessness, looters turned out in force. Local officials were compelled to call on average citizens to arm themselves and help restore order. Eventually, 600 National Guardsmen and 400 federal troops from Fort Bragg arrived to finish the job. "Armed citizens also helped preserve order after Hurricane Andrew hit southern Florida in 1992," notes David Kopel.[14]

The Ultimate Breakdown

In Stephen King's sci-fi horror novel *The Stand*, a killer flu is accidentally released from a biological warfare base, annihilating most of the earth's population in a matter of days. Survivors pick their way through empty cities filled with bloated, decomposing corpses, terrorized by looters, criminals, psychopaths, and other human predators stalking the streets.

The Stand was only a novel. But the danger of biological warfare is real. Regarding the possibility of a bioterrorist attack on the United States, Secretary of Defense William Cohen said, "The question is no longer if this will happen, but when."[15] Col. David Franz (Ret.), former commander of the U.S. Army Medical Research Institute of Infectious Diseases, predicts that "a mass-casualty-producing event" could occur within ten years.[16] Such an attack could theoretically produce conditions like those described in King's novel, over large areas of the United States. Nuclear terrorism—the detonation of suitcase-sized nuclear bombs in major cities—could produce similar devastation.

If a mere blizzard could overwhelm the forces of law and order in Buffalo, New York, what would be the effect of a biological, chemical, or nuclear attack leaving millions dead—a type of attack that our highest officials now tell us is not only likely but also perhaps inevitable? As in Stephen King's *The Stand*, survivors' best hope would lie in arming themselves and banding together for protection against brigands. The ancient traditions of watch and ward, hue and cry, *posse comitatus* and citizen's militia would take on new and urgent life.

THE KISHINEV POGROM

ON EASTER, April 6–7, 1903, angry mobs stormed through the streets of Kishinev, Russia, killing any Jew they could find. When the violence ended, 49 Jews were dead, 500 wounded, and 2,000 families homeless. About 700 houses and 600 businesses had been looted and destroyed.

Under international pressure, the Russian government administered wrist-slaps to some lower-level organizers of the riot. However, the government itself turned out to be the principal conspirator. Government agencies had helped spread anti-Jewish propaganda in the weeks before the riot—some of it written by the local police chief—and the city garrison of 5,000 troops refused to intervene once the violence began.

For many Jews, the Kishinev Pogrom—as the event became known—simply underscored their helplessness. Many packed their bags and fled to America. But one Russian Jew, a young journalist named Vladimir Jabotinsky, drew a far different lesson from the incident.

"JEWISH YOUTH, LEARN TO SHOOT!"

"It's better to have a gun and not need it, than to need it and not have it," admonished Jabotinsky, in what later became one of his most oft-quoted sayings.

Jabotinsky devoted his life to promoting armed self-defense among Jews. He traveled through Europe and Palestine during the 1920s and '30s, urging Jewish youth to "learn to shoot!" and organizing Jewish militias.

With eery prescience, Jabotinsky warned that "time was imperiling the very existence of millions of European Jews." With Nazism on the rise, Jabotinsky urged a mass evacuation of Jews to Palestine. But most Jews mocked Jabotinsky for his alarmism. They listened instead to the soothing words of Rabbi Leo Baeck, who said that "the Nazis like dark clouds will pass."

Jabotinsky was denounced as an extremist and even a "fascist." But, tragically, all his predictions came true. After the war, many of Jabotinsky's fiercest critics admitted their error. "I deeply regret that I had fought against Jabotinsky's evacuation plan," said writer Shalom Asch.

The Ghetto Mentality

Jabotinsky has gone down in history as the founder of the Haganah self-defense force, which he started in 1920. It evolved into the army of the new state of Israel in 1948. Yet his name is obscure. Most of Jabotinsky's fellow Zionists were socialists. They disliked and distrusted Jabotinsky because he did not support their leftist agenda. Consequently, his legacy has been downplayed. Israel's first prime minister, David Ben-Gurion, hated Jabotinsky so intensely that he refused to allow his burial on Israeli soil. Though he died of a heart attack in 1940, Jabotinsky's remains were not moved to Israel until 1964.

Today, it is primarily hardline Jewish militants such as Irv Rubin of the Jewish Defense League who lionize Jabotinsky and keep his name alive. The resistance he encountered from fellow Jews the JDL attributes to the so-called "ghetto mentality."

"Those who suffer from the ghetto mentality are unable to cope with reality," writes Ari Rubin, Irv Rubin's son." They hope by giving into the will of authority, they will be able to avoid punishment."[17]

DENIAL

WHAT ARI RUBIN calls the "ghetto mentality" is not unique to Jews. It afflicts nearly everyone in our society, to one degree or another. Psychiatrist Sarah Thompson calls it "denial." She writes:

> Another defense mechanism commonly utilized by supporters of gun control is *denial.* Denial is simply refusing to accept the reality of a given situation. For example, consider a woman whose husband starts coming home late, has strange perfume on his clothes, and starts charging flowers and jewelry on his credit card. She may get extremely angry at a well-meaning friend who suggests that her husband is having an affair. The reality is obvious, but the wronged wife is so threatened by her husband's infidelity that she is unable to accept it, and so denies its existence.
>
> Antigun people do the same thing. It's obvious that we live in a dangerous society, where criminals attack innocent people. Just about everyone has been, or knows someone who has been, victimized. It's equally obvious that law enforcement can't protect everyone everywhere twenty-four hours a day. There is irrefutable evidence that victim disarmament nearly always precedes genocide. Nonetheless, the antigun folks insist, despite all evidence to the contrary, that "the police will protect you," "this is a safe neighborhood," and "it can't happen here," where "it" is everything from mugging to mass murder.[18]

HUBERT HUMPHREY AND THE SECOND AMENDMENT

OF COURSE, the ultimate danger to public safety is an abusive government. During the twentieth century, more people were murdered by tyrants than died in combat, as political scientist Rudolph J. Rummel noted in his book *Death by Government.* Fresh from their experience fighting the British, the Founding Fathers understood this danger well. They did not suffer from denial. They knew that an armed and vigilant citizenry was an essential check against government abuse.

As recently as 1959, the belief that armed citizens provided the ultimate check against tyranny was so widely accepted in America that even a liberal Democrat such as then-Senator Hubert Humphrey could say, without fear of criticism, "The right of citizens to bear arms is just one more guarantee against arbitrary government, one more safeguard against the tyranny which now appears remote in America, but which historically has proved to be always possible."[19]

It Can't Happen Here . . . or Can It?

Something has changed in America since Hubert Humphrey's day. Many have forgotten the lessons of the Founders. "I do not see a time when we Americans will need our guns at home to stage a coup to reclaim our democracy," writes syndicated columnist Jack Anderson, in his book *Inside the NRA.*[20]

Like the Jews in Nazi Germany, Anderson believes, "It can't happen here." Let us pray that he is correct. But his own writings belie his optimism. While downplaying the seriousness of street crime in Washington during the 1980s, Anderson remarks:

> If I had cause to look over my shoulder when I walked the streets of the nation's capital, it was only because I was accustomed to being tailed by the CIA or FBI agents on assignment from paranoid men in the White House. By 1989 I had even stopped watching for them. I had embarrassed the skulkers and their agencies by exposing them in print often enough that they no longer found it politic to follow me.[21]

Interestingly, Anderson demonstrates in this passage that he is well aware of how easily a president can disregard the Constitution and use government power to intimidate journalists. Yet he is supremely confident that the mere threat of "exposing them in print" will always prove sufficient to deter them.

"Emergency Czar"

Anderson's complacency has a schizophrenic quality. In one part of his mind, he denies the danger. Yet in another part, he seems to recognize it.

In 1984, for instance, Anderson reported a serious attempt by General Louis O. Giuffrida to usurp our Constitution. Giuffrida was then head of the Federal Emergency Management Agency (FEMA), empowered with coordinating government responses to emergencies. According to Anderson, Giuffrida rewrote the rules to give FEMA—and thus himself—near-dictatorial power in the event of a crisis. He would, in effect, become an "emergency czar," wrote Anderson.[22]

Giuffrida prepared "stand-by" legislation enabling the White House, in times of peril, to suspend the Bill of Rights, confiscate property, nationalize industry, and censor all communications. FEMA would then be appointed to run the country.[23]

Major media ignored Anderson's sensational charges. But it appears the problem was addressed behind the scenes. Giuffrida soon resigned amid a flurry of petty allegations, ranging from sweetheart deals with contractors to paying his wife's travel expenses with government funds—the sort of improprieties that would probably have been overlooked in normal times. One has to wonder whether the corruption charges against Giuffrida were but a smokescreen to hide the real reason for his dismissal.[24]

CT—CATASTROPHIC TERRORISM

GIUFFRIDA MAY BE gone, but contingency plans for martial rule continue to proliferate. It is all but taken for granted among government officials today that any great crisis—such as a biological or nuclear attack—must be met with an immediate suspension of civil rights. The sort of "emergency" planning going on in think tanks and congressional committees today represents precisely the sort of threat to American liberty whose existence Anderson denies.

Little noticed by the public, political, military, and academic elites are currently engaged in a historic debate over how America should deal with our seemingly inevitable confrontation with "CT" or "Catastrophic Terrorism."

In a January 15, 2001, article in *Insight* magazine, Jon Basil Utley reviews some of the measures being floated in these high-level discussions, which include "seizure of community and private assets," "utilization of the military for civil control," "warrantless detention of individuals," and "control of access to communications—including restricting media." Juliette Kayyem of Harvard University's School of Government argues that censorship of media—including the Internet—is of crucial importance during a CT event, to prevent mass hysteria and unauthorized flight from affected areas.[25]

THE SPIRIT OF LINCOLN

Americans did not always think in such terms. There was a time when our Constitution was honored in good times and bad alike. In 1864, for instance, in the midst of a bloody civil war, Abraham Lincoln willingly submitted to a free election. As commander in chief, he could have postponed the election on the pretext of a "national emergency." But he put due process first.

In a similar bow to due process, the U.S. Congress refrained from disarming the South after the war. Former rebels willing to take an oath of loyalty to the United States were permitted to keep and bear arms. When Senator Henry Wilson (Republican of Massachusetts) introduced a measure in 1866 to seize Southern arms, it was defeated as unconstitutional. "The idea, by a sweeping enactment . . . of disarming the whole people of the South seemed to me so directly in the face of the Constitution itself, as to strike me as somewhat strange," commented Republican Senator Waitman T. Willey.[26]

Times have changed. The bureaucratic murmurings coming out of Washington in recent years make clear that any "mass-casualty-producing event" today, on the scale of the American Civil War, would be met not with Lincolnesque restraint but with a wholesale abandonment of Constitutional guarantees.

Keeping a Stiff Upper Lip

Most Americans are willing to tolerate a temporary suspension of their liberties. After the attack on Pearl Harbor in 1941, the Hawaiian Islands were put under martial law. Any civilian arrested on so much as a traffic violation was hauled before a military court. Some people resented it, but most kept a stiff upper lip. There was a war on, and most considered it their patriotic duty to keep their complaints to themselves.

It is natural and praiseworthy for people to cooperate with the authorities in times of emergency. However, it is also wise to be vigilant. "Crisis is the rallying cry of the tyrant," said James Madison. Unfortunately, ruthless and ambitious men have always been willing to take advantage of bad times. Like the brigands and looters who fill the streets during earthquakes and blackouts, certain men in high places, in every government that ever existed, would not shrink from exploiting disaster to increase their power and neutralize their opponents.

THE REICHSTAG FIRE

ON THE NIGHT of February 27, 1933, Germany's parliament building, the Reichstag, went up in flames. Police found a Dutch communist named Marinus van der Lubbe inside the building, setting fires. Hitler announced that a communist uprising had begun. He persuaded President Hindenberg to declare a state of emergency, in which civil rights were suspended and thousands of Hitler's opponents rounded up. It was the end of German democracy.[27]

In fact, the alleged communist uprising was a fantasy. Most historians now accept that van der Lubbe was a patsy for Nazi conspirators. A week before the fire, while drinking in a bar, van der Lubbe had boasted of his plan to burn down the Reichstag. Nazi informants reported this to Hitler's henchman Hermann Goering. Instead of stopping van der Lubbe, the Nazis watched and waited.

Some historians even believe that Nazi arsonists actively assisted van der Lubbe in setting the fire. The man was mentally retarded and almost blind. Some maintain that it would have been virtually impossible for him to set such a blaze without help.[28] Whether or not the Nazis participated in the arson, it is clear that they knew about it beforehand, did nothing to stop it, and exploited the panic it created for their own ends.

THE REICHSTAG FACTOR

Suppose America experienced its own "Reichstag fire." Suppose an event occurred, so terrifying, monstrous, and bloody, that any measures taken against it seemed justified—an attack on New York City by nuclear terrorists, say, or the release of anthrax in a dozen major cities. As horrifying scenes of mass graves and burning bodies filled our TV screens, our first impulse would be to keep a stiff upper lip and cooperate with whatever measures the government took to restore order.

But how would we know for sure that the terrorist event had not been a "Reichstag fire," something that the government itself had allowed to happen—or perhaps even quietly facilitated behind the scenes—in order to provide an excuse for repression?

We Americans do not like to contemplate such possibilities. We like to believe that "Reichstag fires" happen only in other people's countries. But, as the Spanish American philosopher George Santayana once observed, "Those who do not remember the past are condemned to repeat it." There would be little point in studying and remembering Nazi Germany, unless we are prepared to learn from the Germans' mistakes.

Can a Militia Resist a Superpower?

Let us suppose a situation in which Americans have been pushed to the brink. Elections have been canceled or postponed. Military rule has been imposed. Mass arrests without warrants are commonplace. Slowly but surely, the reality sinks in that we have been hoodwinked. The "temporary" state of emergency has become permanent. The normal checks and balances, such as courts and elections, no longer function.

What do we do then? According to the antigun crowd, we do nothing. Resistance is futile, they say. We must submit and obey.

"A militia armed with only rifles would not win a war against a federal war-machine equipped with airplanes, missiles and even nuclear weapons," opines graduate student Johan Wanstrom in the *Oklahoma Daily*, the student paper of the University of Oklahoma. Therefore, he concludes, "the reasoning behind the Second Amendment simply does not exist anymore."

Wanstrom is a typical product of today's educational system. He has imbibed from his elders a despair in the Second Amendment. Though he understands perfectly well that "The Second Amendment was written so people could organize a militia and fight against an oppressive and dictatorial regime," Wanstrom has been taught that modern tyrants are too well-equipped to be threatened by a people in arms.[29]

Cost Analysis

Had the Swiss thought that way in World War II, they would certainly have been overrun, like virtually every other country in Europe. Most historians agree that Hitler had the ability to subdue Switzerland in a matter of days or weeks. A blitzkrieg attack with tanks, dive bombers, heavy artillery, and overwhelming masses of infantry would have crushed tiny Switzerland, no matter how valiantly its militiamen fought. Yet Hitler refrained from attacking, because he knew the cost would be high.

He did not hesitate to attack Norway, however. After World War I, Norway had embraced a pacifistic program of disarmament and social programs. Its army numbered only 13,000 when the Nazis struck in 1940. The country fell easily. "Owing to a complete lack of arms, ammunition and organization, the Norwegians have not been able to put up a serious fight," reported the *Times* of London on April 18.

Brave bands of Norwegian guerrillas kept up the fight in the hinterland, but Wehrmacht General Eduard Dietl commented that "one clearly noticed their defective training." They also lacked arms and ammunition. Only after years of Nazi occupation were the Norwegian partisans able to train and outfit 35,000 men with arms smuggled in by British fishing boats.[30]

By preparing for war, the Swiss gained peace. By preparing only for peace, the Norwegians got war. How does this lesson apply to America in the twenty-first century?

Risk Management

Should some tyrant actually succeed in gaining power in America, how would the people resist? Of course, it would be foolish for militiamen, armed only with assault rifles, to march out en masse to engage in pitched battles with federal tanks, tactical bombers, nuclear weapons, and Apache helicopters. They would be wiped out.

However, it is extremely unlikely that such forces would be deployed against them. Even the most ruthless tyrant would hesitate to unleash such massive firepower on his own people. Too much is at risk. Engaging in all-out civil war would shatter the illusion of popular support that even a dictator requires. And no dictator can ever be sure that his troops will obey when ordered to fire on their own countrymen.

A Tyrant's Worst Nightmare

Back in 1978, when I was a student at Leningrad State University in the Soviet Union, I found myself in the midst of a large-scale street disturbance. Some 5,000 young Leningraders had gathered in Palace Square on the evening of July 4th for a scheduled rock concert featuring Santana, Joan Baez, and The Beach Boys. When we arrived, we found that the concert had been canceled without explanation. The square was filled with police, demanding that we disperse.

To my surprise, no one obeyed. Police tried for hours to break up the crowd, using beatings, arrests, and water sprayed from street-cleaning trucks. At one point, I noticed a convoy of military trucks moving down a side street. "Are they going to use soldiers against us?" I asked a Russian companion. "No, never," he laughed. "The army is on our side." In fact, no troops were deployed that night.

My companion must have known something I didn't about the attitude of Soviet fighting men. His words proved prophetic. Thirteen years later, during the attempted coup in 1991, armored units sent to disperse protesters in front of the Russian parliament building in Moscow mutinied and joined the protesters.

Their defection marked a turning point in the coup. The plotters lost their nerve. No attempt was made to strafe or bomb the rebels from the air, though they were sitting ducks for such an attack. The conspirators feared provoking a civil war in which the loyalty of their own troops was uncertain. So they simply called it quits.

The Best Insurance

Here in America, if an armed and determined populace made a show of force during a declared "state of emergency," the would-be usurper would face a terrible choice. He could order an all-out attack—and risk mutiny by his own troops—or he could back down, call off the "state of emergency," and try to pretend that it had all been a misunderstanding.

Neither option is attractive. For that reason, an aspiring Caesar would be unlikely to put himself in such a precarious situation in the first place. As long as significant numbers of Americans are armed, a tyrant would be just as reluctant to provoke them as Hitler was to provoke Switzerland. The worst-case scenario would simply never happen in the first place.

The Guerrilla Option

But suppose it did happen. Suppose a tyrant seized power who was willing to gamble. Suppose he dispatched tanks and helicopters with orders to use maximum force against every pocket of resistance. Could a citizen's militia prevail in such a fight?

It could, using guerrilla tactics: avoiding open engagement; breaking up into small units; hiding out in remote areas; and using stealth, sabotage, and surprise attack. Primitive guerrilla fighters defeated superpowers in Vietnam and Afghanistan. When pushed to the wall, Americans would surely prove no less resourceful than the Viet Cong or the Mujahedeen. In such a fight, it is not the best-armed or best-equipped army that wins, but the side that is willing to fight longest and hardest and to accept death before defeat.

THE POWER OF DETERRENCE

TWENTY YEARS AGO, leftists were demanding that the United States halt its arms race with the Soviet Union. They argued that any conflict with the Russians would annihilate all life on the planet. The only solution, leftists argued, was to lay down our arms and sue for peace, on the Soviets' terms.

Ronald Reagan took a different approach. He accelerated the arms race and made plain in his public statements that he would not hesitate to push the nuclear button, if provoked. The Soviets believed him. Unable to match our defense spending and fearing continued tension with a superior foe, they threw in the towel.

The Doomsday Button

Popular insurrection is like nuclear war. It is a doomsday button that no one wants to push. God forbid that Americans should ever face a test as dreadful as war with their own government. The results of such a conflagration would likely prove as awful for the victors as for the losers. Dictators could emerge from either side.

Yet the surest way to avoid it is to keep our finger on the button at all times and make clear that we are willing to push it. Deterrence works. As horrifying as nuclear war might be, we stand ready for it. Our missiles rest in their silos, ready to fly. Because we are prepared for nuclear war, we have enjoyed fifty-five years of nuclear peace.

So it should be with the armed and vigilant citizenry prescribed by our Founding Fathers. Their readiness to fight provides the best insurance that such a fight will never be necessary.

MYTH 6

WE SHOULD TREAT GUNS THE SAME WAY WE TREAT CARS, REQUIRING LICENSES FOR ALL USERS

"WE HAVE insane gun laws in this country," said New York City Police Commissioner Howard Safir in a March 12, 2000, television interview. "[W]e should . . . license guns the way we license cars. . . . [W]e require somebody who drives a car to have a license. If you own a gun, which is capable of taking somebody's life, you should be required to be licensed, too."[1]

With those words, the commissioner summed up what is perhaps the most popular and universally accepted argument of the gun-ban lobby. According to the antigunners, requiring a license for gun ownership would enable the government to impose safety and training requirements and to keep better track of gun owners. All this would ostensibly save lives.

Moreover, licensing would supposedly not infringe on anyone's Second Amendment rights. Just fill out a few papers, and voila! You can keep and bear arms to your heart's content. At least, so goes the argument.

RIGHTS AND PRIVILEGES

THE PROBLEM IS, when you apply for a firearms license, the government may or may not grant it. Having granted it, the government may later choose to revoke it. What that means, in effect, is that you never really had a right to bear arms in the first place. A right, by definition, cannot be withheld or denied. As Thomas Jefferson put it, "I have a right to nothing, which another has a right to take away."[2]

Those who advocate gun licensing are implicitly acknowledging that Americans have no right to keep and bear arms. Rather, they regard gun possession as a special favor or privilege that can be granted or revoked for almost any reason.

THE HARSH REALITY

We do not need to speculate about how gun licensing would work. It is already in force in several states and cities, and the results are clear: Citizens in those areas have effectively lost the right to keep and bear arms.

In New York City, for instance, prospective gun owners must apply to the police for a permit. The procedure is arduous, time-consuming, and expensive. The cops have six months to act on your application, and, in the end, they usually say no.

In an April 14, 1997, *Business Week* article entitled "Annie Get Your Gun License—Just Try," Paul M. Eng recounts his months-long ordeal in seeking a pistol permit in the Big Apple. The first step was hiring a consultant for $395 to help with the paperwork. This is necessary, because only an expert can tell you how to avoid the hidden booby-traps in the application process. For instance, one of the questions on the application is whether or not you have ever been issued a government license or permit. Many innocently answer no, forgetting that their driver's license falls in that category. The applicant is disqualified for having made a "false statement."

Eng was fingerprinted, charged a $244 fee, and grilled by a police officer over his knowledge of city laws regarding the use of "deadly physical force." Any misstep during that interview would have resulted in an immediate rejection. As he completed each step of the process, Eng was told: "Don't call us." He just had to wait until he was summoned for the next step. "I'm nearing the end of the six-month waiting period, and I still haven't heard from anyone down at One Police Plaza," he worries.[3]

Capricious Bureaucracies

Corruption and favoritism run rampant in bureaucracies, and gun licensing bureaucracies are no exception. In 1997, New York's deputy inspector of pistol permits and his entire command were suspended for giving "preferential treatment to individuals or entities." Stephen P. Halbrook notes in *That Every Man Be Armed* that "In New York City . . . it is common knowledge that licenses to carry handguns are usually not granted except to the rich and the well-connected."[4]

When your ability to exercise a constitutional right is made conditional on the approval of a capricious bureaucracy, it is difficult to argue that that right truly exists.

DOES LICENSING HELP?

But if it saves lives, isn't it all worth it? Can't we surrender a little convenience and freedom, if it means reducing crime and violence? Earlier generations of Americans would have said no. However, even if we accept the argument that safety is more important than freedom, what effect do gun licensing laws actually have on our safety?

"Unfortunately," writes John Lott, "laws requiring the licensing and registration of firearms are more likely to increase crime than to reduce it. . . . There is . . . substantial evidence that even the short waiting periods that go with these laws increase the incidence of rape and that longer waiting periods increase violent crime across the board. Time spent administering these laws is time that the police do not have to do what they normally do to stop crime."[5]

Lott points out that licensing and registration become useful as crime-stopping tools only in cases where a criminal leaves his weapon at the scene of a crime—and then only if he is a sufficiently law-abiding criminal to have bothered with licensing and registration in the first place. In such cases, the serial number on the weapon will enable police to trace it back to its owner. However, as Lott notes,

> [D]espite tens of thousands of man-hours spent by the police administering these laws in Hawaii (the one state with both rules), as well as the efforts of cities like Chicago and Washington, D.C. that have similar laws, there is not even a single case where licensing and registration have been instrumental in identifying someone who has committed a crime.
>
> The reasons for this are simple. Criminals very rarely leave their guns at the scene of the crime. Moreover, would-be criminals virtually never get licenses or register their weapons.[6]

De Facto Gun Ban

Because the gun-controllers know that Lott is correct and that guns used in crimes are virtually never left at the crime scene, they have launched a nationwide push for "ballistic fingerprinting." This requires gun makers or gun sellers to test-fire each weapon they sell and send the spent shell casings to police, so that the tell-tale markings on them can be recorded in a database and used to identify which shells came from which guns.

Implementing such a program has proved so costly and cumbersome in Maryland that it has resulted in a de facto ban on handguns in the state. The cost of "ballistic fingerprinting" made it uneconomical for many gun makers to sell their products in Maryland. Handguns simply began vanishing from the stores.

Politicians scrambled to cover themselves, as public outrage grew. "None of the law was intended by anybody, from the governor on down, to be banning handguns in Maryland," said House Speaker Casper Taylor Jr., a Democrat. Maryland State Police Superintendent Col. David Mitchell declared, "We did not, nor did we ever, intend for this legislation to be a de facto gun ban, nor did we intend this legislation to create an undue hardship on Maryland gun dealers."[7]

Good intentions aside, the effect of the policy was clear. "Ballistic fingerprinting" is a colossally expensive project that will increase the cost of guns and reduce their availability to law-abiding citizens wherever it is implemented. The one thing it will not do is stop criminals, since criminals do not buy their weapons from licensed dealers.

THE REAL PURPOSE OF GUN LICENSING

IF LICENSING does not stop or inhibit crime, what is its actual purpose? A 1995 concealed-carry law in Nevada provides one clue. It requires applicants to take a $100 safety class before obtaining a permit. After passing the class, you are issued a permit—not to carry just any gun, but to carry only the particular weapon that you used in the class, which is identified by serial number.

"The idiocy of contending this has anything to do with 'safety' should be obvious," writes columnist Vyn Suprynowicz. "If I pass my driver's license road test in an old Plymouth with a manual transmission, is that license invalid when I later trade in the Plymouth for a Chevy with an automatic?"

Suprynowicz charges that the only reason for this odd rule is "so police can collect a list of the serial numbers of every weapon out there, and the addresses of the sock drawers in which each one is kept."[8]

The Irish Precedent

It is hard to counter Suprynowicz's logic. In fact, gun-ban lobbyists have long displayed a peculiar obsession with collecting data on law-abiding gun owners. Often it is accomplished surreptitiously under a false pretext, as in the case described by Suprynowicz. David Kopel remarks:

> Notably, anti-gun groups insist that whenever a person passes the federal background check, the government should keep records on the buyer. But what's the point of retaining a list of non-criminals who are just exercising their constitutional rights? Simple. Firearm confiscation is a lot easier when the government has a list of every gun owner, and every gun owned.[9]

Readers will recall the fear that swept the English government when labor unrest after World War I seemed to threaten Red Revolution. Among the measures floated was a bill "for licensing persons to bear arms," a method "which has been useful in Ireland because the authorities know who were possessed of arms."[10] Anyone familiar with Irish history knows that concern for the "safety" of the Irish public was never paramount in the minds of British rulers. Their chief concern was thwarting rebellion—the one purpose for which gun licensing is genuinely effective.

THE WASHINGTON SQUARE MASSACRE

We have all heard of the massacre at Columbine High School. But how many of us remember the Washington Square Park Massacre of April 23, 1992? It happened on a clear, sunlit day in Manhattan's Greenwich Village. The park was filled with students, sunbathers, street musicians, and mothers with children.

Violence struck suddenly at 3:20 P.M. When it was over, four lay dead and twenty-seven wounded. Another would die later in the hospital, bringing the death toll to five. "It was like a surreal experience," remembered twenty-six-year-old Evie Hantzopoulos, a New York University graduate student. "We couldn't believe what was happening. It was like a movie. First we heard noise and it sounded like gunfire. . . . People were just trying to get out of the way."

"It was like war, total war. So violent," said New York University student Sam Catlin, twenty-three. Thirty-year-old bookstall proprietor John Arnold remembered, "There were bodies all lying there. There was a girl lying in the middle of a walkway about twenty feet away from her sneaker. There was a guy lying there with a smile on his face. I don't know if he was dead. It looked like they were asleep."

"There were just people all over the place," remembers paramedic Andrew Margolies. "It was like a bomb had exploded."[11]

"It reminded me of wartime footage, the type of injuries I saw in old Vietnam news clippings," remarked paramedic Mark Honickel.[12]

Out of Control

Who was responsible for this carnage? Some trench-coated teenager brandishing an AK-47? Not at all. It was seventy-four-year-old Stella Maychick, an elderly Yonkers woman out for a drive in her 1987 Oldsmobile.

Mrs. Maychick states that the car accelerated on its own. She could not stop it. The car jumped the curb and burst through a concrete fountain, swerved down a crowded walkway, and plowed through benches and crowds of people at an estimated sixty miles per hour. Screams filled the air as bodies flew and two people were dragged beneath the car.

NYU graduate student Carl Seibert, twenty-six, was still shaking hours later. "People were flying everywhere," he remembers. "It was just a mess. They were like rag dolls. The people were just mangled. They were grotesquely twisted."[13]

When the blood-stained car finally came to a stop against a tree, Maychick emerged in a daze. "People approached her, screaming. At least one person started to attack her," reported the *New York Times*. But then the crowd turned its efforts to trying to free the bodies trapped beneath the car.[14]

Investigators concluded that Stella Maychick had inadvertently stepped on the gas pedal instead of the brake.[15] She was not charged with any crime. And she was allowed to keep her driver's license.[16]

Licensing "Loopholes"

Gun-ban lobbyists are always pointing out "loopholes" in the law that allow questionable people to purchase firearms. But one seldom hears about "loopholes" in the issuance of driver's licenses.

All over the country, cars are being driven by people who, for one reason or another, present a higher-than-usual risk for accidents. Some are elderly, such as Mrs. Maychick. Some have poorly controlled diabetes or heart conditions and may suffer an insulin reaction or heart attack behind the wheel at any time. Some are being medicated for anxiety or depression. Some are suicidal. Some abuse drugs and alcohol. And some are criminals, sex predators, or murderous psychotics. But all have one thing in common. They have perfectly legal driver's licenses.

The fact is, most Americans would not want these "loopholes" closed, even if it were possible to do so. The level of screening that would be required would transform our society into a police state. Everyone's lives would be under constant scrutiny through a government microscope. We would never permit such a massive invasion of our privacy over a mere driver's license. American soccer moms are more than willing to accept bloody horrors such as the Washington Square Massacre, rather than allow Big Brother to pry into their private lives each time they renew their driver's licenses.

PROZAC NATION

ALTHOUGH MOST Americans recoil from the thought of closing every "loophole" in the driver's licensing system, we are slowly but surely being lulled into accepting precisely that sort of police-state intrusion when it comes to gun licensing. For instance, even the staunchest defenders of gun rights generally agree that guns should be withheld from the mentally ill. But how exactly do we determine who is mentally ill and who is not?

On December 14, 1999, the Clinton administration gave a hint as to just how broadly this term can be applied. At a Washington press conference, Surgeon General David Satcher released a report on mental health that, among other things, claimed that 50 million Americans—fully 20 percent of the population—suffered from some form of mental illness.

The nation was facing "a public health crisis," said Health and Human Services Secretary Donna E. Shalala. "The fact is that today mental illness is the second-leading cause of disability, the second-leading cause of premature death in the United States," she said. Satcher urged America's mentally ill to cast aside their embarrassment, ignore the stigma society placed on mental illness, and come forward for the treatment they needed.[17]

A Question of Definition

If some readers are shocked by the notion that one in five Americans could be mentally ill, relax. Satcher was not talking about serious illnesses such as schizophrenia, manic depression, and obsessive-compulsive disorder. *The Diagnostic and Statistical Manual of Mental Disorders* (DSM-IV)—the authoritative guide to mental illnesses used by the psychiatric profession—categorizes many types of human behavior as pathological that most of us would never have considered particularly worrisome, such as cigarette addiction, coffee drinking, and PMS.

It is somewhat unclear where the Clinton administration drew the line in calculating its 50-million figure, but clearly that number included many people who would never have dreamed they were "mentally ill" unless the government told them so. All of these 50 million people have been urged to officially register themselves—that is, put themselves permanently on record—as being in need of mental health services. The press spun the announcement as a compassionate gesture, an attempt to reach out to people in need. But is it possible that it had another purpose?

Let a Hundred Flowers Bloom

In 1957, the Chinese dictator Mao Tse Tung introduced a policy called, "Let a Hundred Flowers Bloom." It was meant to encourage artists and writers to come out from the shadows of self-censorship and express themselves more freely. Many did so.

As Nikita Khrushchev later observed in his memoirs, "Now it's clear to everyone that the slogan was intended as a provocation. It was proclaimed in order to encourage people to express themselves more openly so that any flowers whose blossoms had the wrong color or scent could be cut down and trampled into the dirt."[18]

SECOND-CLASS CITIZENS

Today, we know what happened to those naïve Chinese who accepted Mao's invitation. They stepped forward, expressed themselves, and were subsequently arrested. What will happen to those Americans who accept the invitation of the Clinton administration to step forward and declare themselves "mentally ill"?

Coming from a family that includes several doctors and medical professionals, I have the highest respect for medicine and psychiatry. Many people out there do need care and should be encouraged to shed their fears and apply for it.

Unfortunately, there are also many people in government who will not shrink from exploiting medicine as a tool to control and disenfranchise people. As the baby boom generation grows older, tens of millions of Americans will grow ever more dependent on medical care. They will also find themselves increasingly at the mercy of a growing government health bureaucracy that—like all government entities—is far more concerned with power than it is with helping people.

Strong evidence exists that the excuse of "mental illness" will be used more and more by our government to relegate large numbers of Americans to a kind of second-class citizenship, in which they can be stripped of basic liberties, such as the right to keep and bear arms.

VETERANS DISARMED

This tactic has already been used against military veterans. On June 22, 2000, WorldNetDaily.com reported that the Department of Veterans' Affairs, which runs the nation's VA hospitals, had been turning over private medical records of veterans to the FBI. The information was to be entered into the National Instant Background Check System (NICS), enabling the FBI to bar veterans judged "incompetent" or mentally "defective" from purchasing firearms. As with Bill Clinton's 50-million figure, it is a bit unclear how the line is drawn between those veterans who may or may not possess arms. But considering the large number of combat veterans diagnosed with conditions such as post-traumatic stress disorder, it does not seem far-fetched to predict that the "defective" category will continue growing through the years until it affects substantial numbers of America's best and bravest.[19]

The *New York Times*'s Spin

When this situation was reported on Internet news sites such as WorldNetDaily.com and NewsMax.com, many veterans were horrified to learn that the FBI was receiving reports on their mental health. But, in fact, the *New York Times* had been aware of this situation for quite some time and had already alluded to the practice two months earlier, in an article entitled, "Hole in Gun Control Law Lets Mentally Ill Through."

The *Times* noted that "the Federal Bureau of Investigation, which conducts background checks for the majority of states, has mental health records only on people treated in Veterans Affairs hospitals. . . ."

This was a sad state of affairs, the Times implied—not because veterans were losing their medical privacy, but because everyone else was not being similarly treated. The article complained that "gun background checks of people with psychiatric problems typically fail to turn up their mental health history, a loophole that has contributed to the wave of school and workplace shootings of the last decade."[20]

THE DEATH OF PRIVACY

Nothing is more sensitive and private than the information patients confide to their doctors. But we are fast moving into an era when this sort of privacy will no longer exist. On the contrary, doctors are being gradually manipulated into becoming unwitting government informants against their own patients.

For instance, a group called Doctors Against Handgun Injury (DAHI) has long urged that doctors treat gun ownership as a medical problem, such as smoking or drinking. It encourages doctors to probe their patients for information about their gun use. The American Medical Association, in a booklet entitled "Physician's Guide to Firearms," specifically urges doctors to ask patients whether they keep guns at home.

Dr. Robert Seltzer, executive director of DAHI, pooh-poohs the notion that such questioning might violate patients' rights. "They [physicians] do not report gun ownership to the federal government, the state government, local governments, police, insurance companies, or anyone else. They treat it just the way they do when you go in for a physical and the doctor asks: 'Do you smoke? Do you drink?' But it's not an effort to spy on patients."[21]

Well, maybe not yet. But despite Dr. Seltzer's assurances, physicians are fast losing the right to keep patient information private, even if they wish to do so.

Hillarycare

Most Americans are at least vaguely aware that, in 1993, then–First Lady Hillary Clinton attempted to push through a national health plan. And most are aware that her plan was rejected by Congress. What most Americans do not know—because it was not widely reported in the press—is the reason for her plan's rejection.

Hillarycare, as the plan has been nicknamed, would have given the U.S. government a level of control over the doctor-patient relationship that is unheard of except in socialist societies.

In a July 21, 1999, *New York Post* op-ed piece explaining why he could not support Hillary's run for the New York Senate, Bartle Bull—a prominent New York Democrat who had served as Robert Kennedy's campaign manager—made a rare allusion to some of Hillarycare's more draconian stipulations. "Who recalls the details of her health-care debacle, when in unlawful closed meetings she revealed her authoritarian leftist bent, crafting a compulsory national medical program that literally would have jailed doctors who practiced medicine outside the state-controlled structure she was designing for all 260 million of us?"[22]

National Patient Database

Most people assume that Hillarycare is dead. However, a key facet of the program—the effective abolition of doctor-patient privacy—is alive and well in a new medical regulation quietly signed by Bill Clinton in the last days of his presidency.

The 1,500-page document was presented as a measure for protecting patient privacy. Only by reading it cover to cover, with careful attentiveness to its subtle bureaucratic language, could one discover that it actually did just the opposite.

NewsMax.com senior editor John L. Perry likens the document to a fork-finger fast ball. As it leaves the pitcher's hand, it looks like a fastball coming straight over the plate. But then it drops short and veers to the side, leaving the batter swinging at thin air. Perry writes:

> Whoever drafted this Clinton regulation is a Cy Young Award pitcher. Take this on faith from one who has written his share of federal regs and had to wade through more than he ever wants to remember: This one is a masterpiece—of obfuscation, sleight-of-hand, semantic trickery. . . .

> It took an entire evening, the next day and the better part of another evening just to read through the hundreds upon hundreds of pages of this gobbledegook.
>
> If you don't read the key portions at least twice, you miss the "except as otherwise provided in Section this, that or the other" escape hatches. It's easier to navigate amid the mirrors in the Fun House at the county carnival.[23]

In fact, the new rule effectively gives government agencies wide access to many patient records, including the private notes of psychiatrists. It opens the door for creating a national database of patient records, and requires doctors to turn over patient information on demand, for potential inclusion in that database.[24]

On April 14, 2001, President George W. Bush approved the new rule, without change, giving it the force of law.[25]

Bureaucratic Abuse

Once we accept the notion that basic constitutional liberties can be licensed, where do we draw the line? Is there, in fact, any freedom that we enjoy in this country that could not be seen as potentially dangerous and thus in need of government oversight through a licensing system?

Many libertarians argue that the government should not even have the power to issue driver's licenses. They say that people are just as capable of learning to drive safely, without government meddling, as they are capable of learning to cook with charcoal grills or to use cigarette lighters responsibly. Lighter fluid, after all, can be used to make Molotov cocktails, yet no license is required to purchase it.

Readers may decide for themselves how far down the libertarian trail they wish to go. But whatever one's thoughts may be on the question of limited government, there is no question that licensing, by its nature, offers almost unlimited potential for bureaucratic abuse.

The Slippery Slope

Consider the right to freedom of religion. Like all freedoms, religious liberty creates problems. It allows murderous fanatics such as Jim Jones and Marshall Applewhite to create killer cults like the Peoples' Temple and Heaven's Gate.

It could be argued that a government licensing program might prevent such tragedies. Anyone starting a church could be subjected to psychiatric screening, his beliefs and doctrines vetted by a board of experts. Cult killings might well diminish. But freedom of worship would be dead.

Then there's sex. As any cop can tell you, sexual passions drive a large proportion of serious crimes, from assault to murder. Sex acts also kill by spreading disease and cause great expense to society by generating fatherless children. If all this dangerous activity were regulated, society might arguably become more orderly. The government could limit sexual activity only to those people with a valid license. Such licenses would be awarded only to adults who had been trained in contraceptive techniques and had been screened for AIDS and other diseases, as well as for dangerous personality traits such as a penchant for rape or sexual abuse. Couples meeting in a bar could flash their picture I.D.s before repairing to a more private setting.

How about freedom of speech? Think of all the pornography, hate speech, and dangerous conspiracy theories that could be eliminated by denying "speech licenses" to undesirable Web sites. Hillary Clinton has actually proposed something along these lines. Arguing that cyberspace is too free, she suggests that the Internet needs an "editing or gate keeping function" to control its content.[26]

TOO MUCH LIBERTY?

HILLARY CLINTON aside, most Americans seem to understand that requiring licenses for the exercise of basic liberties is a bad idea. Though they may not articulate it as eloquently as Thomas Jefferson, most would agree with his famous declaration that "I would rather be exposed to the inconveniences attending too much liberty, than those attending too small a degree of it."

Those who push gun licensing would do well to remember Jefferson's words. Whether they personally wish to carry a gun or not, the issue will affect them. For someday they, too, will grow old and infirm. And when the people-controlling bureaucracy they have created comes knocking on their doors to assess their "competency," they may cry aloud, "Leave me alone! I have no guns here." But guns will no longer be the issue. The issue will be you.

MYTH 7

REASONABLE GUN-CONTROL MEASURES ARE NO THREAT TO LAW-ABIDING GUN OWNERS

"POLL AFTER POLL shows that this is not a partisan issue," said Sarah Brady, chair of Handgun Control Inc., in a July 1999 press release. "Republicans and Democrats alike want to see stronger gun laws." She claimed further that "The overwhelming majority of Americans—gun owners and non-gun owners alike" are united in their desire for "sensible gun laws"—which Brady defined as laws that "make it more difficult for children and criminals to get guns."[1]

Whether the term used is "sensible" gun laws, "reasonable" gun laws, or "common-sense gun laws," the message is always the same: No one in his right mind could possibly oppose such laws; law-abiding gun owners have nothing to fear from them; they will not infringe on anyone's legitimate gun rights; and anyone who opposes them must be a "gun nut," an "extremist," or perhaps even a criminal.

Is Sarah Brady correct? Are the demands of the gun controllers as "reasonable," "sensible," and "common-sensical" as they appear? Or do they, in fact, represent a real and present danger to the gun rights of Americans?

THE LION AND THE WOODSMAN

IN THE EARLY phases of the War Between the States, many of Abraham Lincoln's advisers pressed him to compromise with the South, by giving in to its demands. One Virginian counseled him to give up all federal forts and property in the Southern states. Lincoln responded by recounting Aesop's fable of the Lion and the Woodsman. He said:

> A lion was very much in love with a woodsman's daughter. The fair maid referred him to her father and the lion applied for the girl. The father replied: "Your teeth are too long." So the lion went to a dentist and had them extracted. Returning, he asked for his bride. "No," said the woodsman, "your claws are too long." Going back to the dentist he had them drawn. Then he returned to claim his bride, and the woodsman, seeing that he was unarmed, beat out his brains.

"May it not be so with me," asked Lincoln, "if I give up all that is asked?"

LINCOLN'S QUESTION

Americans today need to ask Lincoln's question. If we continue "compromising" with the gun controllers, will we meet the same fate as the lion in Aesop's fable? Once we have submitted to universal licensing, registration, and background checks, will we be helpless to prevent the next step: confiscation?

Once the new gun-control bureaucracy is in place, it will be a simple matter for the government to start tightening the screws. Background checks can be used to disqualify more and more people. Licensing requirements can be made stricter, more expensive, and more cumbersome, until it becomes practically impossible to get a license, as in Japan. Ultimately, the remaining guns can simply be confiscated, using the national database of registered gun owners as a guide.

Step by Step

In their public statements, antigun groups seldom admit that they seek a total gun ban. But, from time to time, loose-lipped activists let the cat out of the bag.

Take Nelson T. "Pete" Shields, founder of Sarah Brady's organization, Handgun Control Inc. In 1976, when he was executive director of its predecessor, the National Council to Control Handguns (NCCH), Shields told the *New Yorker*, "We're going to have to take one step at a time, and the first step is necessarily—given the political realities—going to be very modest."

Here's how the process would work. After getting one federal gun law in place, Shields said, "we'll have to start working again to strengthen that law, and then again to strengthen the next law and maybe again and again."

The first step would be "to slow down the increasing number of handguns being produced and sold in this country." The second would be "to get handguns registered," while "the final problem is to make the possession of *all* handguns and *all* handgun ammunition—except for the military, policemen, licensed security guards, licensed sporting clubs, and licensed gun collectors—totally illegal."[2]

The Fabian Strategy

The gradualistic approach described by Shields has a long tradition among activists of the Left. It is sometimes known as the Fabian strategy, after the Roman general Fabius Cunctator—Fabius the Delayer. When a Carthaginian army under Hannibal invaded Italy in the third century B.C.,

Fabius worried that Rome's entire army might be annihilated if he confronted the invaders in open battle. So instead, Fabius picked away at the edges of Hannibal's army, wearing him out with many small attacks and avoiding direct confrontation. The strategy saved Rome.

Some British socialists in the 1880s likewise feared that a direct confrontation with capitalism—that is, a revolution—might end in total defeat for their movement. So they opted instead for a "Fabian" strategy, of gradually and peacefully introducing socialist "reforms" through the parliamentary system, one law at a time. That way, the radical nature of their goals would be concealed, and they could move, step by step, toward a socialist society. The so-called Fabian Society, founded in 1884, has been extremely influential in British politics and led to the foundation of today's Labour Party.

"We Are Not Anxious to Rouse the Opposition"

Fabianism has been a key strategy for gun prohibitionists from early on. In 1969, for instance, J. Elliott Corbett, secretary and board member of the National Council for a Responsible Firearms Policy—an influential antigun group of the time—wrote a letter to a correspondent who had complained that the group was not tough enough on guns. Corbett wrote:

> I personally believe that handguns should be outlawed. . . . Our organization will probably officially take this stand in time but we are not anxious to rouse the opposition before we get the other legislation passed. It would be difficult to outlaw all rifles and shotguns because of the hunting sport. But there should be stiff regulations. . . . We thought the handgun bill was a step in the right direction. But, as you can see, our movement will be towards increasingly stiff controls.

Like the Fabian socialists, gun-ban lobbyists understand that pushing for too much too soon can "rouse the opposition." But if you push step by step, asking only for a few small, "reasonable," "sensible" compromises at a time, the opposition will lower its guard.

HAVE THINGS CHANGED?

SARAH BRADY is perhaps the leading antigun activist today. Do we have any reason to believe that her views differ from those of her Fabian predecessors, Pete Shields and J. Elliott Corbett? Not at all. In fact, Brady has made clear that her goals are very much in line with theirs. "To me, the only reason for guns in civilian hands is for sporting purposes," she told the Tampa Tribune.[3]

Gun prohibitionists have managed to convince many Americans that "reasonable" gun-control measures, such as waiting periods, one-gun-a-month limits, trigger locks, "smart" technology, and so on, do not threaten the rights of legitimate gun owners. But this only holds true if you presume that guns will be used exclusively for sport. Virtually every gun-control measure currently being pushed as "reasonable" and "sensible" seriously impedes the use of firearms for self-defense.

SMART GUNS

Take "smart" guns. These contain electronic systems that prevent anyone except a designated user from firing the gun—in some cases, by requiring that the user wear a special ring or wristband with a magnetic actuator or radio transponder.

Let's say you wake up in the dead of night. Your husband is on a business trip, and a serial rapist is standing in your bedroom. This is not the time to be fumbling around in the dark, undoing the trigger lock and trying to remember where your husband put the transponder.

Another problem with computerized guns is that computers get glitches. "You want to have to call an 800 number to get your gun to work when your life's on the line?" asks John Risdall, president of Magnum Research in Minneapolis, which makes the .357 Magnum.[4]

ELECTROMAGNETIC INTERFERENCE

MICROCHIPS IN guns can also be disabled on purpose, through the use of electromagnetic interference. Sophisticated criminals and tyrannical governments would have little trouble obtaining and using such technology.

During her race for the New York Senate, Hillary Clinton raised eyebrows by proposing to use federal money to set up high-tech scanners that would monitor the streets to reveal which pedestrians were carrying firearms.[5] Theoretically, a surveillance system of this sort could be equipped not only to locate guns, but also to disable them by remote control. Such remote controls would only disable smart guns, however. Ordinary guns would be immune.

Showing off a .45-caliber revolver to his interviewer, Risdall comments, "A hundred years from now, this gun will still work." The same cannot be said of any smart gun now under development.

WAITING PERIODS

WAITING PERIODS can also be deadly. In September 1990, Catherine Latta, a mail carrier in Charlotte, North Carolina, requested permission to buy a handgun. She had been robbed and raped by her ex-boyfriend, and assaulted by him several times. The clerk at the sheriff's office told her that there would be a two- to four-week wait for the permit.

"I'll be dead by then," Latta told her. She left the sheriff's office and bought a $20 semiautomatic pistol illegally that same afternoon. Her ex-boyfriend attacked just five hours later, outside her house, and Latta shot him dead. Luckily for her, the county prosecutor decided not to press charges. Latta could easily have ended up in jail for nothing more than defending her own life.[6]

An August 2000 study in the Journal of the American Medical Association found "no evidence that implementation of the Brady Act was associated with a reduction in homicide rates." On the contrary, many women have been raped and killed, because the Brady Law and other mandated waiting periods prevented them from obtaining guns when they needed them.

According to John Lott, waiting periods prevent "people who are being stalked or threatened from quickly obtaining a gun for protection. . . . While research shows that even short waiting periods increase rape rates, waiting periods longer than 10 days increase all categories of violent crime."[7] He notes that rapes increased 3.6 percent and aggravated assaults against women 3 percent, over and above what they would have been without passage of the Brady Law.[8]

ONE-GUN-A-MONTH RULES

ATTEMPTS TO limit the number of guns a person can purchase at one time seem reasonable to most people. But, like virtually all other "reasonable" gun controls, they impede people's ability to respond to deadly emergencies.

When riots or natural disasters strike, looting and brigandage present a real danger. People in such situations often band together in groups to defend themselves and their communities.

They have a need to stockpile arms quickly for their families, neighbors, and employees.

Assault Weapons Ban

Perhaps the least sensible of all antigun efforts is the drive to ban "assault weapons." Although many people have heard this term in the news, few know what it means. Most assume that an "assault weapon" is the same as a military "assault rifle," such as the Russian AK-47 or the American M-16, weapons that can fire automatically. But this is not what the term means at all. This confusion has been deliberately fostered by gun prohibitionists.

"Assault weapons . . . are a new topic," states a report by the antigun Violence Policy Center. "The weapons' menacing looks, coupled with the public's confusion over fully automatic machine guns versus semiautomatic assault weapons—anything that looks like a machine gun is assumed to be a machine gun—can only increase the chance of public support for restrictions on these weapons."[9]

Assault Rifles vs. Assault Weapons

In fact, the assault weapons ban enacted in 1994 did not affect ownership of fully automatic assault rifles. Automatic weapons had been all but banned from civilian use since passage of the National Firearms Act of 1934.

It banned *semi*automatic weapons—weapons that can fire as fast as you can pull the trigger. The problem is that most modern hunting rifles are semiautomatic. Are those assault weapons, too? Well, not yet. For the time being, gun prohibitionists are simply picking and choosing which semiautomatic weapons to take off the market, concentrating on those that resemble military models. For instance, they have targeted the Chinese AKS rifle because it looks like a Russian AK-47, and the Colt AR-15 because it looks like the military M-16. In both cases, however, the proscribed guns are semi-automatic and cannot fire automatically like the military guns they resemble.

Trojan Horse

More than anything else, the attack on "assault weapons" appears to be a Trojan Horse, a continuation of the Fabian strategy, whereby Americans are slowly but surely acclimated to the idea that rifles and shotguns, like pistols, can now be banned. More and more types of guns will surely be added to the "assault weapon" category, as the years go by.

Another point to keep in mind is that "assault weapons" such as the Colt AR-15 and the Chinese AKS, are precisely the guns best suited for use by a citizen's militia. As David Kopel explains:

> "Assault weapons" are not essential to resistance to tyranny. Freedom-fighters around the world have, with very low-quality weapons, fought effectively against powerful modern armies. But "assault weapons" use light ammunition that is easy to carry long distances. They are rugged, easy to maintain, and easy to shoot accurately. They would be the best guns with which to resist tyranny.[10]

As the brave Korean grocers discovered during the LA riots, they are also the best guns for defending one's home or property during a large-scale civil disturbance. By banning these weapons, the gun prohibitionists seem to be making a calculated move to undermine Americans' ability to survive and function during catastrophic breakdowns in civil order.

THE THIRD WAY

A May 23, 1999, article in the *New York Times* declared that a "third way" had appeared in the once sharply polarized gun debate. Writer David E. Rosenbaum argued that, in the past, there had been two "extremes"—those who wanted to ban handguns and require licensing and registration for all other guns, and those who wanted "the right to own and carry guns more or less at will."

Now both sides had found a "third way," a middle ground, Rosenbaum declared. Both had embraced the "common sense" view that some gun control was necessary. The only question was how much.

Appeasement and Compromise

In his article, Mr. Rosenbaum drew analogies between the gun debate and other hard-fought political battles. He noted, for instance, that there had once been two "extreme" views on health care, with one side advocating a national health insurance system and the other opposing all government meddling in health care. Eventually, writes Rosenbaum, the two sides compromised, and we got Medicare and Medicaid.

What Mr. Rosenbaum failed to mention is that, having achieved this compromise, the national health insurance extremists continued pushing for more. As this book goes to press, Senator Hillary Clinton has vowed that creating a national health care system in the United States will be her top priority. The "extremists" on the other side—those who want no government involvement in health care at all—are nowhere to be heard. They have become an extinct species.

The March of Fabius

When Hitler marched into the Rhineland, the Allies did nothing. When he occupied the Sudetenland and then Czechoslovakia, they did nothing again. At each step, the Allies hoped that they could satisfy Hitler by "compromising." But Hitler had a long-term plan. He meant to swallow Europe whole. Like Fabius, he avoided open confrontation and proceeded one step at a time. Though he declared at each stage that "this is positively my last territorial demand," every victory only whetted his appetite for more.

So it is with the gun prohibitionists. It is noteworthy that Mr. Rosenbaum's article characterizes as "extremists" those Americans who believe, like our Founding Fathers, that the right to keep and bear arms should not be infringed. Also noteworthy is the fact that, while Republicans, NRA officials, and other traditionally progun forces have embraced "compromise," the antigun forces—epitomized by Sarah Brady—do not appear to have retreated one step from their commitment to universal licensing and registration of firearms.

In the final analysis, Mr. Rosenbaum's "third way" seems just another name for the strategy of Fabius Cunctator. It remains to be seen whether the defenders of gun rights in America will, like Hannibal, succumb to this strategy or whether, like the Allies in World War II, they will finally wake to the danger in the nick of time.

EPILOGUE

THE END OF MANHOOD

PREVIOUSLY, IN Myth 3, I recounted an incident that I had witnessed at a Kinko's copy shop, in which a number of hip, "sensitive," countercultural young men employed by the shop stood by with glazed eyes and did nothing while their manager—a five-foot-tall woman—confronted a potentially dangerous man.

I raised the question of what this sort of behavior implied about the state of American manhood today. And I suggested that the real question underlying the gun-control debate was whether or not we wish to remain a warrior society.

Should we continue—as past generations of Americans have always done—to raise our children as fighters? Or should we teach them to fear weapons, to stifle their aggression, and to submit meekly to the demands of enemies, bullies, and tyrants?

What is at stake in the gun debate goes far beyond issues of crime and safety. It goes to the question of manhood itself. In this final section, we will address the subject of guns, men, women, and warriorship, and grapple with the fundamental issues that make this debate the most important of our generation.

THE SPIELBERG PERSPECTIVE

THE FILM *Jurassic Park* has a scene in which a number of characters are barricaded in a building, while the dinosaurs rampage outside. It becomes clear that someone must go out to throw the circuit-breaker in order to restore the electricity. The Laura Dern character volunteers. But in a burst of chivalry, the elderly billionaire, played by Richard Attenborough, offers to go in her stead.

"Why?" asks the woman.

"Well, I'm a . . . and you're a . . ." he stammers.

It is one of the strangest moments in cinema. The elderly billionaire is just old-fashioned enough to think that a man should not let a woman risk her life while he sits around doing nothing. But he is just modern enough to feel embarrassed about saying so. And so he stutters and stammers, unable to pronounce the words *man* and *woman*.

The Dern character perceives his plight. With the weary look of a schoolteacher dealing with a stupid child, she says, "Look, we can discuss sexism in survival situations when I get back."

With that, she shoulders a rifle and troops out the door to face what seems certain death. And the man lets her go. Just like the clerks in Kinko's that night.

Ideological feminists have long taught that it is insulting and demeaning for a woman to accept a man's protection. That notion has now filtered into the mainstream. A frail old man's offer to sacrifice his life may or may not be useful in a survival situation. But there was a time when a woman receiving such an offer might at least have thought it appropriate to say, "Thank you."

THE "M" WORD

THAT TONGUE-TIED billionaire in *Jurassic Park* was fictional. But some men in real life have just as much trouble pronouncing the "m" word. An article in the March 1998 issue of *Los Angeles Magazine* talked about "power trippers"—high-powered Hollywood executives who take death-defying adventure vacations.

It opened with a description of movie producer Charles Schlissel inching his way up the 6,000-foot, near-vertical face of the Eiger Nordwand in the Swiss Alps, against a wind-chill factor of forty degrees, with a bruised tendon in his foot.

"Outward Bound–style action-adventure vacations like this have become a required Super Male ritual for some of the most influential and highly paid executives, producers, agents and managers in the entertainment industry," said the article.

Why do they do it?

Warner Brothers executive vice president of production Tom Lassally offered this explanation: "I don't want to feel like some pampered pussy. I want to feel—not like a 'man'—but I don't want to feel like some Hollywood executive who gets manicures and pedicures and facials."[1]

Notice the phrase "not like a man." It doesn't take an Einstein to figure out that feeling "like a man" is precisely what Mr. Lassally and his fellow "power trippers" are after. But they can't say it. Mr. Lassally feels perfectly comfortable pronouncing the word *pussy*, which is both obscene and offensive to many people. Yet he shrinks from the word *man*. As a film producer, Mr. Lasally's pop culture barometer is sufficiently well-attuned to warn him that pronouncing the "m" word in a magazine interview might be a bad public relations move. In today's society, manhood is practically a taboo subject.

THE MEN'S MOVEMENT

MANY READERS will remember a brief flurry in the press during the late 1980s and early 1990s about the so-called Men's Movement. Groups of men would betake themselves to the woods in an attempt to get in touch with their masculinity.

They would beat drums, paint their faces, do war dances around bonfires, and cry on each others' shoulders, grasping for some hint of what it meant to be a "warrior" in modern society.

Poet Robert Bly was a pioneer of the Men's Movement. He led many of those retreats and probably did more than anyone to popularize the movement, appearing on public television with Bill Moyers and writing a bestselling book in 1990 called *Iron John: A Book About Men.*

The Soft Male

Bly was a man of the Left. Though a Navy veteran of World War II, he became an antiwar activist during the '60s and later gave feminist seminars promoting New Age goddess worship. In the course of his ramblings through the hippie counterculture, however, Bly saw many things that disturbed him. One was a steady erosion of the toughness of the American male. He writes:

> In the seventies I began to see all over the country a phenomenon that we might call the "soft male." Sometimes even today when I look out at an audience, perhaps half the young males are what I'd call soft. They're lovely, valuable people—I like them—they're not interested in harming the earth or starting wars. There's a gentle attitude toward life in their whole being and style of living. But many of these men are not happy. You quickly notice the lack of energy in them.[2]

Showing the Sword

These men had tried to live by the feminist code. They had attempted to suppress all traces of aggression and drive within them. In so doing, they had lost their spirit. Bly's retreats were an attempt to mend such broken souls, but it was an uphill battle. Many seemed to regard *manhood* almost as a dirty word.

In *The Odyssey*, the enchantress Circe turned Odysseus's men into swine. Odysseus set out to confront her. On his way to the meeting, the god Hermes appeared and counseled Odysseus that when Circe attempted to cast her spell upon him, he should draw his sword and raise it against her. Odysseus did as he was told. Instead of turning him into a pig, Circe took Odysseus to her bed.

Bly attempted to reproduce Odysseus's gesture in his men's groups through a simple, confidence-building exercise. He asked each man to take a sword and hold it boldly aloft. But many had been so conditioned to suppress aggressive feelings that they recoiled even from this harmless, symbolic act.

"In those early sessions it was difficult for many of the younger men to distinguish between showing the sword and hurting someone . . . ," writes Bly. "One man . . . found himself unable to extend his arm when it held a sword."[3]

Few men in America have been brainwashed to quite this extreme. But the trend is clear. The "soft" male is making inroads at every level of society. And it's going to take a lot more than face-painting, drum-beating, and symbolic sword-holding to turn the tide.

Initiation

What is missing in our society, says Bly, is a rite of initiation. In traditional cultures, a clear ritual marks the moment when a boy becomes a man. After that, he is recognized as an adult, with all the privileges and responsibilities that accrue to his status. He becomes a warrior. In the most literal sense, he stands ready to fight in defense of his people or homeland, should the need arise.

Our society has no rite of male initiation. A man goes through life unsure, at every stage, whether he has attained manhood. Does it happen when he turns twenty-one? When he sleeps with a girl for the first time? When he gets his first full-time job? When he marries or fathers a child? Nobody knows.

Perhaps that is the question those Hollywood "power trippers" are seeking to answer. Each time they test their mettle in death-defying adventure vacations, they seek some reassurance, some connection with the heroes of past ages. Yet no matter how hard they seek, they come back empty-handed. They may scale the Alps or scuba dive off the shark-infested coast of Australia. But they cannot say the words "I am a man" without irony, embarassment, or apology.

The Fading of the Warrior

In *Iron John*, Robert Bly quotes a Russian woman of the World War II generation. She offered these observations on the subject of manhood:

> I know that women in the United States are angry with the men because they are too aggressive, and so on. We don't feel that way. If the Russian men had not had great aggression in them, the Germans would be in Moscow right now. The matter of aggression looks very different if you have been invaded.[4]

Bly observes that American men have tried too hard to be "sensitive" and soft. "If his wife or girlfriend, furious, shouts that he is a 'chauvinist,' a 'sexist' . . . he doesn't fight back, but just takes it. . . . He feels, as he absorbs attacks, that he is doing the brave and advanced thing. . . ." However, as Bly notes later in the book, dangers lurk in such passivity. "The fading of the warrior contributes to the collapse of civilized society. A man who cannot defend his own space cannot defend women and children."[5]

Warriors Without War

Bly has done an admirable job of identifying the problem. But, in some ways, his pacifist views have prevented him from seeing the solution. In Bly's view, the time for real warriors is over. Modern men should aspire to warriorship only in some symbolic, intellectual sense, he implies.

Bly's seminars reflect this attitude. Most of us would feel silly partaking in such exercises as painting our faces, dancing around bonfires, chanting, drum-beating, and so forth. Though we all enjoyed playing Indian as children, we rightly feel that there comes a time to stop playing at being a warrior and to start being a real one. That is where Bly's seminars seem to fall short.

A different situation attains in Switzerland. There, warriorship is a practical matter. Young Swiss men experience no confusion about when the moment of "initiation" comes. Just as in primitive, tribal societies, the Swiss man becomes a warrior at a certain, definite age. He enters basic training at about age twenty and enrolls in the militia. He learns small-unit tactics, hand-to-hand fighting, wilderness survival, and the care and handling of his assault rifle. He learns everything he needs to know in order to fight for his homeland. He becomes a warrior.

Yet he never seems to find it necessary to put those deadly skills to work. Feminist Cassandras warn that a heavily armed society of testosterone-charged warriors would soon lead to a bloodbath. But Switzerland has demonstrated just the opposite. It has avoided the wars, revolutions, dictatorships—and even the street crime—that plague its neighbors ceaselessly. It has shown the world that a man can be a warrior without necessarily having to wage war.

THE INDIAN WAY

One of our most popular columnists at FrontPage Magazine.com is a Comanche Indian named David Yeagley. A graduate of Yale Divinity School, with additional degrees in music, art, and ancient humanities, Yeagley serves, at this writing, as an adjunct professor of humanities at the College of Liberal Studies, University of Oklahoma.

His first column for FrontPage was entitled, "Warriors and Weapons." In it, Yeagley puzzled over America's sudden obsession with disarming its own people. He wrote: "Long ago, the government took away the Indian's weapons and put him on reservations. That is history. Indians know all about broken promises. But why would the White Man betray himself? Why would the U.S. government take the weapons away from its own good citizens?"

What follows is worth quoting at length. Dr. Yeagley wrote:

> I've found myself wondering why Indians have not played a bigger role in the gun rights debate.
>
> Weapons are an integral part of our culture. In Indian country, it's taken for granted that everyone shoots and hunts. Perhaps the use of arms is so fundamental to us that we don't even think of it as a right that can be lost.
>
> Recently, I visited Indian friends of the Salish-Kootenay Reservation in Montana. It was a few days before a funeral. Extra food was needed for the mourners. "I've got to go get a deer," my friend Terry said, as simply as most Americans would say, "I've got to go to the store."
>
> Among Indians, the weapon is a symbol of honor. In Comanche tradition, the young man grew up with the bow. Its mastery was a test of manhood. The relationship of man and weapon was intimate and lifelong.
>
> Every Comanche learned to fight and hunt. If you weren't waging war, you were preparing for war. It was the duty of every member of the tribe to be ready, just in case.
>
> In modern America, women seem to have turned against their own men over the gun issue, judging by the polls and the Million Mom March.

Indian women have a different mindset. It was the women who taught Comanche boys how to use their weapons. Long before anyone ever heard of Xena the Warrior Princess, a woman called the "adiva," or governess ran the Comanche training camps.

Americans nowadays seem to be forgetting what it means to be a warrior. They don't value preparedness. They think the government will always be there to defend them from enemies and criminals.

But that's not the Indian way. That's not the way of a man.[6]

AN ANTIMALE AGENDA

DR. YEAGLEY made a crucial point when he wrote, "In modern America, women seem to have turned against their own men over the gun issue." Women have, in fact, formed the backbone of the modern gun-ban movement. And ideological feminists have provided much of the leadership.

The feminist position on guns was expressed with unusual candor by Alana Bassin in a 1997 article in the *Hastings Women's Law Review*, entitled, "Why Packing a Pistol Perpetuates Patriarchy." Bassin bluntly confessed that the antigun agenda was really an antimale agenda.

"Firearms are a source of male domination—a symbol of male power and aggression," she wrote. "First, the gun is phallic. Just as sex is the ultimate weapon of patriarchy used to penetrate and possess women, the gun's sole purpose is to intrude and wound its victim. Historically, men have used guns to conquer and dominate other people." Bassin concluded that women needed to oppose gun rights, in order to "curb the perpetuation of patriarchy."[7]

SEX AND GUNS

The link between antigun and antimale attitudes was further documented by H. Taylor Bruckner, in a 1994 paper entitled, "Sex and Guns: Is Gun Control Male Control?" From surveys of Canadian college students, Bruckner concluded:

> Men and women have different patterns of motivation for being pro gun control. The men who favor gun control are those who reject traditional male roles and behavior. They are opposed to hunting, are pro homosexual, do not have any experience with or knowledge of guns and tend to have "politically correct" attitudes. The women who support gun control do so in the context of controlling male violence and sexuality. Gun control is thus symbolic of a realignment of the relation between the sexes.[8]

Bruckner's findings imply that there is more to the antigun movement than meets the eye. Publicly, it presents itself as a reasoned response to problems of crime and safety. But the movement's true vitality may spring from its ability to tap into the deep, unconscious ambivalence that some women feel toward men and sex.

THE WISH TO CASTRATE

On June 23, 1993, a Venezuelan immigrant named Lorena Bobbitt hacked off her husband's penis with a knife while he lay drunk in bed, then fled, throwing his severed member out the car window. Bobbitt later explained that she had acted in self-defense, fearful of her husband's physical abuse. She failed to explain how amputating his penis was supposed to make him less violent toward her. But the jury bought Bobbitt's argument and, in January 1994, found her not guilty on grounds of "temporary insanity."

At the news of her acquittal, the *Washington Post* reported, "Women cheered and whooped brazenly as they crowded around office televisions; men crossed their legs and made nervous jokes about sleeping on their stomachs."[9] ABC's Cokie Roberts seemed greatly amused by the whole affair. On *This Week with David Brinkley*, she taunted men for their discomfort, implying that they were only getting what they deserved. "You've been lording it over us for 5,000 years," she laughed.[10]

The desire to castrate men may not be quite as widespread as the mass media would have us think. But for those women who share the fantasy—such as Cokie Roberts, apparently—gun control may provide a convenient and socially acceptable metaphor for an otherwise taboo act. According to psychiatrist Sarah Thompson, women's anxieties toward men and sex can often manifest themselves in an unconscious identification of guns with the male sex organ. In the case of Alana Bassin, cited previously, the identification is quite explicit. For such women, Dr. Thompson observes, "opposing gun rights is likely a displacement of the desire to castrate."[11]

Guns and Men

Castration is a peculiarly appropriate metaphor for gun control. The urge to fight, defend, and protect lies at the core of male identity. Strip him of his warrior status, and a man is broken.

On an everyday level, guns are actually more useful to women than to men. Only with a gun can a woman defeat a larger, stronger male adversary. As previously noted, a woman who offers no resistance to an attacker is 2.5 times more likely to suffer serious harm than one who resists with a gun.[12]

But men cherish their firearms in a way that goes beyond the practical. Deep in their hearts, men see themselves as warriors. In the mastery of weapons, they find completion and peace. "In Comanche tradition, the young man grew up with the bow," writes Dr. Yeagley. "Its mastery was a test of manhood. The relationship of man and weapon was intimate and lifelong."

When the Indian man was stripped of his arms and corralled in reservations, the Indian woman wept, for she knew that her power faded with his. She knew that when the warriors lost heart, the whole people suffered.

Many women today seem to have forgotten this basic rule of life. They have come to view men as rivals in a struggle for jobs, money, and status. Some even view men as foes to be disarmed and defeated. How did this happen? What force could have been strong enough to sunder the bonds of love, trust, and need that have drawn men and women together since the dawn of time?

"A COMFORTABLE CONCENTRATION CAMP"

MOST HISTORIANS agree that modern feminism began in 1963, with the publication of a bestselling book called *The Feminine Mystique* by Betty Friedan. The conventional account holds that Friedan was a suburban housewife who became bored with her life, realizing that her marriage was nothing more than "a comfortable concentration camp." Three years later, in 1966, she founded the National Organization for Women (NOW) and became its first president. Friedan's struggle to break free of the deadening routine of childrearing and housekeeping was held up as an example for other women to follow.

This story, while widely accepted, gives a misleading view of Friedan's life and motivations. In 1999, Smith College professor Daniel Horowitz (no relation to my boss David Horowitz, by the way) published a book called *Betty Friedan and the Making of the Feminine Mystique.* It revealed what had previously been known only to the small circle of hard-core leftists who knew her: that Friedan had never in her life been a normal housewife or, indeed, a normal anything.

Hardline Stalinist

Beginning in college, Friedan—then known by her maiden name of Betty Goldstein—was already a hardline Stalinist, active in the communist movement. Though Jewish, she supported Stalin's 1939 nonaggression pact with Hitler. When orders went out from Moscow to all Communist Parties worldwide to treat Hitler as a friend, many communists couldn't stomach it and broke ranks with Stalin. But Friedan was among the loyal few who obeyed.

"Friedan's secret was shared by hundreds of her comrades on the Left," writes David Horowitz, "though not, of course, by the unsuspecting American public—who went along with her charade presumably as a way to support her political agenda."[13]

Friedan later married a fellow leftist, Carl Friedan, and devoted her life to the cause of Marxist revolution. Friedan spent her married years working as a "labor journalist"—a professional propagandist for the Left. Her full-time maid did the housework. As her ex-husband, Carl, later noted, Friedan "was in the world during the whole marriage" and "seldom was a wife and mother."[14]

The "Woman Question"

The conventional account implies that Friedan developed her feminist views in a spontaneous, trial-and-error fashion, based upon her experience with the "comfortable concentration camp" of middle-class married life. In fact, Friedan had no need to invent this philosophy. Feminism—or what we call feminism today—had been a standard feature of Marxist thought at least since the publication of the *Communist Manifesto* in 1848. David Horowitz observes:

> Not at all a neophyte when it came to the "woman question" (the phrase itself is a Marxist construction), she was certainly familiar with the writings of Engels, Lenin, and Stalin on the subject and had written about it herself as a journalist for the official publication of the communist-controlled United Electrical Workers union.[15]

The Abolition of Marriage

In the *Communist Manifesto*, Karl Marx and Friedrich Engels had shocked the world by calling for the abolition of marriage and family, which they viewed as oppressive institutions. They wrote:

> What is the present family based on? On capitalism, the acquisition of private property. It exists in all of its meaning only for the bourgeoisie . . . and will vanish when capitalism vanishes. Are you accusing us that we want to end the exploitation by parents of their children? We confess to that crime. . . . The bourgeois sees in his wife nothing but an instrument of production.

Marx and Engels argued for free love, in which everyone would have sexual access to everyone else. They mocked the "moral outrage of our bourgeois," who found the notion scandalous.

> Our bourgeois find their main amusement in mutually seducing their wives.

> The bourgeois marriage is in reality the community of the wives. One could at best accuse the communists that instead of a hypocritical, hidden one, they want to introduce an official, open-hearted women's community.[16]

Male Chauvinism

Of course, Marx and Engels were men. One has to wonder whether the notion of communal lovemaking appealed to them for reasons other than ideological. Be that as it may, generations of Marxists strove dutifully to put the curious teachings of their founding fathers into practice. Few went so far as to embrace the extreme of free love. However, a deep ambivalence toward marriage and family was instilled in every Marxist heart.

During the 1920s, it was considered "reactionary" among communists to have any children at all, since family responsibilities might dampen one's revolutionary zeal. "When years passed and there was no revolution, people became frustrated with the situation and began to start families," writes David Horowitz in his autobiography *Radical Son.*[17]

Horowitz's parents were part of that generation. Growing up in a communist household in the 1940s, Horowitz remembers that his mother and father were always on guard against something called "male chauvinism"—a communist buzz phrase that has now entered the mainstream.[18] He was taught to view men as oppressors and women as victims. This early conditioning led to problems later on, when Horowitz started a family of his own.

Consciousness-Raising

At one point, Horowitz pressured his wife into joining a "consciousness-raising" women's group, thinking it his duty as a "progressive" husband to encourage her independence. He writes:

> Elissa came home from the first session in a state of agitation, vowing never to return. "They hate me because I'm a mother," was all she said. Years later, I learned from other members of the group that they had berated her for allowing me to "oppress" her by "making" her assume the housewifely role. They also told me that within a year of the group's formation, every marriage in it had dissolved.[19]

In fact, Elissa had embraced the role of wife and mother quite willingly. But Horowitz's Marxist conditioning would not allow him to accept her choice. The first time Elissa announced that she was pregnant, Horowitz says his reaction was "ambivalent." She had not yet finished her graduate degree, and Horowitz felt guilty about interfering with her studies. He writes:

> As the male and the sexual aggressor, I was sure that I was the source of the conflicts she now had to face. A maternal state was part of woman's oppression. I had made it harder for her to become independent and achieve a status beyond motherhood. This progressive but abstract understanding prevented me from entertaining the idea that her will might be as forceful in this situation as mine.[20]

When "Right" Is Wrong

Years later, Elissa confronted Horowitz about his failure to offer emotional support during her pregnancies. He writes:

> I was bewildered . . . my guilt at "getting her pregnant" had caused me to let her down. I had done the "right" thing but somehow it had turned out wrong. For the first time, I began to resent the progressive ideas that had shaped my reactions and, in this instance, separated me from her.[21]

The same sort of "progressive" ideas underlay Betty Friedan's 1963 bestseller *The Feminine Mystique*. After wreaking havoc in the personal lives of generations of communist activists, the genie of "progressive" thought was now unleashed to work its black magic in mainstream America.

A RUDE AWAKENING

IN THE November 19, 1990, issue of *Newsweek*, a freelance writer named Kay Eberling ruffled many left-wing feathers with a column entitled, "The Failure of Feminism." She wrote:

> To me, feminism has backfired against women. In 1973 I left what could have been a perfectly good marriage, taking with me a child in diapers, a 10-year-old Plymouth and Volume 1, Number One of *Ms. Magazine*. I was convinced I could make it on my own. In the last 15 years my ex has married or lived with a succession of women. As he gets older, his women stay in their 20s. Meanwhile, I've stayed unattached. He drives a BMW. I ride buses.

Eberling had accepted the feminist teaching that men were disposable, easily replaceable, and perhaps not even necessary at all. But in practice, it turned out to be women who were left out in the cold, once men were released from the traditional obligation to protect and provide for them.

"Sometimes on Saturday nights I'll get dressed up and go out clubhopping or to the theater," Eberling wrote, "but the sight of all those other women my age, dressed a little too young, made up to hide encroaching wrinkles, looking hopefully into the crowds, usually depresses me."[22]

"Worse Is Better"

For women like Eberling, feminism proved to be a disaster. But for the left-wing ideologues who invented the movement, Eberling's suffering was irrelevant.

There is a saying among activists of the Left that "worse is better." The more alienated and unhappy people feel, the more susceptible they are for recruitment into the revolutionary cause. For that reason, many leftists deliberately promote policies that they know will cause misery, suffering, and chaos.

For instance, in *Radical Son*, David Horowitz recalls a series of discussions with '60s activist Tom Hayden, in which the Chicago Seven conspirator revealed his true motive for inciting riots during the 1968 Democratic Convention. Horowitz paraphrases Hayden:

> If people's heads got cracked by police, he said . . . it "radicalized them." The trick was to maneuver the idealistic and unsuspecting into situations that would achieve the result.

In short, the Chicago Seven had deliberately lured their followers into situations where they could be hurt or killed. The bloodier things got, the better for the cause. Horowitz writes: "It was the extrapolation of a familiar radical idea: 'The worse, the better.'"

The same principle applied to more subtle disruptions, such as the promotion of promiscuous sex and drug use. Radicals "welcomed the subversive element in the counterculture, its challenges to prevailing norms, and—in the case of drugs—open defiance of the law," writes Horowitz. "Such attitudes were creating a disaffected generation that, given time, could be recruited for revolutionary goals."[23]

State-Run Baby Farms

On April 7, 2000, I attended a conference entitled, "The Legacy and Future of Hillary Rodham Clinton." Held at the American Enterprise Institute in Washington, D.C., the event was cosponsored by David Horowitz's Center for the Study of Popular Culture.

Betty Friedan was one of the panelists. Instead of talking about Hillary, as expected, Friedan launched into a discourse on the future of feminism. "Modern feminism has transformed our society for the better," she said. According to Friedan, women were now getting the same number of advanced degrees as men, and their pay was roughly equal to men's, at least up to midlevel management. But equality broke down at the top ranks. Why was that?

"When you analyze that," said Friedan, ". . . you see the gap begins in the childbearing, childrearing years and it is never made up. The question is not simple discrimination. That may not even be the main point anymore."

What was now holding women back, Friedan explained, was motherhood itself. The solution was to implement a massive state-managed day care system, into which babies as young as six weeks could be deposited, while their mothers worked. "This is the next step," proclaimed the founder of modern feminism.[24]

A Telling Confrontation

It is said that Friedan retreated from her hardline "Stalinist" position while in her mid-thirties. That may be so. But her teachings still clearly reflect the Marxist worldview, especially when it comes to issues of family.

During the question-and-answer period, a woman in the audience stood up to confront Friedan. She was Mallory

Millett—whose sister Kate Millett had written the 1970 feminist bestseller *Sexual Politics*. Mallory had been converted to feminism by her sister but later renounced it. The exchange between Millett and Friedan is worth quoting in some detail:

Millett: I would like to charge Betty Friedan with a question. . . . You and my sister Kate Millett . . . and all of you gathered together in 1968 to create this great women's movement. . . . It was right around that time that all of us left-wing radical feminists gathered together and decided we were going to change the face of the American family. . . . You use the word *society* a lot, Betty, and I would like to know what you think society is comprised of. For me, society is comprised of families and children. And from what I can see, since the great radical changes that were inserted into our culture in 1970, for thirty years now we've had a total deterioration of the American family and the absolute ruination of the American child. . . . If you think society is so much better off in the last thirty years, explain the deterioration of the family and the ruination of the children.

Friedan: I do not see great evidence of the deterioration of the family at all. What happened to the family is that . . . we don't have a single model of the family anymore. We have single-parent families and we have traditional families, of wife and wage-earner husband and we have many many many more growing numbers, a majority of two-paycheck families. And from every evidence. . . .

Millett: And children run wild.

Friedan: No, and there is no evidence of children running wild. This is, you're making it up.

Millett: They're shooting each other in the schools.

Friedan: The children in this country are doing better than they ever did.[25]

As the exchange grew more heated—and ever less relevant to the subject of Hillary Clinton—the moderator stepped in and ended it. However, Friedan had made her point. In her view, the skyrocketing divorce rate and the rise in single-parent families in recent decades were not bad things at all. On the contrary, they represented a widening of women's choices, a major step in the right direction.

The Bourgeois Enemy

As any child of divorced or separated parents can tell you, the dissolution of a family is a heartbreaking tragedy. Yet it is easy to see why left-wing radicals such as Betty Friedan welcome and encourage this development. As the power of the family declines, the power of the Left grows.

Marx and Engels intuited more than 150 years ago that the family was the basic building block of the "bourgeois" order—by which they meant the peaceful, orderly community of hard-working, tax-paying, middle-class citizens. Marxists have always recognized the middle class as their enemy. Wherever communist regimes have taken power, middle-class people have been systematically exterminated by the millions.

The problem with the middle class—from a Marxist point of view—is that it has a strong stake in preserving stable, democratic government and in resisting revolution and disorder. That is why, when the British government feared a communist uprising in 1919, some officials suggested that the lower classes be disarmed, while the middle classes—stockbrokers, clerks, university students, and the like—be provided with weapons.[26] The British government felt confident that the middle class would be its ally in any revolutionary outbreak.

DISARMING THE MIDDLE CLASS

LEFT-WING STRATEGISTS have long understood that the "bourgeois" classes oppose them. For that reason, the disarming of the "bourgeoisie" has been a longstanding project of the Left.

This goal was clearly expressed by the socialist writer H. G. Wells in the 1930s. Wells believed that mankind was moving inexorably toward a global, socialist government that he called the "new world order." He believed passionately in this movement, but he knew that many would resist it.

Eventually, Wells predicted, "We shall find ourselves almost abruptly engaged in a new system of political issues in which the socialist world-state will be plainly and consciously lined up against the scattered vestigial sovereignties of the past."

To ensure the success of global socialism, Wells advised that all potential pockets of resistance be disarmed. "Life is conflict and the only way to universal peace is through the defeat and obliteration of every minor organization of force," he wrote. "Carrying weapons individually or in crowds, calls for vigorous suppression on the part of the community."[27]

DIVIDE AND CONQUER

"A government that robs Peter to pay Paul can always depend upon the support of Paul," observed George Bernard Shaw. "Divide and conquer" is a time-honored tactic of the Left. The poor are turned against the rich. Blacks are turned against whites. Women are turned against men. It is easier to control and subdue people when they are fighting among themselves.

In a stable, middle-class society, men and women work together to provide a good home and education for their children and a secure retirement for themselves. Working as a team, they achieve a high rate of success. But in a society where men and women are locked in ideological combat, the system breaks down. Energies are consumed in power struggles, infidelities, divorce, and child-custody battles and finally in managing the parade of lovers, therapists, and angry bill-collectors who enter one's life after divorce.

This is bad news for the families involved but good news for the Left. After all, "worse is better" when seeking revolutionary change. Frightened, lonely, aging divorcées—or soccer moms who fear divorce, since they see it happening all around them—make far better recruits for the Left than women happily ensconced in stable, loving families.

THE MARRIAGE GAP

IN THE 1970s, feminists used to joke, "A woman needs a man like a fish needs a bicycle." They neglected to point out, however, that if a woman chooses to live without a man, she will eventually have to find a replacement. For many women, that replacement has turned out to be the government.

During the 2000 presidential campaign, a *Los Angeles Times* poll showed a startling "marriage gap." While Gore enjoyed three-to-one support among single women, Bush led among married women by 51 to 40 percent.[28] Single women perceived, in Gore's Big-Government policies, a kind of Super Husband who would protect and provide for them. "The promise of a safety net counts for more with those who don't have a male version of one," writes Samuel Silver in *Liberty Magazine*.[29]

Thus, America finds itself dividing into rival camps, with sex being an ever-more-important indicator of who will choose which side. As Ann Coulter pointed out in the August 7, 2000, issue of *Jewish World Review*, "Except in the landslide election in 1964, Democrats haven't been able to get a majority of men to vote for their candidate in any presidential election since 1944."[30]

Some men spend weekends in the woods, beating drums and painting their faces as a substitute for real warriorship. Likewise, some women who lack real warriors in their lives seek substitutes—often in the form of a sterile bureaucracy that produces Medicare and Social Security checks on demand but that will never be able to hold them in its arms or wipe the tears from their eyes.

THE GREAT FEAR

FEW THINGS are more frightening to women than the mass shootings in today's schools. As noted previously, violent crime—and youth crime in particular—has been in steep decline since 1994. The 1999 arrest rate for juveniles on murder charges was the lowest since 1966.[31] Yet, the relative rarity of school shootings does not make them less threatening to the soccer moms who view them on television.

The horror evoked by such shootings is a great boon for the Left. Remember, "worse is better." Millions of middle-class mothers, terrified that their child may be next, provide easy recruits for the antigun cause. Back in 1968, the same was true of young demonstrators beaten by police during the Chicago Democratic Convention. Their heads bleeding from police billy clubs, their eyes burning from tear gas, they were finally ready to hear the revolutionary rhetoric of extremists such as Tom Hayden. Little did they suspect that Hayden had set them up, deliberately provoking the police and maneuvering demonstrators into positions where they were bound to get hurt.

A MANUFACTURED PROBLEM?

MIKE A. MALES of the Center on Juvenile and Criminal Justice at the University of California, Santa Cruz, has noted that random school shootings by white kids can be traced back at least to 1974, when seventeen-year-old honor student Anthony Barbaro opened fire at his school in Olean, New York, killing three.[32]

To what extent such shootings have become more common in recent years is hard to discern. As Males notes, there have simply not been enough cases to chart any clear statistical trend. Yet, it seems plain that such incidents did not form a part of American life as recently as a generation ago. And therein hangs a mystery.

However rare these shootings might be today, the question is, Why are they happening at all? More than a few experts have suggested that the same left-wing educators now calling for a "zero-tolerance" crusade against guns and aggression may themselves—however unwittingly—have helped instigate the violence that now makes such policies seem necessary.

The Masculinity Crisis

Guns have always been with us, writes Mona Charen. But school shootings have apparently not. They are a relatively new phenomenon, requiring a new explanation. Charen writes:

> Many American men over the age of fifty today were first taught to handle a gun at age eleven or twelve. . . . Yet those people would no more have taken a gun to school and shot their classmates than they would have shown up at school naked.
>
> If we accept the premise that human nature has not changed in the past forty years, we must conclude that some change in American life over the past several decades has removed inhibitions that worked well for centuries.

But what was that change? Charen suggests that it was the decline in traditional notions of masculinity. Our society is in the throes of a "masculinity crisis," she says.

THE WAY OF THE GENTLEMAN

CITING SENATOR Daniel Patrick Moynihan, Charen notes that "every civilization faces an invasion of barbarians every couple of decades. The barbarians are adolescent boys. With testosterone coursing through their veins and aggression hard-wired into their brains, boys can be dangerous."

Successful societies harness and restrain male aggression by teaching boys to be "gentlemen"—teaching them that a man's honor depends on such things as "getting and staying married, providing for and protecting one's family, protecting all women and children, serving one's country in the armed forces . . . ," and so on.

In the past, these values were reinforced with "adventure stories" of "death-defying heroes" whose sense of honor, chivalry, and warrior spirit would inspire the emulation of young boys. Competitive sports offered physical release for male aggression and also built the fitness, discipline, and team spirit essential to military preparedness.[33]

MANLY VIRTUE

Carleton University political scientist and philosopher Waller Newell concurs. In researching his book *What Is A Man? 3,000 Years on the Art of Manly Virtue*, Newell studied the concept of manhood through thousands of years of literature. He notes:

> I think the main thing that surprised me is the consistency of these concepts of male virtue from Homer to Winston Churchill and Teddy Roosevelt. I didn't find shifts and changes in that time period. There is more difference in my generation of men than in the 3,000 years of writings on honor and reputation, the art of good manners, courage and ambition. There is an impressive body of work about man-

> hood that gives us signposts to follow. The continuity is very powerful. It is truly a case where heeding the past can save our future.

What are those virtues to which men have aspired for at least 3,000 years? Newell writes: "Our fathers and their fathers won women with heroism, honor, bravery and commitment to family life. . . . We are now raising a generation of fatherless men who do not have those role models."[34]

The Role of the Father

It was from their fathers that little boys traditionally learned to become "gentlemen." But more and more boys today do not have fathers. And those who do, may have fathers so out of touch with their own manhood that they have no power to guide their sons.

"Thirty years of research suggests that the . . . boys who are most at risk for juvenile delinquency and violence are boys who are *physically* separated from their fathers . . . ," writes Clark University philosophy professor Christina Hoff Sommers, author of "The War Against Boys." "As the phenomenon of fatherlessness has increased, so has violence."

In a 1965 study for the Labor Department entitled, "The Negro Family: The Case for National Action," Senator Daniel Patrick Moynihan issued a prophetic and now-famous warning about the breakup of families among the urban underclass. He wrote:

> A community that allows a large number of young men to grow up in broken families, dominated by women, never acquiring any stable relationship to male authority, never acquiring any rational expectations about the future—that community asks for and gets chaos.

Sociologist David Blankenhorn writes in *Fatherless America* that "the weight of evidence increasingly supports the conclusion that fatherlessness is a primary generator of violence among young men."[35]

The arguments of Moynihan, Newell, Sommers, and Blankenhorn exert a strong appeal to common sense. But the Left has proposed a different solution to the problem of male violence—a solution that could not have been more perfectly tailored to make the problem worse if that had been its deliberate purpose.

BOYS IN SKIRTS

In 1998, two hundred teachers and school administrators attended a training seminar at the Wellesley Center in New England. The subject was "gender equity for girls and boys." Nancy Marshall, associate director of the Center, told the group, "When babies are born, they do not know about gender." Only later, between the ages of two to seven do they learn what it means to act like a boy or act like a girl."

It was the mission of the schools, she said, to do all in their power to counteract this gender programming. The very idea that some behavior was appropriate for boys and some for girls was wrong. Teachers must actively strive to stamp out all differences between the sexes.

But how could this be done?

Marshall and her fellow presenters offered some suggestions, via slide show. One of their favorite slides—judging by the number of times they returned to it—showed a preschool boy decked out in high heels and a dress. "It's perfectly natural for a little boy to try on a skirt," said the presenters. Apparently, this method was already known to some of the participating teachers. One kindergarten teacher told the group that she had had great success in persuading little boys in her class to wear skirts. Other activities recommended for little boys by modern educators are sewing quilts and playing with dolls.[36]

A Method to the Madness

Ordinary people imbued with common sense might look upon these exercises with bewilderment. Why would anyone wish to stamp out the differences between boys and girls? Do parents actually want their sons to wear dresses and play with dolls? Most, I suspect, do not.

Yet there is a method to this madness. The current war against masculinity has deep roots in the Marxist doctrine of class struggle. According to the Left, women are an oppressed class, much like poor people. The way to help poor people achieve equality with the rich, according to leftists, is to impoverish the rich, so that everyone can be poor together. Likewise, the way to obviate any unfair advantages that men allegedly have over women is to strip men of their ability to be masculine.

Undermining Capitalism

Carol Gilligan, professor of gender studies at Harvard University, has played a major role in developing the antimale agenda now standard in today's schools. One purpose of this program, as she clearly states, is to undermine "capitalism."

Gilligan says that boys from three to seven years of age are compelled by society to "take into themselves the structure or moral order of a patriarchal civilization: to internalize a patriarchal voice." The key to overcoming "patriarchy"—that is, male dominance—is to train little boys to reject "cultures that value or valorize heroism, honor, war, and competition—the culture of warriors, the economy of capitalism."[37]

In short, Gilligan's prescription is exactly the opposite of Waller Newell's. Where Newell advises instilling little boys with a yearning for "heroism, honor, bravery, and commitment to family life," Gilligan specifically targets "heroism" and "honor" for elimination. Why? Because boys imbued with these qualities—with the "culture of warriors," as Gilligan puts it—tend to support the "economy of capitalism."

"Raise Boys Like We Raise Girls"

In order to abolish "honor" and "heroism," Gilligan recommends radical measures.

Christina Hoff Sommers explains:

> Carol Gilligan calls for a fundamental change in child rearing that would keep boys in a more sensitive relationship with their feminine side. We need to free young men from a destructive culture of manhood. . . . We must change the very nature of childhood: we must find ways to keep boys bonded to their mothers.[38]

In Gilligan's view, boys must be discouraged from wanting to be "one of the boys," from segregating themselves into all-male groups such as the Cub Scouts and Little League, from bonding with male authority figures.[39] In short, they must be prevented from becoming men.

"Raise boys like we raise girls," advises Gloria Steinem.[40]

THE WAR AGAINST BOYS

As bizarre as Gilligan's guidelines may seem, today's schools have little choice but to follow them. Those who fail to cooperate may be accused of violating federal sex-discrimination laws and may lose their public funding. Thanks to such federal intervention, radical feminism has become a major force in today's educational system.

"It's a bad time to be a boy in America," writes Christina Hoff Sommers in *The War Against Boys.* The attitude of many educators toward boys ranges from disapproval to outright hostility. Sommers writes:

> An unacknowledged animus against boys is loose in American society. We have allowed socially divisive activists, many of whom take a dim view of men and boys, to wield unwarranted influence in our schools. They write anti-harassment guides, gather in workshops to determine how to change boys' "gender schema," and barely disguise their anger and disapproval. . . . Many popular writers and education reformers think ill of boys. Gang rapists and mass murderers become instant metaphors for everyone's sons. The false and corrosive doctrine that equates masculinity with violence has found its way into the mainstream. Only by raising boys to be more like girls, critics argue, can we help them become "real boys."

Demonizing Masculinity

In today's schools, boys are taught to fear and distrust their own masculinity. They learn in history class about the evils of male domination. Their behavior toward girls is constantly scrutinized for evidence of sexual harassment.

In September 1996, first-grader Johnathan Prevette—age six—was accused of sexual harassment and suspended from school in Lexington, North Carolina, because he kissed a girl on the cheek.[41] His case became a national scandal, but it was only one among many. Sommers writes:

> In another case, a mother who came to pick up her three-year-old son was told he had been reprimanded and made to sit in the "timeout chair" for having hugged another child. "He's a toucher," she was told. "We are not going to put up with it."

> A nine-year-old boy in Virginia who had been caught drawing a picture of a naked woman in art class (following a school trip to the National Gallery of Art) was accused of deliberately rubbing up against a girl in the cafeteria queue. School officials told the police. The boy was charged with aggravated sexual battery, and was handcuffed and fingerprinted.[42]

Competition Banned

Little boys are also taught to suppress and feel guilty about their natural, competitive urges. Mona Charen writes:

> Competitive play and learning are frowned upon. Teachers and administrators encourage "cooperative learning," in which teams of students help one another "discover" the answers, and stark distinctions between right and wrong answers are blurred. Even on the playground, competition is discouraged, and games "where no one keeps score" are recommended.[43]

Boys on Drugs

If all the previous methods fail to extinguish masculinity in little boys, today's gender warriors have a secret weapon: drugs. "It is not uncommon in many classrooms today to find the percentage of children on Ritalin to be 25 percent or greater and the numbers are climbing," charges Parents Against Ritalin (PAR).

Ritalin is the drug of choice for treating hyperactivity or Attention Deficit Disorder (ADD). A great deal of controversy exists over ADD. Experts differ on how to define it and even on whether it should really be called a disease. But one thing is sure. According to the National Institute of Mental Health, boys are diagnosed with ADD three times more often than girls. Forty percent of Ritalin prescriptions in the United States are for children between the ages of three and nine. Within that group of Ritalin-taking tikes, 80 percent are boys.[44]

Fidgeting and Squirming

How do you know if a child has ADD? According to the Diagnostic and Statistics Manual of the psychiatry industry, some of the symptoms include "fidgeting, squirming, distraction, difficulty waiting turns, blurting out answers, losing things, interrupting and ignoring adults."

ADD affects grown-ups, too. Columnist Maggie Gallagher writes:

> Do you often get excited by projects and then not follow through? Do you have a hard time relaxing? Do you smoke or drink? Do you drum your fingers? Do you like to gamble? Are you particularly intuitive? Are you a maverick? As a kid, were you a klutz at sports? Do you let the bank balance your checkbook? Do you love to travel? Do you laugh a lot? Do you get the gist of things very quickly?
>
> If you answered yes to many of the above, then the gist is you, too, may have attention deficit disorder. I kid you not. These questions are from a list developed by [Edward] Hallowell and [John] Ratey to "offer a rough assessment as to whether professional help should be sought to make the actual diagnosis of ADD."[45]

"You'll See It Everywhere"

In their book *Driven to Distraction*, psychiatrists Hallowell and Ratey write, "There is no clear line of demarcation between ADD and normal behavior." As a result, "Once you catch on to what this syndrome is all about, you'll see it everywhere."[46]

Well, not quite "everywhere." You will see it especially in little boys. Indeed, the grossly disproportionate rate at which boys are diagnosed with ADD has caused some critics to wonder whether, in many cases, it is just a fancy new way of describing boyish behavior.

Boys have always been a discipline problem for teachers. They squirm. They fidget. They fight. They interrupt. Such antics seem to be hardwired into their genes. In past years, such behavior was controlled through scolding and punishment. But modern pharmacology has given teachers a new tool for controlling male unruliness.

"For millions of satisfied teachers (who at this point are the chief pushers of Ritalin), the proof of the pudding is in the eating: Kids on Ritalin become more focused and more compliant in the classroom. So what's the problem?" writes Maggie Gallagher.[47]

The problem is that being a boy is not a disease and therefore should not require medication. "Boys need discipline, respect, and moral guidance," writes Sommers in *The War Against Boys*. "They do not need to be pathologized."[48]

Boys at Risk

The war against boys being waged in today's schools has already begun yielding enormous casualties. Sommers writes:

> The typical boy is a year and a half behind the typical girl in reading and writing, he is less committed to school and less likely to go to college. In 1997 college full-time enrollments were 45 percent male and 55 percent female. . . . Girls . . . now outnumber boys in student government, in honor societies, on school newspapers, and in debating clubs. . . . At the same time, more boys than girls are held back and more drop out. Boys are three times as likely to receive the diagnosis of attention deficit hyperactivity disorder. More boys than girls

> are involved in crime, alcohol, and drugs. . . . In 1997, a typical year, 4,483 young people aged five to twenty-four committed suicide: 701 females and 3,782 males.[49]

The Drug Connection

If quelling male violence is a goal for today's gender warriors, their efforts may have backfired in a spectacular way. A growing number of critics have hypothesized that psychotropic drugs such as Ritalin, Prozac, and Luvox may be contributing factors in the rash of motiveless, unexplained school shootings that have received wide publicity since 1996.

The autopsy of Columbine shooter Eric Harris, for instance, showed that he was heavily medicated with the antidepressant Luvox, a relative of Prozac. Fourteen-year-old Kip Kinkel, who killed two students and wounded twenty-two when he opened fire in a school cafeteria, had prescriptions for both Ritalin and Prozac.

"The list of these cases goes on and on," writes Deborah Carson in the *Las Vegas Review-Journal.* She notes that the manufacturer of Ritalin has admitted that "psychotic episodes can occur." Carson continues:

> Today at least 6 million kids are now on mind-altering drugs such as Ritalin, Luvox and Prozac. In some classrooms, 20 percent of the students are on Ritalin. Yet no research has shown that such psychoactive drugs are safe for minors nor that they remedy any brain-chemistry imbalance.

Not surprisingly, Carson observes, many "Americans increasingly see a link between the torrent of seemingly senseless acts of violence by school-age children and prescription psychotropic drugs—many of which have been known for years to cause serious adverse effects when given to minors."[50]

EMOTIONAL FLOODWATERS

ARE PSYCHOTROPIC drugs really causing kids to become mass shooters? Or do mass killers simply happen to be taking psychotropic drugs because of their existing instability? Only further research can shed light on this question.

There can be little doubt, however, that the attempt to eradicate little boys' competitive and aggressive urges—rather than providing constructive outlets for them—has contributed greatly to the problem of school violence. Psychiatrist Sarah Thompson explains:

> All people have violent, and even homicidal, impulses. For example, it's common to hear people say "I'd like to kill my boss," or "If you do that one more time I'm going to kill you." They don't actually mean that they're going to, or even would, kill anyone; they're simply acknowledging anger and frustration. All of us suffer from fear and feelings of helplessness and vulnerability. Most people can acknowledge feelings of rage, fear, frustration, jealousy, etc. without having to act on them in inappropriate and destructive ways.[51]

But suppose you are not allowed to acknowledge those feelings. Suppose any attempt to do so will put you in instant violation of a "zero-tolerance" policy and get you suspended from school or worse. Then your aggressive impulses have no constructive outlet. Like floodwaters rising against a levy, they will seek a way out, one way or another. And the ways they find will quite likely be "inappropriate" and "destructive," in Dr. Thompson's words. She continues:

> [E]ducation "experts" commonly prohibit children from expressing negative emotions or aggression. Instead of learning that such emotions are normal, but that destructive behavior

needs to be controlled, children now learn that feelings of anger are evil, dangerous and subject to severe punishment. To protect themselves from "being bad," they are forced to use defense mechanisms to avoid owning their own *normal emotions*. Unfortunately, using such defense mechanisms inappropriately can endanger their mental health; children need to learn how to deal appropriately with reality, not how to avoid it.[52]

The Psychology of Gun Control

Schoolchildren are not the only victims of today's "zero-tolerance" culture. The antiaggression crusaders themselves, in many cases, may be suffering deeply from the unexpected consequences of their own rules.

"In my experience, the common thread in anti-gun people is rage," says Sarah Thompson, who writes frequently on the subject of psychology and gun rights and is Executive Director of Utah Gun Owners Alliance. "Either anti-gun people harbor more rage than others, or they're less able to cope with it appropriately. Because they can't handle their own feelings of rage, they are forced to use defense mechanisms in an unhealthy manner."

As an illustration, Thompson cites an anonymous e-mail she once received from a person opposed to gun rights. She did not know whether the sender was male or female, but in her article "Raging Against Self-Defense: A Psychiatrist Examines the Anti-Gun Mentality," Thompson referred to the e-mailer as a man, for convenience. This correspondent opined that he opposed the carrying of firearms because he did not want to be murdered by some neighbor who just happened to be having a "bad day."

"I responded by asking him why he thought his neighbors wanted to murder him, and, of course, got no response," writes Thompson.

Statistically speaking, this person was far more likely to be shot accidentally by a policeman than by a neighbor with a concealed-carry license. His fear was not realistic. But that did not make it any less real for him. Thompson writes:

> How does my correspondent "know" that his neighbors would murder him if they had guns? He doesn't. What he was really saying was that if *he* had a gun, *he* might murder his neighbors if he had a bad day, or if they took his parking space, or played their stereos too loud. This is an example of what mental health professionals call *projection*—unconsciously projecting one's own unacceptable feelings onto other people, so that one doesn't have to own them.[53]

Rage and Aggression

Projection is a defense mechanism, Thompson explains. It is a way for people to deal with unconscious emotions that they cannot allow themselves to feel consciously. She writes:

> Some people . . . are unable consciously to admit that they have such "unacceptable" emotions. They may have higher than average levels of rage, frustration, or fear. Perhaps they fear that if they acknowledge the hostile feelings, they will lose control and really will hurt someone. They may believe that "good people" never have such feelings, when in fact all people have them.

Such a person may cope with his anger or rage by "projecting" those feelings onto others—by imagining that people around him are the ones who actually suffer from such emotions. Thus a person who feels unconsciously tempted to mow down his neighbors or co-workers with an AK-47 might become convinced that it is really other people—such as gun owners or NRA members—who are actually inclined to do so. The objects of his projection may be perfectly harmless people. But in his mind, they are deadly threats who must be disarmed before they hurt someone. "Because they wrongly perceive others as seeking to harm them, they advocate the disarmament of ordinary people who have no desire to harm anyone," writes Thompson.[54]

The Poisoned Crusader

Another defense mechanism is *reaction formation*, in which the unacceptable feeling or desire is transformed into its opposite. "For example, a child who is jealous of a sibling may exhibit excessive love and devotion for the hated brother or sister," writes Thompson. "Likewise, a person who harbors murderous rage toward his fellow humans may claim to be a devoted pacifist and refuse to eat meat or even kill a cockroach."

People who adopt this strategy can do great harm to others, without even knowing it. They become poisoned crusaders, preaching love, peace, and gentleness while using their crusade as a cover for venting their rage and inflicting harm on others. An environmentalist who professes a love for trees may advocate acts of sabotage that could hurt or kill lumberjacks. An animal rights activist might take violent action against hunters or fur trappers. "In the case of anti-gun people," writes Thompson, "reaction formation keeps any knowledge of their hatred for their fellow humans out of consciousness, while allowing them to feel superior to 'violent gun owners.' At the same time, it also allows them to cause serious harm, and even loss of life, to others by denying them the tools necessary to defend themselves."

Sarah Thompson's fascinating theory is presented in easy-to-understand layman's terms in a booklet entitled, "Do Gun Prohibitionists Have a Mental Problem?" Interested readers can obtain the booklet through jpfo.org, the Web site of Jews for the Preservation of Firearms Ownership, or by calling (800) 869-1884.

Million Mom Mayhem

If Thompson's theory is correct, many antigun activists who imagine that they are battling to save the world from mad gunmen may, in fact, be driven by a secret fear that they themselves will one day go berserk with a gun. In some cases, these fears turn out to be well-founded.

Take Million Mom Marcher Barbara Graham. After her son was gunned down at a 1999 Martin Luther King Day rally, Graham became active in the antigun cause. She joined a Washington, D.C., group called "Mothers on the Move Spiritually," which helped sponsor the Million Mom March. Graham spoke at the March on Mother's Day, 2000.

Two months later, she was arrested—and subsequently convicted—on a charge of assault with intent to kill. Enraged by the failure of police to find her son's murderer, Graham had sought her own vengeance. She had gunned down twenty-three-year-old Kikko Smith with three shots from a .45-caliber pistol, on January 26, 2000. Unfortunately, Smith was the wrong man. He had had nothing to do with her son's murder. Yet he is now paralyzed and bound to a wheelchair for life.

After Graham's arrest, police found "three handguns and a TEC-9 submachine gun at her home," according to the *Washington Post*.

Graham's case is a classic example of what journalists call a "man-bites-dog" story. When an urban gang-banger shoots someone, it is not news but rather an ordinary event, a case of "dog bites man." When a Million Mom Marcher does it, however, journalists, under normal circumstances, would be expected to take notice. Every talk show in the land should have jumped on the story. Yet they did not. The case has been kept out of the public eye, perhaps because of what it might reveal about the smoldering, violent rage that animates so many anti-gun crusaders.

The Madness Within

"Lethal violence even in self defense only engenders more violence," Betty Friedan once preached.[55] These are strange words, coming from a woman who long defended a Soviet regime that murdered 61 million people. But Sarah Thompson's theory may help explain the paradox. Like the pistol-packing Million Mom Marcher Barbara Graham, Friedan exhibits many of the classic symptoms of a poisoned crusader.

In her book *Life So Far*, Friedan accused her ex-husband, Carl, of having beaten her, a charge that was quickly picked up by the media. He "started beating up on me . . . ," Friedan wrote. "I realize now he must have been desperate with rage and envy."[56]

After thirty years of silence, her ex-husband—an eighty-year-old retired ad man—was forced to respond. On his Web site, CarlFriedan.com, he wrote: "I recount all this that follows with considerable reluctance, having never expected to reveal these episodes of Betty Friedan's extreme irrational behavior—ever. But I have no intention of going to my reward labeled a wife beater. . . ."

He stated that Betty suffered from serious mental illness, characterized by "episodes of uncontrollable hysteria and physical violence during our marriage." Carl said that his wife had come after him, at various times, with knives and shards of broken glass from a mirror she had shattered. He writes:

> Being with her was like walking a field of land mines. Bang! She'd explode unexpectedly, often out of the clear blue sky with no provocation at all. She was the most violent person I

> have ever known. . . . In the mid-sixties one psychiatrist of hers, Dr. Dalmau, prescribed the drug Thorazine which she took for a week or two until she discovered it was widely used at that time to subdue hysterical mental patients. She stopped taking it, insulted that a doctor would consider her nuts.

It Takes a Monster

As in all such cases, it is easy to dismiss the war of words between Carl and Betty Friedan as a case of he-said, she-said. However, as Howard Kurtz of the *Washington Post* noted on June 5, 2000, Betty "seemed to be backing off her charge" in a subsequent appearance on *Good Morning America.* She said, "I almost wish I hadn't even written about it, because it's been sensationalized out of context. My husband was no wife-beater and I was no passive victim of a wife-beater. We fought a lot, and he was bigger than me."

David Horowitz has noted, "If I am more inclined to believe Mr. Friedan's side of the story, it is only because his ex-wife has a long and well-documented history of lying."[57]

To this day, Carl Friedan remains true to his left-wing ideals. He laments his ex-wife's behavior, but insists that "I am proud of what she did for the world." Carl recalls:

> About six years ago I was interviewed by a writer working on a biography of Betty Friedan. In the course of our talk she said, "Everywhere I went I've heard one description of Betty over and over—a monster!" Betty being monstrous in the pursuit of her goals doesn't bother me at all. She changed the course of history almost singlehandedly and it took a "monster" perhaps, a driven, super-aggressive, egocentric, almost lunatic dynamo to rock the world the way she did. Unfortunately, she was that same person at home, where this kind of conduct doesn't work. She simply never understood this.[58]

PUBLIC GOOD OR PRIVATE DEMONS?

CARL FRIEDAN may be proud of his ex-wife's work. But it is worth pondering to what extent the antigun movement—and the radical feminism that drives it—may reflect not so much a vision for the public good as the private demons of a troubled woman.

If the last century has taught us anything, it is that the question of how men and women can best live in harmony remains an open one. Relations between the sexes have come a long way since the time when women could be dragooned into the harems of lustful pashas. I am optimistic that further improvements lie ahead.

How those improvements will come about and what form they should take remains an unresolved question to open and inquiring minds. Perhaps it always will be, to some extent. But nearly forty years after the publication of *The Feminine Mystique*, one thing seems undeniable: The model of "class warfare" between the sexes, promoted by angry, leftist revolutionaries such as Karl Marx, Friedrich Engels and Betty Friedan is not the sort of "improvement" we need.

COOL HEADS NEEDED

BY A WEIRD coincidence, an epidemic of mass school shootings broke out simultaneously in England, Australia, and America, all in the same year, 1996. England and Australia responded immediately with massive gun confiscations. They acted on emotion, without stopping to ask what the real problem might be. As a result, their citizens have lost an important right, and, as previously noted, both countries have experienced enormous increases in violent crime.

Americans still have a chance to avoid their fate. But we need cool heads to accomplish it. Unfortunately, cool heads are rare in the antigun community. For reasons that may have a lot to do with the pathologies identified by Dr. Sarah Thompson, passion and hysteria seem to rage unchecked among gun-ban lobbyists.

Rosie's Rage

Rosie O'Donnell provides a prime example. In June 1999, a *National Enquirer* headline caught my eye. It said: "Rosie's Rage: The Murder Secret Behind Her Gun Furor." Intrigued, I purchased the tabloid, expecting to read that some friend or loved one of Rosie's might have been killed by gunfire. But the story presented a far more puzzling scenario.

The *Enquirer* quoted an anonymous friend of Rosie's who said that the roots of Rosie's antigun activism lay in "a very painful story that she has told only her closest friends." Rosie was watching television late one night, while cuddling her newly adopted son Parker. Suddenly, says the *Enquirer*, she got "a terrible shock."

A news story came on about a boy who had found his grandmother's gun, taken it to the school playground, and accidentally shot and killed his best friend. "It deeply affected Rosie," said the friend. "Rosie told me, 'How can any mother go on after their child is killed? I just couldn't bear it. I looked down at little Parker and thought to myself: I can do something to help save the lives of children.' And that's when Rosie got involved in supporting gun control."

It's quite a story, but it may not convey quite the picture that Rosie's friend intended. Assuming that the account is true, it suggests that Rosie's antigun stand results from an emotional reaction grossly out of proportion to the event that supposedly inspired it—the viewing of a single televised news story. That Rosie allows herself to be swayed so dramatically by her emotions raises questions about her judgment and objectivity. A greater degree of sobriety would seem appropriate for a person who presumes to lead the nation in a debate as serious and far-reaching as that over gun rights.

No More Tears

"When it comes to talking about guns, responsible women should adopt Johnson & Johnson's Baby Shampoo pledge: No more tears." Thus wrote syndicated pundit Michelle Malkin in a June 23, 1998, column. She continued:

> Alas, the sopping feminization of political debate continues to drown out sober analysis of gun-control laws. . . . In our Oprah-fied culture, overwrought women . . . are deified while accomplished scholars such as John Lott are demonized. The question is no longer "Which policy will save the largest number of lives?" but "Who can shed the most tears?" Therein lies the real tragedy: Instead of arming the nation's youth with the intellectual tools they need to pursue the truth, we are teaching them to deal with crucial public policy problems by burying their heads at the bottom of a Kleenex tissue box.[59]

Raw Emotion

Malkin's observation is on target. The gun control debate has not only been drowned by tears, but also in many ways, it is defined by them. John Lott, David Kopel, and other researchers have long since demonstrated that the facts and figures used by gun control lobbyists are, to a shocking extent, lies, distortions, and fabrications. But what the gun-banners lack in factual justification, they make up for in raw emotion.

New York Congresswoman Carolyn McCarthy provides a case in point. Her husband was slain in 1993, when a black gunman named Colin Ferguson, consumed by hatred for whites, got on the Long Island Railroad and began picking off commuters, one by one, with a 9-mm pistol. He shot twenty-six commuters, killing six. McCarthy ran for Congress three years later as a one-issue candidate. Her single goal was to crack down on guns. She was swept into power on a tide of antigun hysteria.

"This Is Not a Game to Me"

On June 18, 1999, when it appeared that a bill she was pushing to regulate gun shows was going to fail, a weepy McCarthy mounted the podium of the U.S. House of Representatives to beg for support. "This is not a game to me," she sobbed, tears welling in her eyes.[60]

Of course, the battle over gun rights is hardly a "game" to the rest of us either. It is a grave issue of Constitutional liberty. Awash in emotion and tears, McCarthy seems insensitive to such subtleties.

No compassionate person can ignore the tears of a Carolyn McCarthy or a Sarah Brady (the latter joined the antigun crusade, as chair of Handgun Control Inc., after an assassin's bullet left her husband with severe brain damage). Their personal tragedies seem to lend weight and dignity to their cause. Yet the fact that these women suffered personal traumas does not make them right. Sometimes people draw the wrong lessons from the tragedies in their lives.

A Poor Mix

Some years ago, my Aunt Vera died a horrible death from breast cancer. I watched her die. Month after month, she lay in bed, screaming and moaning in agony.

She did not have to die that way. Vera had placed her trust in an "alternative" doctor who persuaded her to forgo chemotherapy and even pain killers. I do not know whether Vera would have survived longer under conventional treatment. But she certainly would have suffered less pain.

If I were to follow Carolyn McCarthy's example, I might feel justified in devoting the rest of my life to an impassioned crusade against alternative medicine. I might lobby ceaselessly and tearfully for the legal abolition of all treatments not specifically endorsed by the American Medical Association.

Such a campaign might satisfy some emotional need to give purpose to my Aunt Vera's death. But in the process of indulging my feelings, I would be robbing other people of the freedom to treat their health problems as they see fit. It is precisely because of such conflicts that emotion and legislation make a poor mix.

A DIFFERENT SOLUTION

A COOL-HEADED APPRAISAL of the Long Island Railroad massacre might have suggested a different solution than Carolyn McCarthy's.

Israel is a country that has dealt very effectively with the problem of mass public shootings. Like Switzerland, Israel has a citizen's militia. Its people are well-armed with government-issued weapons, including fully-automatic Uzis and Galils.[61]

In 1984, a terrorist group concocted a plan to carry out several mass shootings in crowded public areas in Israel. Their plan failed on the first attempt. Three terrorists opened fire on a Jerusalem crowd with machine guns. But they succeeded in killing only one person. The moment they began firing, shopkeepers and pedestrians—perhaps as many as half a dozen—pulled pistols from belts and holsters and returned fire. One terrorist was shot dead by a jewelry store proprietor. The other two fled the scene and were later captured. "We didn't expect to find armed civilians," one of the gunmen later admitted. Israel still suffers its share of bombings, but, for obvious reasons, mass shootings have not been favored by terrorists in Israel since that 1984 incident.[62, 63, 64]

It is highly probable that Ferguson—like the Jerusalem terrorists—would have refrained from attacking those LIRR commuters had he believed they were likely to shoot back. John Lott notes that the mean per-capita death rate from mass public shootings fell by 69 percent in states that passed concealed-carry laws.[65]

"It Would Have Been Worse"

It happens that my wife and I personally knew one of the people gunned down by Colin Ferguson on the Long Island Railroad. Her name was Amy Federici. She was shot in the head point-blank.

After the massacre, her father, Jacob Locicero, became an antigun activist. Many people in the New York City area began pressing for a concealed-carry law to prevent future incidents. But Locicero spoke out against it. "It would have been worse," he said, if even one commuter on that train had been able to shoot back. More people would have been killed, shot by mistake, or caught in the crossfire, he claimed.[66]

Mr. Locicero's antigun activism has no doubt helped him deal emotionally with his daughter's death. But the fact is, Amy might well be alive today if commuters on that train had been allowed to carry guns.

"Totally Unprepared"

An assistant district attorney named Thomas McDermott witnessed Amy's death. He was reading the *New York Times* on the train when he heard the first shots. Turning, he saw Colin Ferguson coming toward him down the aisle. "He made eye contact with me just after he shot Lisa Combatti, who was pregnant. I'd heard her beg him not to fire, because of her baby. He fired anyway. He then drew out a fresh ammunition clip."

A Vietnam combat veteran, McDermott instinctively turned to expose less of his body as a target. The move may have saved his life. When the bullet came, it only hit him in the arm. Others on the train were not so quick-thinking.

"The civilians who had never heard gunfire before were totally unprepared," he said. "Many just froze in their seats. Amy was one of them. Ferguson walked over and shot her in the head at point-blank range. She fell to the floor beside me.

"I had seen combat wounds before. I knew she was not going to make it. I've at least been able to reassure her parents that Amy didn't suffer for long."[67]

Helpless

Witnesses say that Colin Ferguson made his way methodically down the aisle, facing each victim before he fired. Many remarked on the calm, unhurried manner with which he executed his task. "The gunman was pressing the trigger every half second or so," recalls William A. Warshowsky. "Going side to side shooting people. Not rapid fire, but pressing the trigger steadily—pop, pop, pop."[68]

Ferguson could afford to take his time. The eighty people trapped in that railroad car with him were helpless. Like the terrorists who opened fire on that Israeli crowd in 1984, Ferguson was confident that no one would shoot back. Unlike those terrorists, however, he turned out to have been correct in his assumption. People screamed, froze, or stampeded for the next car, clogging the doorway. But they could not defend themselves. All they could do was wait their turn as the killer calmly and methodically worked his way toward them, reloading each time his fifteen-round clip ran out.

Many still argue that the carnage would have been worse that night had commuters been able to shoot back. They are entitled to their opinions. But I ask each reader, if it were you cowering in your seat that night, with nowhere to hide, watching Ferguson work his way toward you, calmly and methodically, and knowing that your turn was coming next, would you really have felt safer knowing that neither you nor anyone else on that train could shoot back?

Heroes

In the final moments of the shooting, witnesses say the car was in pandemonium. Bloody bodies were slumped in the seats or lying on the floor. Surviving passengers were crowded at one end of the car, screaming and trying to get out.

At that moment, Ferguson stopped to reload for the third time. Kevin Blum, 42, Michael O'Connor Jr., 32, and Mark McEntee, 34, were watching him. "Let's get him!" said Blum. The three men tackled Ferguson and held him until police arrived.

"They are the real heroes here," said Andrew Roderick, the first cop to arrive on the scene. "It was their quick thinking that saved this from becoming even more of a tragedy than it is."[69] Ferguson was carrying 160 additional rounds of ammunition at the time he was captured. Plenty more killing would have taken place that night if those three commuters had not stopped him.

Days later, President Clinton met with the three heroes. "I just wanted to see them and talk to them . . . and figure out, why did these guys do this?" he said.[70] Why, indeed? According to Carol Gilligan and other antiaggression educators, heroism is undesirable. Children—and boys, in particular—should be discouraged from emulating and identifying with the deeds of a Blum, an O'Connor, or a McEntee. According to Gilligan, boys need to be insulated from "cultures that value or valorize heroism. . . ." Fortunately for the commuters on the Long Island Railroad that night, at least three men on board had not yet gotten Gilligan's message.

SWITZERLAND BESIEGED

ADMIRATION FOR HEROES runs deep in every human heart. The antiaggression crusaders may never succeed in stamping it out completely. But they can do a lot of damage while trying.

Throughout this book, Switzerland has been cited for its great success in addressing the issue of warriorship and weapons in modern society. No nation better epitomizes the peaceful, prosperous middle-class ideal. For that very reason, leftists have worked overtime, in recent years, to disrupt and discredit this Alpine utopia whose very existence defies their dogma.

The memory of Switzerland's heroic stand against the Nazis has faded among the young. Taking advantage of this fact, the Left has agitated relentlessly for the weakening and dismantling of the militia system that made it possible. In 1977, a proposal was floated to allow Swiss men to choose hospital or social work in place of military service.[71] It was voted down. But the Left persisted. Their efforts bore fruit in 1989, when the Socialist Youth of Switzerland succeeded in pushing through a nationwide vote on whether or not to abolish the militia. To everyone's surprise, 35.6 percent voted "Yes" for abolition. This was not enough to carry the motion, but it was enough to plunge the nation into an orgy of introspection and self-doubt.[72]

THE END OF HEROISM

Swiss culture was changing. For years, leftist intellectuals had been chipping away at the foundations of Swiss identity. They argued that the legendary founding of Switzerland by armed rebels in 1291 was a myth. They claimed that the national hero, William Tell, never existed. "At the end of the twentieth century heroic acts by single, male figures have lost their fascination," explains Jonathan Steinberg in *Why Switzerland?*[73]

Consequently, Swiss men had begun losing interest in the idea of being heroes. A national security report by the Swiss Federal Council following the 1989 referendum noted that "The will to self-defense (*Selbstbehauptungswille*) is not as marked as it was."[74] A generation gap had arisen, in which more and more young people looked upon military service as a burden. Steinberg describes the problem thus:

> [T]he Swiss officer corps faces the turbulence of the young dissidents with very little inner confidence. The historic language of command has lost its purchase. The values embedded in words like *Ehre* (honour), *Pflicht* (duty) or *Zucht* (discipline) have evaporated so completely that contemporary young people can hardly make sense of the terms at all. There are no words to use which are common to both sides of the generation gap or which transcend the division in styles of life.[75]

"What does a true Swiss man need?" asks the old folk song. "A clean little gun on the wall, and a cheerful song for the Fatherland." The song remains the same, but there are signs that Switzerland's warrior culture may not.

Honor, Duty, and Discipline

What happens to a country when its young men disdain honor, duty, and discipline? One thing that happens is that they lose interest in honoring their commitments to wives and children. The Swiss divorce rate has climbed sharply in recent years.

As the bonds of love and marriage dissolve, so does agreement between Swiss men and women on fundamental issues of liberty. A substantial number of Swiss women now object to the requirement that militiamen keep their assault rifles and live ammunition at home.[76] It remains to be seen whether the society of proud and peaceful warriors that is Switzerland can long withstand this new and intimate assault.

Hearth and Home

In a crucial scene in the film *Dances with Wolves*, the Kevin Costner character breaks his oath to the U.S. Army and distributes rifles to his adopted Indian tribe so they can defend themselves from a Pawnee war party. The Indians slaughter their foes easily. Afterward, the Costner character reflects:

> It was hard to know how to feel. I'd never been in a battle like this one. There was no dark political objective. This was not a fight for territory or riches or to make men free. It had been fought to preserve the food stores that would see us through the winter, to protect the lives of women and children and loved ones only a few feet away. . . . I felt a pride I had never felt before. . . . I knew for the first time who I really was.

Swiss men have felt that pride for centuries. They have stood ready to fight, not for some "dark political objective" but in defense of hearth and home, alongside their friends and neighbors. For the time being, the old ways are holding out. On March 4, 2001, the Swiss voted overwhelmingly against entering into membership talks with the European Union (the "Yes to Europe!" proposal had been pushed, predictably, by the far-left Green Party).

"Even though they are surrounded by EU countries, the Swiss are fiercely independent . . . ," observed the *Associated Press*. "Switzerland is not even a member of the United Nations because of deep mistrust of outside interference."[77]

Of course, the Left will keep on pushing. It always does. Switzerland may yet be persuaded to lay down its sovereignty. If it does, then Swiss men, for the first time in centuries, would be compelled to don a foreign uniform—the blue helmet of the UN—and they would die far from home in places like Kuwait and Kosovo, not to protect friends and family but to serve the "dark political objectives" of bureaucrats and power-brokers in distant lands.

ENOUGH IS ENOUGH

ON APRIL 19, 1994, Bill Clinton appeared on an MTV broadcast entitled "Enough Is Enough" to push his anticrime and antiviolence agenda. Speaking to a group of 200 young people, ages sixteen to twenty, Clinton promoted a number of extreme measures, including his new plan for allowing police to conduct random gun searches in public housing projects without warrants.

A twenty-year-old named Richard Dyer posed a question. Pointing to the low crime rate in Singapore—an Asian dictatorship where basic rights such as free speech do not exist—Dyer asked whether America might be better off adopting a Singaporean-type system. "Is our system outdated? Does it need to be changed?" he asked.

Bill Clinton's reply to this question is worth recounting in detail. He said:

> Well, that's not where I thought you were going with the question. Good for you. (Laughter.) . . . My own view is that you can go to the extreme in either direction. And when we got organized as a country and we wrote a fairly radical Constitution with a radical Bill of Rights, giving a radical amount of individual freedom to Americans, it was assumed that the Americans who had that freedom would use it responsibly. . . .

> But it assumed that people would basically be raised in coherent families, in coherent communities, and they would work for the common good, as well as for the individual welfare.
>
> What's happened in America today is, too many people live in areas where there's no family structure, no community structure, and no work structure. And so there's a lot of irresponsibility. And so a lot of people say there's too much personal freedom. When personal freedom's being abused, you have to move to limit it. That's what we did in the announcement I made last weekend on the public housing projects, about how we're going to have weapon sweeps and more things like that to try to make people safer in their communities. So that's my answer to you. We can have—the more personal freedom a society has, the more personal responsibility a society needs, and the more strength you need out of your institutions—family, community, and work.[78]

Just in case any readers failed to get the point, what President Clinton said was that the system of "radical . . . individual freedom" passed down to us by our Founding Fathers was no longer working. It had been designed for a situation in which people were "raised in coherent families, in coherent communities." But now that these structures were breaking down—as in public housing projects inhabited largely by single-parent families on welfare—violence and disorder were on the rise. In such circumstances, said President Clinton, we can no longer afford the kind of "radical freedom" bequeathed to us by our forefathers. We must "move to limit" freedom.

And for those who might ask precisely how he meant to "limit" freedom, Clinton offered the specific example of his "weapon sweeps" policy, which allowed police to invade people's homes whenever they wished, without search warrants, in order to find and confiscate guns.

Worse Is Better

It is hard to find a better illustration of the "worse is better" principle in action. Widely known as the "first feminist president," Clinton helped channel tens of millions of taxpayer dollars into leftwing and feminist organizations such as NOW that are ideologically committed to weakening and breaking up the traditional family.[79]

Yet in that MTV broadcast, he pointed to family breakdown as a chief cause of violence and disorder. Without "coherent families," said Clinton, the Constitution itself could not function. It would be drowned out in a rising tide of chaos—a tide that could only be stemmed by massive, unrestrained police force.

Could it be that America's first feminist president understood what he was doing as clearly as Tom Hayden understood when he lured young students into harm's way in Chicago, 1968? Could it be that, given a choice between a "bourgeois" society of happy, prosperous families and an authoritarian police state, Bill Clinton actually preferred the latter? I leave the question to each reader to ponder.

SOUL SEARCHING

"There is nothing so good and lovely as when man and wife in their home dwell together in unity of mind and disposition," says Odysseus in Homer's *Odyssey*. "A great vexation it is to their enemies and a feast of gladness to their friends."[80]

America has vexed her foes and gladdened her friends for over 200 years. But what of the future? Children hunger today for their parents' teaching. Yet they hear only silence. They yearn to know how our freedom was won, and what they must do to keep it. But we cannot teach what we ourselves have forgotten. We cannot inspire when we ourselves have lost heart.

THERE IS HOPE

YET THE ANSWERS are available, for those who know where to look.

Our Comanche columnist, David Yeagley, once told me about a project he had conducted in his class at Oklahoma State University-OKC. He had organized his students into a formal debate on the question of patriotism and whether or not it should be taught in schools (a pet cause of Yeagley's is to promote patriotism classes in public schools).

Many of his students seemed bewildered. One young man confessed, "Dr. Yeagley, I don't think we have a clue of what you're talking about. When I think of patriotism, all I can think of is my grandfather who fought in World War II. I think of old people."

ASK THE ELDERS

ON ONE LEVEL, this young man's statement seems discouraging. What will become of our republic if young people don't "have a clue" what it means to love their country and fight for their liberties?

Yet Yeagley found cause for hope. Despite his bewilderment, this student had shown that he knew instinctively where to look for his answers. "I think of old people," he had said. And he was right. Yeagley notes that it has always been the elders' role to preserve and pass on the stories of the tribe.

"If an Indian wants to know what it means to be Indian, he asks his elders," says Yeagley. "If you want to know what it means to be American, ask your grandfather. He'll tell you."[81]

All over America, in every community, the elders are among us. They have seen war and peace, good times and bad. They knew America before any gun-control law was passed. They knew it before crime had exploded in our cities, before divorce and easy sex had filled the streets with fatherless boys, bent on mayhem. They knew America before anyone ever heard of a school shooting. They knew an America that worked. Ask the elders. Ask them what we must do. If anyone knows the answer, surely they will.

ENDNOTES

FRONTMATTER

1. Stephen P, Halbrook, *That Every Man Be Armed* (San Francisco, CA: Liberty Tree Press, 1984), pp. 118–119.
2. David B. Kopel, *The Samurai, the Mountie, and the Cowboy* (Amherst, New York: Prometheus Books, 1992), pp. 338.
3. Ibid, p. 340.
4. Myles Kantor, "The Present Slavery," FrontPageMagazine.com, April 26, 2001

   http://www.frontpagemag.com/columnists/kantor/mk04-26-01.htm

INTRODUCTION

1. Brian Melley, "Rural Terror: Stranger Stabs Children to Death with Pitchfork," Associated Press, April 25, 2000. (The rest of this story is based upon wire and newspaper accounts, as well as e-mail interviews with Tephanie Carpenter.)
2. Mike Feinsilber, "Over Six Months, Bush Has Edged Away from Reagan Policies," Associated Press, July 18, 1989.
3. Yohuru R. Williams, "In the Name of the Law: The 1967 Shooting of Huey Newton and Law Enforcement's Permissive Environment," *Negro History Bulletin* 61, no. 2 (April 1, 1998).
4. Jack Anderson, *Inside the NRA* (Beverly Hills, CA: Dove, 1996), p. 94.
5. "New York City Police Commissioner Howard Safir Discusses Whether He Has Done Enough to Reform NYPD," *News Forum* with Gabe Pressman, WNBC-TV, March 12, 2000.
6. Pat Milton, "NY Governor Signs Sweeping Gun Law," *Associated Press*, August 10, 2000.

7. Frank Lombardi, Timothy J. Burger, and Bill Hutchinson, with Kenneth R. Bazinet and Joe Mahoney, "Pataki Triggers NRA Anger," *New York Daily News*, March 16, 2000, p. 8.
8. William Safire, "Rewriting the Second Amendment," *Seattle Post-Intelligencer*, June 20, 1999.
9. Tanya Metaksa, "Showdown," FrontPageMagazine.com, December 19, 2000.

   http://www.frontpagemag.com/archives/guest_column/metaksa /metaksa12-19-00.htm
10. Tanya Metaksa, "Global Gun Grab," FrontPageMagazine.com, September 13, 2000.

    http://www.frontpagemag.com/archives/guest_column/metaksa /metaksa09-13-00.htm

MYTH 1, ASSUMPTION 1

1. Rudolph J. Rummel, *Death by Government* (Somerset, NJ: Transaction Pub., 1994), chap. 1. (Internet edition)
2. Rudolph J. Rummel, *Statistics of Democide*, 1997, chap. 13 (prepublication edited manuscript). (Internet edition)
3. Jonathan Cohn, "Guns 'n Moses," *The New Republic*, June 22, 1988.
4. Dr. Henry Picker, ed., *Hitler's Table-Talk at the Fuhrer's Headquarters 1941–1942* (Bonn: Athenaum-Verlag, 1951).
5. Aaron Zelman, "Holocaust Survivor Denounces Anti-Gun Movement," jpfo.org.

   http://www.jpfo.org/Survive.htm
6. Stephen P. Halbrook, *Target Switzerland* (Rockville Centre, New York: Sarpedon, 1998), pp. 184–185.
7. E. J. Dionne Jr., "A Culture of Violence," *Chicago Tribune*, September 21, 1999.
8. Clayton E. Cramer and David B. Kopel, "Shall Issue: The New Wave of Concealed Handgun Permit Laws," October 17, 1994 (Internet edition) http://uhavax.hartford.edu/~kdowst/competen.html].
9. Roger D. McGrath, *Gunfighters, Highwaymen and Vigilantes*, 2d Ed., (Berkeley and Los Angeles: University of California Press, 1987), p. 157.
10. Robert A. Dykstra, *The Cattle Towns: A Social History of the Kansas Cattle Trading Centers* (1968), pp. 144–147 (cited in Cramer and Kopel, 1994).

11. W. Eugene Hollon, *Frontier Violence: Another Look* (1974), p. x. (quoted in Cramer and Kopel, 1994).
12. Cramer and Kopel, 1987.
13. Samuel Francis, "Clues About Guns and Crime," *Washington Times*, May 10, 1994, p. A19.
14. John Perazzo, *The Myths That Divide Us* (Briarcliff Manor, New York: World Studies Books, 1999), pp. 81–82.
15. Ibid., p. 89.
16. Walter Williams, "What About Hate Crimes By Blacks?," *Cincinnati Enquirer*, August 22, 1999, p. DO2; and e-mail interview with John Perazzo, May 5, 2001.
17. Mike A. Males, e-mail interview, May 10, 2001.
18. Mike A. Males, "Leave the Kids Alone," p. 24.
19. Males, e-mail interview.
20. Males, "Leave the Kids Alone," *In These Times*, June 12, 2000, Page 24.
21. Perazzo, *The Myths That Divide Us*, p. 180.
22. Larry Elder, "Littleton and the Brando Rule," JewishWorldReview.com, April 30, 1999 (citing David Whitman, "White-Style Urban Woes," *U.S. News & World Report*, December 9, 1996).
23. George Will, "'Right to Bear Arms' Out of Date," *Seattle Post-Intelligencer*, March 21, 1991, p. A15.
24. Males, e-mail interview.
25. Mike A. Males, *Kids and Guns: How Politicians, Experts, and the Press Fabricate Fear of Youth* (Monroe, ME; Philadelphia, PA: Common Courage Press, 2001), p. 3.
26. Michael J. Sniffen, "Juvenile Murder Rate Down 68 Percent From 1993 to 33-Year Low," *Associated Press*, December 14, 2000.
27. Mark Lorando, "Pet Rock," *Times Picayune*, July 12, 1999, p. C1.
28. Michael James and Erin Texeira, "Shootings' Racial Aspect Examined by NAACP," *Baltimore Sun*, April 22, 1999, p. 11A.
29. "Morbidity and Mortality Among US Adolescents: An Overview of Data and Trends," *American Journal of Public Health*, 86, no. 4 (April 1996).
30. Jack E. White, "A Real, Live Bigot," *Time* 154, no. 9 (August 30, 1999).
31. David Horowitz, *Radical Son* (New York: The Free Press, 1997), p. 54.
32. Ibid., pp. 53–54.
33. Ibid., p. 55.

34. Scott Sherman, "David Horowitz's Long March," *The Nation*, July 3, 2000.
35. Ibid., p. 247.
36. Ibid., p. 259.
37. Ibid., p. 253.
38. Ibid., p. 258.
39. Ibid., p. 269.
40. Ibid., p. 315.
41. Ibid., p. 288.
42. David Horowitz, *Hating Whitey and Other Progressive Causes* (Dallas, TX: Spence Publishing Company, 1999), pp. 13–14.
43. Murray N. Rothbard, *For a New Liberty* (New York: Collier Books, 1978), p. 27.
44. John R. Lott Jr., *More Guns, Less Crime* (Chicago: University of Chicago Press, 1998), p. 68.
45. Patricia Alex, "Debate Sweeping Public Housing: Privacy vs. Safety. Some Welcome Surprise Inspections," *The Record*, September 6, 1994, p. B-1.
46. Halbrook, *Target Switzerland*, p. 56.
47. Stephen P. Halbrook, *That Every Man Be Armed* (San Francisco: Liberty Tree Press, 1984), p. 97.
48. Ibid., pp. 143–144.
49. Ibid., p. 147.
50. Don Temy, "Chicago Project in Furor About Guns and the Law," *New York Times*, April 8, 1994, sect. A, p. 12.
51. Ibid.
52. William G. Blair, "Good Samaritan's Victim Said to Have Fled," *New York Times*, August 17, 1990, sect. B, p. 3.
53. Halbrook, *That Every Man Be Armed*, p. 100.
54. Flynn Roberts, "CHA Has Clinton's Attention: Anti-Crime Bill, Sweeps Touted," *Chicago Tribune*, June 18, 1994.
55. "Jackson Asks Greenville Residents to Keep Guns Off Streets," *Associated Press*, August 20, 1999.

MYTH 1, ASSUMPTION 2

1. David B. Kopel, *The Samurai, the Mountie, and the Cowboy* (Amherst, NY: Prometheus, 1992), pp. 20–21.
2. Ibid., 1992, pp. 23–25.
3. Ibid., 1992, pp. 25–27.
4. Ibid., 1992, pp. 29–30.
5. Ibid.
6. Ibid., 1992, p. 23.
7. Ibid., 1992, pp. 20, 37.
8. Ibid., 1992, p. 45.
9. Ibid., 1992, p. 39.
10. Tanya K. Metaksa, "Global Gun Grab," FrontPageMagazine.com, September 13, 2000.

    http://www.frontpagemag.com/archives/guest_column/metaksa/metaksa09-13-00.htm
11. Stephen P. Halbrook, "Armed to the Teeth and Free," *Wall Street Journal Europe*, June 4, 1999.
12. Kopel, 1992, p. 290.
13. Kopel, 1992, p. 285.
14. Kopel, 1992, p. 20.
15. Kopel, 1992, p. 27.
16. Stephen P. Halbrook, *Target Switzerland* (Rockville Centre, NY: Sarpedon, 1998), pp. 18–20.
17. Ibid., pp. 95–96.
18. Halbrook, 1999.
19. Kopel, 1992, p. 282.
20. Jonathan Steinberg, *Why Switzerland?* (New York: Press Syndicate of the University of Cambridge, 1996), p. 236.
21. Kopel, 1992, p. 286.
22. Kopel, 1992, p. 292.
23. Kopel, 1992, p. 286.
24. Kopel, 1999.
25. Kopel, 1992, p. 281.
26. Halbrook, 1999.
27. Kopel, 1992, p. 291.

28. Halbrook, 1998, pp. 11–12.
29. Ibid., p. 11.
30. Tom Bradley, "Ethnic Narcissism and Infertility in Japan," FrontPageMagazine.com, January 2, 2001
    http://frontpagemag.com/archives/miscellaneous/bradley01-02-01.htm
31. R. J. Rummel, *Death by Government*, chap. 13 (Internet edition)
    http://www2.hawaii.edu/~rummel/SOD.CHAP13.HTM
32. Halbrook, 1998, p. 52.
33. Halbrook, 1998, p. 47.
34. Halbrook, 1998, p. 25.
35. Halbrook, 1998, p. 33.
36. Halbrook, 1998, p. 129.
37. Steinberg, 1996, p. xii.
38. Steinberg, 1996, pp. xi–xii.

MYTH 1, ASSUMPTION 3

1. "Million Mom March and Rosie O'Donnell's Gun Control Views," *ABC News* with Cokie Roberts and Sam Donaldson, May 14, 2000.
2. Adam Miller and Bill Hoffmann, "Heat's on Rosie over Bodyguard's Gun Permit," *New York Post*, May 26, 2000, p. 3.
3. Ibid.
4. "Rosie's Kid to Have Bodyguard," *Associated Press*, May 25, 2000.
5. Chris Weinkopf, "Guns 'n Rosie," *Los Angeles Daily News*, May 30, 2000.
6. Brad Bennett, "Rosie a Hypocrite?" Letters to the Editor, *Washington Post*, May 31, 2000.
7. Weinkopf, 2000.
8. John R. Lott Jr., *More Guns, Less Crime* (Chicago: University of Chicago Press, 1998), p. 5.
9. Ibid.
10. Ibid., pp. 4–5.
11. Ibid., p. 5.
12. A. D. Hopkins, "Concealed Weapons: Writer Says More Reduces Crime," *Las Vegas Review-Journal*, September 17, 2000, p. 3B.
13. Lott, 1998, p. 19.
14. Lott, interview, January 12, 2000.

15. Lott, 1998, p. 164.
16. Robert Stacy McCain, "Concealed Arms Deter Crime, Says Researcher's Book," *Washington Times*, April 29, 1998, p. A8.
17. Lott, 1998, p. 122.
18. Lott, 1998, pp. 123–128.
19. McCain, 1998, p. A8.

MYTH 1, ASSUMPTION 4

1. Dominic Mohan, "Madonna: I'm Gonna Marry My Guy Next Year and We'll Live in Britain," *The Sun*, November 22, 2000.
2. Charlie Bain, "Madonna's Raid Terror," *The Mirror*, December 2, 2000, p. 1.
3. Lucy Panton, "Lock, Stock and One Stolen Barrel," *The People*, December 3, 2000, p. 7.
4. Nicholas Rufford, "Official: More Muggings in England Than US," *Sunday Times* (London), October 11, 1998.
5. David B. Kopel, *The Samurai, the Mountie, and the Cowboy* (Amherst, NY: Prometheus, 1992), pp. 72–77.
6. Ibid., pp. 76–77.
7. "Muggers Terrorize London Celebs," *New York Post*, January 1, 2000.
8. Michael Brown, "Results Are in on British Gun Laws," NewsMax.com, January 20, 2000.
9. Jon Ungoed-Thomas, "Killings Rise as 3mm Illegal Guns Flood Britain," *Sunday Times*, January 16, 2000.
10. "42 Deaths as Use of Handguns Hits Seven-Year High," *Guardian*, January 11, 2001.
11. John R. Lott Jr. (interview, January 12, 2000). Also, Australian Bureau of Statistics Web site, www.abs.gov.au.
12. Jon Dougherty, "Britain, Australia Top U.S. in Violent Crime," WorldNetDaily.com, March 2, 2001.

    http://www.worldnetdaily.com/news/article.asp?ARTICLE_ID=21902
13. Australian Bureau of Statistics Web site, www.abs.gov.au, May 10, 2001.
14. Dougherty, 2001.

    http://www.worldnetdaily.com/news/article.asp?ARTICLE_ID=21902
15. "Underclass Britain Is More Violent Than US," *Sunday Times*, February 13, 2000.
16. Ungoed-Thomas, 2000.

MYTH 2

1. Jack Anderson, *Inside the NRA* (Beverly Hills, CA: Dove, 1996), pp. 9–17.
2. Ibid., p. 148.
3. Jeffrey R. Snyder, "A Nation of Cowards," *The Public Interest*, no. 113 (fall 1993).
4. Clayton E. Cramer and David B. Kopel, "Shall Issue: The New Wave of Concealed Handgun Permit Laws," October 17, 1998 (Internet edition). http://uhavax.hartford.edu/~kdowst/competen.html
5. John R. Lott Jr., *More Guns, Less Crime* (Chicago: University of Chicago Press, 1998), p. 11.
6. Joan Treadway, "Judgment Against Son's Killer Applauded," *Times Picayune*, January 17, 1996, p. A1.
7. Lott, 1998, p. 1.
8. Cramer and Kopel, 1998.
9. Cramer and Kopel, 1998.
10. Snyder, 1993.
11. Lott, p. 2.
12. Scott Harris, "Call Me Blockhead, Take Your Best Shot," *Los Angeles Times*, January 28, 1997, p. B-1.
13. Lott, 1998, p. 4.
14. Valerie Richardson, "Kansas Tries to Keep the Peace By Keeping Murder Case Quiet," *The Washington Times*, May 7, 2001; Ron Sylvester, "Survivor Tells of Grisly Night: Woman Recounts Her Friends' Final Hours," *The Wichita Eagle*, April 17, 2001; Valerie Richardson, "Wichita Horror Fuels Debate Over Hate Crimes," *Washington Times*, February 11, 2001; Scott Rubush, "The Wichita Horror," FrontPageMagazine.com, January 12, 2001.
15. Walter Williams, "What About Hate Crimes By Blacks?" *Cincinnati Enquirer*, August 22, 1999, p. D-2.
16. David Horowitz, *Hating Whitey and Other Progressive Causes* (Dallas, TX: Spence Publishing Company, 1999), p. 26.
17. Richard Poe, "Priests in the Temple of Hate," FrontPageMagazine.com, July 27, 2000.
18. "7-Eleven Hero Clerk Fired," *Associated Press*, August 2, 2000.
19. Snyder, 1993.

MYTH 3

1. Matt Drudge, "'Patriot' Scene Stuns Audience; Producer, Gibson Defends Children Shooting Guns in Film," *The Drudge Report*, June 11, 2000.
2. "Million Mom March and Rosie O'Donnell's Gun Control Views," *ABC News* with Cokie Roberts and Sam Donaldson, May 14, 2000.
3. David B. Kopel, "An Army of Gun Lies," *National Review*, April 17, 2000.
4. John R. Lott, Jr., *More Guns, Less Crime* (Chicago: University of Chicago Press, 1998), p. 9.
5. *Larry King Live*, CNN, June 2, 1999.
6. Natalie Angier, "The Purpose of Playful Frolics: Training for Adulthood," *New York Times*, October 20, 1992.
7. "Family of Boy Suspended for Cops and Robbers Sues Sayreville Schools," *Associated Press*, June 2, 2000.
8. "Boy Suspended for Pointing Chicken Finger," *Associated Press*, February 1, 2001.
9. Scott Rubush, "Public Schools Are 'Clueless' About Guns," FrontPageMagazine.com, December 7, 2000.

   http://frontpagemag.com /archives/education/rubush12-07-00.htm
10. Miguel Navrot, "Candidate Wants Squirt Gun," *Albuquerque Journal*, July 28, 2000, p. 2.
11. Gerald Mzejewski, "Dodge Ball Targeted for Elimination at Schools," *Washington Times*, December 8, 2000.
12. "Howitzer Picture Cut from Yearbook," *Associated Press*, October 28, 1999.
13. David B. Kopel, *The Samurai, the Mountie, and the Cowboy*, (Amherst, NY: Prometheus, 1992), pp. 389, 404.
14. Tanya Metaksa, "Gun Grabbers Use the 'Safety' Scam," FrontPage Magazine.com, February 15, 2001.

    http://www.frontpagemag.com/columnists/metaksa/2001/ metaksa02-15-01.htm
15. Guji Yukitaka Yamamoto, "The Way of the Kami: The Life and Thought of a Shinto Priest" (Internet edition), Tsubaki America, 1988.

    http://www.csuchico.edu/~georgew/tsa/Kami_no_Michi_1.html

MYTH 4

1. Tony Mauro, "Scholar's Views on Arms Rights Anger Liberals," *USA Today*, August 27, 1999, p. 4A.
2. Sanford Levinson, "The Embarrassing Second Amendment," *Yale Law Journal*, vol. 99 (1989):637–659.
3. Ibid.
4. Dr. Michael S. Brown, "Clinton vs. the Constitution," NewsMax.com, June 19, 2000.

   http://www.newsmax.com/commentarchive.shtml?a=2000/6/19/081701
5. Tanya Metaksa, "Showdown," FrontPageMagazine.com, December 19, 2000.

   http://www.frontpagemag.com/archives/guest_column/metaksa /metaksa12-19-00.htm
6. Levinson, "The Embarrassing Second Amendment," pp. 637–659.
7. Tanya Metaksa, "Disarming America," FrontPageMagazine.com, October 20, 2000.

   http://www.frontpagemag.com/columnists/metaksa/2000 /metaksa10-20-00.htm
8. Joyce Lee Malcolm, *To Keep and Bear Arms* (Cambridge: Harvard University Press, 1994), p. 135.
9. David B. Kopel, *The Samurai, the Mountie, and the Cowboy* (Amherst, HY: Prometheus 1992), p. 61.
10. Stephen P. Halbrook, *That Every Man Be Armed* (San Francisco: Liberty Tree Press, 1984), p. 100.
11. Malcolm, *To Keep and Bear Arms*, p. 139.
12. Ibid., p. 139.
13. Ibid., p. xi.
14. Halbrook, *That Every Man Be Armed*, p. 13.
15. Kopel, *The Samurai, the Mountie and the Cowboy*, p. 66.
16. Malcolm, *To Keep and Bear Arms*, p. 169.
17. Halbrook, *That Every Man Be Armed*, p. 47.
18. Halbrook, *That Every Man Be Armed*, p. 47.
19. Malcolm, *To Keep and Bear Arms*, p. 145.
20. Halbrook, *That Every Man Be Armed*, p. 68.
21. Ibid., p. 69.

22. Ibid., p. 72.
23. Ibid., p. 76.
24. Tanya Metaksa, "The 'Gun Nut' Smear," FrontPageMagazine.com, January 15, 2001.

    http://www.frontpagemag.com/columnists/metaksa/2001/metaksa01-15-01.htm
25. Halbrook, *That Every Man Be Armed*, p. 77.
26. Ibid., p. 82.
27. Ibid., p. 86.
28. Walter Williams, "Was a Bill of Rights Necessary?" *Jewish World Review*, June 28, 2000.

    http://www.jewishworldreview.com/cols/williams.html
29. Kopel, *The Samurai, the Mountie and the Cowboy*, p. 319.
30. Eugene Volokh, "Rule of Law: Guns and the Constitution," *Wall Street Journal*, April 12, 1999.
31. Halbrook, *That Every Man Be Armed*, p. 73.

MYTH 5

1. *Larry King Live*, CNN, June 2, 1999.
2. Russ Smith (Mugger), "Gun Control Solves Everything," *New York Press*, p. 3.
3. George Will, "'Right to Bear Arms' Out of Date," *Seattle Post-Intelligencer*, March 21, 1991, p. A15.
4. Jack Anderson, *Inside the NRA* (Beverly Hills, CA: Dove, 1996), p. 52.
5. "Loose Lips," *Buffalo News, Buffalo Magazine*, June 19, 1994, p. 14.
6. Larry Elder, "The Sweet Smell of Hypocrisy," FrontPageMagazine.com, July 5, 2000.

   http://www.frontpagemagazine.com/elder/2000/le07-05-00.htm
7. G. Witkin et al., "This Is 911 . . . Please Hold," *U.S. News & World Report*, June 17, 1996, cited in Aaron Zelman, "Will Gun Control Make You Safer," Jews for the Preservation of Firearms Ownership, 2000, p. 6).
8. Richard W. Stevens, *Dial 911 and Die* (Hartford, WI: Mazel Freedom Press, 1999), pp. 149–150.
9. "Dial 911 and Die," Jews for the Preservation of Firearms Ownership (online report).

   http://www.jpfo.org/Dial911.htm

10. "Dial 911 and Die," Jews for the Preservation of Firearms Ownership (online order page).

    http://www.dial911.itgo.com

11. Clayton E. Kramer and David B. Kopel, "Shall Issue: The New Wave of Concealed Handgun Permit Laws," October 17, 1994), Internet edition.

    http://uhavax.hartford.edu/~kdowst/competen.html.

12. John R. Lott Jr., *More Guns, Less Crime* (Chicago: University of Chicago Press, 1998), pp. 13–14.

13. "What It's Like—Living in a City Drowning in Snow," *U.S. News & World Report*, February 14, 1977, p. 21.

14. David B. Kopel, *Guns: Who Should Have Them?* (Amherst, NY: Prometheus, 1995), p. 195.

15. "Terror for the 21st Century," *Japan Times*, November 23, 1999.

16. "Are 'Bioterrorists' Ready to Strike? Reader's Digest Warns U.S. Is Unprepared to Meet Threat," *Business Wire*, January 19, 1999.

17. Ari Rubin, "Heroism and Fear: Lessons Learned from the Holocaust," jdl.org, November 26, 2000.

    http://www.jdl.org/misc/heroes/heroism_v_fear-jab.html

18. Sarah Thompson, "Raging Against Self-Defense: A Psychiatrist Examines the Anti-Gun Mentality," *Bill of Rights Sentinel*, Jews for the Preservation of Firearms Ownership, fall 2000.

    http://www.jpfo.org/ragingagainstselfdefense.htm

19. Kopel, *Guns: Who Should Have Them?*, p. 195.

20. Anderson, *Inside the NRA*, pp. 156–157.

21. Ibid., p. 9.

22. Jack Anderson, "Washington Merry-Go-Round: FEMA Wants Total Control in Case of U.S. Emergency," *United Feature Syndicate*, September 7, 1984.

23. James Ridgeway, "From the Man Who Brought You SWAT: Return of the Night of the Animals," *Village Voice*, February 26, 1985, pp. 30–31.

24. "House Unit Finds Misconduct at U.S. Emergency Agency," *Associated Press*, July 25, 1985.

25. Jon Basil Utley, "Preparing for the Terrorist Threat," *Insight on the News*, January 15, 2001, p. 14.

26. Stephen P. Halbrook, *That Every Man Be Armed* (San Francisco: Liberty Tree Press, 1984), pp. 135–137.

27. Robert T. Elson, *Prelude to War* (World War II series) (Richmond, VA: Time-Life Books, 1999), pp. 94–95.
28. Ibid., p. 93.
29. Johan Wanstrom, "Some Aspects of the Bill of Rights Outdated Now," *Oklahoma Daily*, via University Wire, July 11, 2000.
30. Stephen P. Halbrook, *Target Switzerland* (Rockville Center, NY: Sarpedon, 1998), pp. 92–93.

MYTH 6

1. "New York City Police Commissioner Howard Safir Discusses Whether He Has Done Enough to Reform the NYPD," *News Forum* with Gabe Pressman, WNBC-TV, March 12, 2000.
2. Saul K. Padover, ed., *Thomas Jefferson on Democracy* (New York: Mentor, 1939), p. 47.
3. Paul M. Eng, "Annie Get Your Gun License—Just Try," *Business Week*, April 14, 1997, p. 14.
4. Stephen P. Halbrook, *That Every Man Be Armed* (San Francisco: Liberty Tree Press, 1984), p. 5.
5. John R. Lott, Jr., "Controlling Guns," *Commentary* 110, no. 5 (December 1, 2000): 18.
6. Ibid., 18.
7. "Strict Law Amounts to Gun Ban in Maryland," CNSNews.com, February 23, 2001.
8. Vyn Suprynowicz, "An Organization Without Honor, Principle or Integrity," *The Libertarian Enterprise*.
9. David B. Kopel, "Defending Gun Shows," *National Review Online*, March 15, 2001.

   http://www.nationalreview.com/kopel/kopel031501.shtml
10. Joyce Lee Malcolm, *To Keep and Bear Arms* (Cambridge: Harvard University Press, 1994), p. 172.
11. Dean Baquet, "Crash in Washington Square," *New York Times*, April 24, 1992, p. A-1, col. 1.
12. William M. Reilly, "Four Killed, 24 Injured as Car Runs into Park," *United Press International*, April 23, 1992.
13. Ibid.
14. Dean Baquet, "Crash in Washington Square."

15. Salvatore Arena, "Trial Revisits Village Horror," *Daily News*, August 3, 1997, p. 12.
16. Patricia Edmonds and Bethany Kandel, "Seniors Fighting for Their Licenses and Independence," *USA Today*, July 9, 1992.
17. Marc Kaufman, "Mental Illness in America: 50 Million People a Year," *Washington Post*, December 14, 1999, p. A-3.
18. Nikita Khrushchev, *Khrushchev Remembers* (Strobe Talbott, trans. and ed.) (New York: Bantam, 1971), p. 518.
19. Jon E. Dougherty, "VA Gives FBI Health Secrets," WorldNetDaily.com, June 22, 2000.

    http://www.worldnetdaily.com/news/article.asp?ARTICLE_ID=15399
20. Fox Butterfield, "Hole in Gun Control Law Lets Mentally Ill Through," *New York Times*, April 11, 2000, p. A-1.
21. "Doctors Group Accused of Playing Politics with Patients, Gun Control," CNSNews.com, April 3, 2001.

    http://www.newsmax.com/archives /articles/2001/4/2/185453.shtml
22. Bartle Bull, "Lady MacBeth Comes to New York," *New York Post*, July 21, 1999.
23. John L. Perry, "The Hoax That Keeps on Hoaxing," NewsMax.com, March 29, 2001.

    http://www.newsmax.com/commentarchive.shtml ?a=2001/3/29/194505
24. Wes Vernon, "Medical Group: Regs Would Create National Database of Patient Records," NewsMax.com, March 28, 2001.

    http://www.newsmax .com/archives/articles/2001/3/27/173207.shtml
25. John L. Perry, "'Privacy' Rules Open Door to Socialized Medicine," NewsMax.com, April 23, 2001.

    http://www.newsmax.com/archives/articles/2001/4/23/144851.shtml
26. Joyce Milton, *The First Partner: Hillary Rodham Clinton* (New York: William Morrow and Company, Inc., 1999).

MYTH 7

1. Sarah Brady, "Statement of Sarah Brady, re: Gore and Bradley Gun Control Plans," Handgun Control Inc. press release, July 12, 1999.

    http://www.handguncontrol.org/press/1999/hci/071299.html
2. Richard Harris, "A Reporter at Large 'Handguns,'" *New Yorker*, (July 26, 1976), pp. 53–58.

3. David B. Kopel, "Taking It to the Streets," *Reason* (November 1, 1999).
4. Carla Crowder, "'Smart' Guns," *Denver Rocky Mountain News*, January 23, 2000.
5. "New York City Police Commissioner Howard Safir Discusses Whether He Has Done Enough to Reform the NYPD," *News Forum* with Gabe Pressman, WNBC-TV, March 12, 2000.
6. David B. Kopel, (ed.), *Guns: Who Should Have Them?* (Amherst, NY: Prometheus Books, 1995), page 65.
7. John R. Lott Jr., "Some Time To Kill: In Waiting Periods, Gun Buyers Are At Mercy of Criminals," *Investor's Business Daily*, March 2, 2001, p. 26.
8. Betsy Hart, "Brady Bill Actually Increased Crime," *The Deseret News*, August 4, 2000, p. A13.
9. Dr. Michael S. Brown, "Violence Policy Center Contradicts Gore," NewsMax.com, September 25, 2000.

   http://www.newsmax.com/commentmax/print.shtml?a=2000/9/25/092702
10. David B. Kopel, *Guns: Who Should Have Them?* p. 200.

EPILOGUE

1. Catherine Jordan, "Power Trippers," *Los Angeles Magazine*, March 1998, pp. 92–97, 158.
2. Robert Bly, *Iron John: A Book About Men* (New York: Addison-Wesley, 1990), pp. 2–3.
3. Ibid., p. 4.
4. Ibid., p. 156.
5. Ibid., pp. 63, 156.
6. David A. Yeagley, "Warriors and Weapons," FrontPageMagazine.com, January 26, 2001.
7. Alana Bassin, "Why Packing a Pistol Perpetuates Patriarchy," *Hastings Women's Law Journal* (fall 1997).
8. H. Taylor Bruckner, "Sex and Guns: Is Gun Control Male Control?" Presented in the Deviance and Control: Quantitative Studies session of the American Sociological Association 89th Annual Meeting, Los Angeles, August 5, 1994.

   http://teapot.usask.ca/cdn-firearms/Buckner/sex+guns.html
9. Quoted in Walter Berns, "Getting Away with Murder," *American Jewish Committee Commentary* 97, no. 4 (April 1994): 25.

10. Mona Charen, "Jury Verdicts Relieve Burden of Responsibility," *Fresno Bee*, January 28, 1994, p. B7.
11. Sarah Thompson, M.D., e-mail interview, March 3, 2001.
12. John R. Lott Jr., *More Guns, Less Crime* (Chicago: University of Chicago Press, 1998), p. 4.
13. David Horowitz, "Feminist Icon Debunked," FrontPageMagazine.com, January 19, 1999.

    http://frontpagemag.com/dh/1999/dh01-19-99.htm
14. Ibid.
15. David Horowitz, "Feminism's Dirtiest Secret," FrontPageMagazine.com, June 9, 2000.

    http://frontpagemag.com/dh/2000/david06-09-00.htm
16. Karl Marx and Friedrich Engels, *The Manifesto of the Communist Party*, trans. Walter H. Schneider.

    http://forever.freeshell.org/cm.htm
17. David Horowitz, *Radical Son* (New York: The Free Press, 1997), p. 171.
18. Ibid., p. 48.
19. Ibid., p. 171.
20. Ibid., p. 118.
21. Ibid., p. 118.
22. Kay Eberling, "The Failure of Feminism," *Newsweek*, November 19, 1990, p. 9.
23. Horowitz, *Radical Son*, p. 173.
24. "The Legacy and Future of Hillary Rodham Clinton," American Enterprise Institute, Washington, D.C., April 7, 2000, tape transcript.
25. Ibid.
26. David B. Kopel, *The Samurai, the Mountie, and the Cowboy* (Amherst, NY: Prometheus, 1992), p. 74.
27. Samuel L. Blumenfeld, "The Open Conspiracy," WorldNetDaily.com, August 11, 1999.
28. Ronald Brownstein, "Campaign 2000: The *Times* Poll," *Los Angeles Times*, September 27, 2000, p. 1.
29. Samuel Silver, "The Gender Gap Explained," *Liberty Magazine*, April 2001.
30. Ann Coulter, "The Democratic Party's White Face," JewishWorld Review.com, August 7, 2000.

31. Michael J. Sniffen, "Juvenile Murder Rate Down 68 Percent From 1993 to 33-Year Low," *Associated Press*, December 14, 2000.

32. Mike A. Males, e-mail interview, May 10, 2001.

33. Mona Charen, "Girls Will Be Boys, and Boys Will Be Girls," *American Outlook Magazine* (summer 2000).

    http://www.hudson.org/American_ Outlook/articles_sm00/charen.htm

34. "Interview: Waller Newell," *The Dallas Morning News* (online edition), July 30, 2000.

    http://www.dallasnews.com/sun_reader/120657_newellq&a_30su.html

35. Christina Hoff Sommers, "The War Against Boys," *The Atlantic Online*, May 2000.

    http://www.theatlantic.com/issues/2000/05/sommers.htm

36. Christina Hoff Sommers, "The War Against Boys," *Sunday Times* (London), June 18, 2000.

37. Christina Hoff Sommers, "The War Against Boys," *The Atlantic Online*, May 2000.

    http://www.theatlantic.com/issues/2000/05/sommers.htm

38. Ibid.

39. Ibid.

40. Ibid.

41. "Mother Wants Changes After Son's Kiss Is Called Sexual Harassment," *Associated Press*, September 25, 1996.

42. Christina Hoff Sommers, "The War Against Boys," *Sunday Times* (London), June 18, 2000.

43. Mona Charen, "Girls Will Be Boys, and Boys Will Be Girls."

44. Guy Clavel, "Ritalin Gets a Second Look as US Use Climbs Dramatically," *Agence France Presse*, October 9, 2000.

45. Maggie Gallagher, "Why Ritalin Rules," UExpress Online, April 12, 1999.

    http://www.uexpress.com/ups/opinion/column/mg/text/1999/04 /mg9904127149.html

46. Ibid.

47. Ibid.

48. Guy Clavel, "Ritalin Gets a Second Look."

49. Christina Hoff Sommers, "The War Against Boys," *The Atlantic Online*, May 2000.

    http://www.theatlantic.com/issues/2000/05/sommers.htm

50. Deborah Carson, "Children 'At Risk' from the Mental Health Cartel," *Las Vegas Review-Journal* (March 19, 2000).
51. Sarah Thompson, M.D., "Raging Against Self-Defense: A Psychiatrist Examines the Anti-Gun Mentality," *Bill of Rights Sentinel* (Jews for the Preservation of Firearms Ownership—JPFO), fall 2000.

    http://www.jpfo.org/ragingagainstselfdefense.htm
52. Ibid.
53. Ibid.
54. Ibid.
55. Ibid.
56. Howard Kurtz, "Abuse Reports That Smack of Unfairness," *Washington Post*, June 5, 2000, p. C-1.
57. David Horowitz, "Feminism's Dirtiest Secret," FrontPageMagazine.com, June 9, 2000.

    http://frontpagemag.com/dh/2000/david06-09-00.htm
58. Carl Friedan, "Living with Insanity," CarlFriedan.com, June 2000.
59. Michelle Malkin, "Feminization of Gun Debate Drowns Out Sober Analysis," *Seattle Times*, June 23, 1998.
60. David Shimm (or Robert Dreyfuss?), "Dark Days for Gun Control," *Rolling Stone*, September 12, 1999.
61. Kopel, *The Samurai, the Mountie, and the Cowboy*, p. 301.
62. Lott, *More Guns, Less Crime*, p. 6.
63. "Pistol Packers of Jerusalem," *The Economist*, April 7, 1984, p. 48.
64. David K. Shipler, "3 Arabs with Guns and Grenades Wound 48 in Jerusalem Crowds," *New York Times*, April 3, 1984, p. A-1.
65. Michelle Malkin, "Feminization of Gun Debate Drowns Out Sober Analysis," *Seattle Times*, June 23, 1998.
66. Steve Abubato Jr., "Concealed Weapons Won't Make New Jersey a Safer Place," *Asbury Park Press*, May 27, 1996.
67. Daniel Jeffreys, "Shoot to Kill," *The Independent* (London), November 21, 1994, p. 20.
68. Francis X. Clines, "Death on the L.I.R.R.," *New York Times*, December 9, 1993, p. A-1, col. 3.
69. Robert Dvorchak, "In Darkest Moment, Three Heroic Commuters Step Forward," *Associated Press*, December 9, 1993.

70. "Clinton Praises Three Who Tackled Train Gunman," *Press Association Newsfile*, December 14, 1993.

71. Kopel, *The Samurai, the Mountie, and the Cowboy*, p. 285.

72. Jonathan Steinberg, *Why Switzerland?* (New York: Press Syndicate of the University of Cambridge, 1996), p. 234.

73. Ibid., pp. 15–16.

74. Ibid., pp. 246, 249.

75. Ibid., pp. 246.

76. Kopel, *The Samurai, the Mountie, and the Cowboy*, p. 287.

77. Clare Nullis, "Swiss Reject EU Membership Talks," *Associated Press*, March 4, 2001.

78. "Transcript of Remarks by President Clinton in MTV's 'Enough Is Enough' Forum on Crime," *U.S. Newswire*, April 19, 1994.

79. "Taxpayers Subsidize Attacks on Ashcroft," NewsMax.com, January 16, 2001,

    http://www.newsmax.com/archives/articles/2001/1/15/162020.shtml.

77. T. E. Lawrence, trans., *The Odyssey of Homer* (Oxford University Press, 1991), book IV, p. 89.

81. Richard Poe, "A Comanche Patriot Tries to Save the White Man," FrontPageMagazine.com, January 17, 2001.

    http://www.frontpagemag.com/poesnotepad/2001/pn01-17-01.htm

INDEX